DENNIS O'KEEFFE is one of the nation's leading performers of Australian traditional songs, and has been a successful songwriting teacher for more than ten years. For as many years, he has led the Australian traditional song sessions at the National Folk Festival in Canberra. Dennis plays an anglo-concertina, an instrument that came to Australia during the goldrushes of the 1850s and was the most popular instrument in the Australian outback until the turn of the century. Regrettably, there are very few concertina players left in Australia. Dennis has been at the birth of literally hundreds of songs, having written some forty songs about Australian history and nurtured many songwriters from their first idea through to the first public performance of their work. Twenty years of painstaking research into the origins of 'Waltzing Matilda', combined with his knowledge of Australian traditional songs and proven songwriting ability, gives Dennis an intimate understanding of how the song was written, and what Paterson was writing about.

This popular version of 'Waltzing Matilda', arranged by Marie Cowan in 1903, was used to promote Billy Tea. (National Library of Australia)

Waltzing MATILDA

THE SECRET HISTORY OF AUSTRALIA'S FAVOURITE SONG

Dennis O'Keeffe

ALLEN&UNWIN

Allen & Unwin
Sydney, Melbourne, Auckland, London
83 Alexander Street
Crows Nest NSW 2065
Australia

Phone: (61 2) 8425 0100
Fax: (61 2) 9906 2218
Email: info@allenandunwin.com
Web: www.allenandunwin.com

Cataloguing-in-Publication details are
available from the National Library of Australia
www.trove.nla.gov.au

ISBN 978 1 74237 706 3

Internal design by Bookhouse, Sydney
Index by Jon Jermey
Set in 11.7/16.2 pt Adobe Caslon Pro by Bookhouse, Sydney
Printed and bound in Australia by Griffin Press

10 9 8 7 6 5 4 3 2 1

For Anne, Joel and Ryan

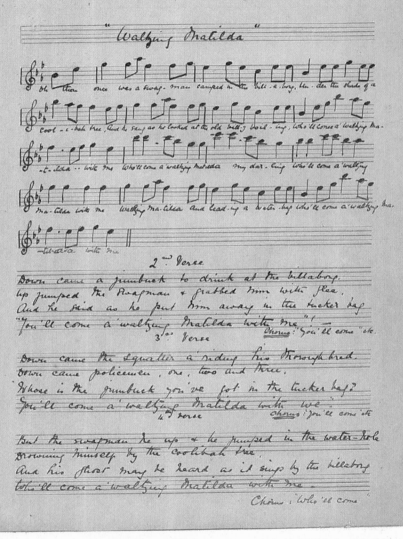

One of Christina Macpherson's original handwritten manuscripts of 'Waltzing Matilda', copied out in 1895. (National Library of Australia)

Contents

Preface   ix

 1 Australia's Song for the World   1

 2 The Backdrop for a Song   13

 3 Clancy and the Man from Snowy River   27

 4 There Once Was a Swagman   37

 5 Up Rode the Squatter   59

 6 'The Banjo'   83

 7 The Old Billy Boiling   107

 8 Warrnambool to Winton   129

 9 Australia for the Australians   143

10 The Fight Begins   165

11 The Burning of the *Rodney*   181

12 Dagworth Burns   199

13 The Cover-Up   211

14 Christina's Tune   223

15 The Love Affair   231

16 The 'Jolly Swagman' Song   245

17 And His Ghost May Be Heard   259

Bibliography   276
Notes   279
Index   288

Preface

THE BATTLE OF MUAR was the last major battle in the Malayan campaign in 1942. During the vicious fighting on 20 January the Australian soldiers of 2/29th were fighting near Parit Sulong along the Muar Road. Japanese soldiers with six heavy machine-guns had pinned down 'C' Company of the 2/19th, who were under intense attack, with mounting dead and wounded. Lieutenant William Picken Carr led a forward attack through a swamp with a platoon from the 2/29th and reached a point within sixty yards of the machine-guns. Under orders to divert gunfire from the 2/19th, who were being slaughtered, they were ordered to charge—the attack was impossible. Carr and his men rose as one and charged the enemy guns, all singing 'Waltzing Matilda'. They were mown down.

This made a lasting impression on the Japanese soldiers, who would many times speak of the Australian soldiers who had advanced singing an Australian song, and had gone to certain death.

On an honour board erected by the Japanese commemorating the Imperial citation, which their 5th Division received for their part in the Muar Road battle, they were commended for completely wiping out a force of well over two thousand men. The honour board was erected at the place where Lieutenant Carr and his men from the 2/29th charged, singing 'Waltzing Matilda'.

1

Australia's Song for the World

WHEREVER THERE ARE AUSTRALIANS, it seems 'Waltzing Matilda' is there. In fact, it seems 'Waltzing Matilda' has always been there. It holds a unique place in our culture. Quite simply, it is part of Australia and part of being Australian.

Our famous folk song has found its way from the remote Queensland plains to every corner of the earth, and the swagman, or 'jolly swagman' as he is now known, has become a symbol of the Australian identity.

Today, Australians live in a global society, where songs are as expendable as cars, television sets, mobile phones and computers. Yet 'Waltzing Matilda', after one hundred and fifteen years, continues to capture the imagination, not only of Australians, but of people throughout the whole world.

'Waltzing Matilda' is truly one of the greatest folk songs ever written and is widely recognised around the world as 'the Australian song', sometimes better known than the national anthem. Like 'La Marseillaise' for the French, 'Danny Boy' and 'Amhrán na bhFiann' for the Irish, 'Flower of Scotland' or 'Loch Lomond' for the Scots, 'Land of Hope and Glory' for the English, or 'The Star-Spangled Banner' and 'This Land is Your Land' for the Americans, 'Waltzing Matilda' is synonymous with the country itself and embodies the spirit of the people. It is 'the people's song'.

'Waltzing Matilda' was performed at the closing ceremony of the 2000 Olympic Games in Sydney and at the opening ceremony of the 1982 Commonwealth Games in Brisbane, and was played as Australia's official song for the Montreal Olympics in 1976. It is the anthem of Australia's rugby team and is performed at every AFL grand final. 'Waltzing Matilda' has marched Australians home from several wars, walked Prime Ministers into office, echoed around every schoolroom and been sung by Aussies at Earl's Court. It is played as the quick march of the 1st Battalion, Royal Australian Regiment, and is the official song of the US Army 1st Marine Division, commemorating the time the unit spent in Australia during World War II. And who could forget the Aussie sailors singing 'Waltzing Matilda' as they returned to dock after winning the America's Cup on *Australia II* in 1983? Today, the song is still preferred by many Australians to 'Advance Australia Fair', the current national anthem. When more than 2000 people trooped into an auditorium on the Via Conciliazione in Rome, it was sung as a tribute to Mary MacKillop. On the eve of her canonisation by Pope Benedict XVI in St Peter's Square, the ceremony finished with a triumphant rendition of 'Waltzing Matilda'—in Italian.

'Waltzing Matilda' has a place in almost every Australian heart, even though most Australians have no real idea what they are singing about. It is difficult to imagine Australia without 'Waltzing Matilda'. Granted, there are many great Australian songs. Who can deny the strong emotions of 'I Still Call Australia Home' or 'Tenterfield Saddler', both written by Peter Allen, or many great ballads penned by John Williamson, including 'True Blue' and 'Raining on the Rock'? The list goes on: 'Along the Road to Gundagai' to a land 'Down Under' where there's 'The Pub with No Beer'. But then, on a sweaty Saturday night in the local pub, you will hear many a call for 'Khe Sanh' or 'Working Class Man' as the greatest Australian songs ever written. But none of them can replace 'Waltzing Matilda', which has stood the test of time, and is by far the most recorded Australian song.

Although 'Waltzing Matilda' was born in January 1895 on a remote homestead in western Queensland, it never really gained popularity for another eight years, when in 1903 the Inglis Tea Company decided it wanted a catchy advertising jingle. The advertising gurus of the time decided to include the words and sheet music of 'Waltzing Matilda' in every packet of their tea. The promotion was apparently to convince the discerning tea-drinking public that they would be transformed into the same 'jolly' state as our legendary swagman camped by his billabong, who resided somewhere out in the Australian bush.

While it is difficult to gauge the popularity 'Waltzing Matilda' achieved throughout the country due to the Inglis 'Billy Tea' promotion, we do know that the song achieved enough acceptance to be sung by Australian diggers in the muddy trenches of the Western Front and the bloody trenches of Gallipoli. One can only imagine the pride of the author, Andrew Barton 'Banjo' Paterson, while attending an army staging camp at Randwick Racecourse at the beginning of World War I, when the parading troops began to sing 'Waltzing Matilda'. He wryly commented to Sir Daryl Lindsay, 'Well Daryl, I only got a fiver for the song, but it's worth a million to me to hear it sung like this.'[1]

The song was first recorded in 1927, thirty-two years after it was written. However, it was not until 1938 that 'Waltzing Matilda' achieved any real international recognition, when Peter Dawson's recorded version was played on radio all around the world. Again the Australian soldiers would continue to sing the song on all fronts during World War II.

Over the next seven decades, 'Waltzing Matilda' would be recorded by thousands of artists throughout the world, in countless different languages, making it one of the most recorded songs in history. There are more than 700 individual recordings in the National Film and Sound

Archive. The universal acceptance of the song on the public stage is further enhanced by performances in almost every different musical genre—from the country singing of the legendary Slim Dusty, the classic pop of Olivia Newton-John, the virtuoso guitar playing of Tommy Emmanuel and breathtaking operatic performances of Dame Nellie Melba, to name just a few. Recently recorded in Australia was the utterly delightful version 'Waltjim Bat Matilda', sung in Kriol by Ali (Arjibuk) Mills from Darwin. There has been a multitude of choral and orchestral arrangements, as well as versions by jazz musicians from solo pianists to Dixieland bands, accordion orchestras, children's entertainers, a Filipino rondalla orchestra, and it is inevitably sung in curious accents by every choir that visits Australia.[2]

'Waltzing Matilda' made its film debut in 1949 in *Once a Jolly Swagman*, starring Dirk Bogarde, and was then used for *On the Beach* in 1959. Since then the song has been used in countless Australian productions and is currently touring the world as part of the score in the 2008 Baz Luhrmann film *Australia*.

Today, 'Waltzing Matilda' is not our song alone, with many international artists claiming it as theirs too, from masculine Welsh choirs to trendy Rod Stewart and the gravel voice of Tom Waits fitting the phrase into 'Tom Traubert's Blues'. Even Chubby Checker recorded a version of our song when the twist craze took over the world between 1960 and 1962. I will never forget the exhilaration I experienced in 2007 when the best-selling Universal artist, violinist André Rieu, backed by 100 Scottish pipers, played 'Waltzing Matilda'. I, along with 30,000 Melburnians, stood, applauded and sang every word.

Unfortunately, the song's international acclaim has caused one problem for Australians. The song was copyrighted by an American publisher, Carl Fischer Music, in 1941. Although no copyright applies in Australia, the Australian Government had to pay royalties to Carl Fischer Music when the song was played at the 1996 Summer Olympics held in Atlanta. Research in recent times, however, has cast doubt on the claim of Carl Fischer Music to have the original composition rights to 'Waltzing Matilda'.

The controversy over the rights to 'Waltzing Matilda' is just one of the many mysteries of the absorbing history of our national song.

Although 'Waltzing Matilda' was written 115 years ago, debate still rages about its origins, and why Banjo Paterson wrote it. Many historians and authors have written about 'Waltzing Matilda'. Some writers like Peter Forrest believe 'the wonderful thing about Waltzing Matilda is that its words have no real meaning',[3] while historian Dr Jonathan King, during the centenary celebrations at Winton in 1994, claimed Waltzing Matilda was a 'harmless ditty'.[4] On the surface it appears to be a happy-go-lucky song about a jolly swagman, a petty thief who gets caught stealing a sheep and would rather jump into a billabong and drown than be taken alive. Many people have no idea what the idiom 'waltzing matilda' really means; most think it has something to do with a dance, but none of this really seems to matter. The song just sounds good and as Australians, we relate to it—it brings out the larrikin in us all.

Embodied mythically is a cultural connection that could only be Australian. 'Waltzing Matilda' could never have attained such universal acceptance if it had been a 'harmless ditty'. To believe this is to undermine the character and literary genius of Australia's most loved poet, Banjo Paterson.

'Waltzing Matilda' has proven its bona fides. No-one can really identify the secret ingredients, or set out purposefully to write a song that will come to represent the spirit of a nation. These great songs seemingly write themselves, and are absorbed into the culture as belonging to the people. 'Waltzing Matilda' is one of these great songs. It belongs to us. There is no other nation that sings of such strange things as swagmen, squatters, jumbucks, billabongs and 'waltzing matilda'.

On 6 April 1995, at the centenary celebration for the first public singing of 'Waltzing Matilda' in Winton, the then Prime Minister Paul Keating commented:

> I suspect there is no one here who has not at some time, somewhere in the world, heard or remembered the tune and felt deeply affected by it. I'm sure it had brought Australians home before they intended to, and given others the strength to stay away a bit longer. For a century it has caused Australian hearts to beat faster. I venture to say it has caused more smiles and tears, and more hairs to stand

up on the backs of Australian necks than any other thing of three minutes' duration in Australian history. It has long been our unofficial national song. Not our anthem—one can't sing too solemnly about a jumbuck. But 'Waltzing Matilda' is Australia's song and it always will be . . .

But what does this strange phrase 'waltzing matilda' really mean?

There is little doubt the origins are German, and that the idiom came across to Australia with German settlers, in one form or another. But it truly found favour with the swagmen-shearers of the outback.

'Waltzing' is derived from the German term *auf der Walz*, meaning 'on the tramp'. In Germany, apprentices in various trades or crafts were required to spend an allotted period travelling around the country, or even outside Germany, gaining experience and new techniques for their trade. They were *auf der Walz*, taking only what they could carry in a roll or swag: their tools, a change of clothes and any bare necessities. During this period, the apprentice gained employment with master craftsmen in various towns, earning his living as he went, sleeping where he could. The traditional *Walz* of the journeyman (itinerant tradesman) lasted at least three years and one day, and he never stayed in any one place for more than three months.

The apprentice was required to carry a special book, a *Handwerksbuch*, in which each master who employed him had to enter the particulars of the work he learnt, its duration and his conduct. After completing his allotted time 'on the tramp' the apprentice could return to his village and practise his trade. All this was part of the guild system for apprentice tradesmen, and was not done away with officially until about 1911. The revival of the custom in Germany through newly established journeyman guilds or brotherhoods during the 1980s admitted women for the first time, and increasing numbers of journeymen are *auf der Walz* again.

The name 'Matilda' also has a Teutonic origin, meaning 'Mighty Battle Maiden'. Over the years the name was given to the female camp followers who accompanied the soldiers in a brutal European religious conflict, the reformation (1618–1648), also known as the Thirty Years' War, which was fought mostly in present-day Germany.

These 'Matildas' would sleep with the soldiers and keep them warm at night. Because of the warmth the Matildas provided the name was then used to describe the grey army coats that the soldiers wore or carried with them. In Australia, the name was given by the workers in the bush to the 'swag' or blanket that they carried, usually over the shoulder, to keep them warm at night.

In the Australian vernacular, then, 'waltzing matilda' means to go walkabout, looking for a job, with your tools of trade and whatever keeps you warm at night. What a wonderful expression!

Many thousands of German settlers came to Australia in the mid-1800s, settling by the River Torrens and around the Barossa Valley area; by the 1850s as many as 6000

German-born people were on the Victorian goldfields. By 1880 there were very tight-knit German settlements along the Murray River and northwards into New South Wales, to Henty and Temora and eastwards to Cooma. In 1885, 1000 Germans had settled in the Moreton Bay district; their numbers reached 14,000 by 1891. Other settlements in Queensland were at Maryborough, Wide Bay, Bundaberg, Rockhampton, Mackay, Townsville and Kennedy.

A large proportion of the Germans on the goldfields had come out independently of the community migration, hoping to win a fortune from gold. Others were working-class refugees who came to escape the political upheavals of the 1848 European revolutionary movements. It is possible to assume that a number of the young men among them were still *auf der Walz*, and would have sacrificed their apprenticeships to come to Australia. If this were so, they could have described themselves as still being *auf der Walz* in Australia, or at least used that expression to describe their involvement in the 'rushes' from one goldfield to another.

During World War I, many good citizens of the Australian Germanic population were interned for the duration of the war, for fear of an attack from within. Although some German-named towns still exist, such as Hahndorf in the Adelaide Hills, most Germanic town names were wiped from all Australian maps. Fortunately, the phrase 'waltzing matilda' had already been printed in the *Bulletin* newspaper, and was sufficiently well known in the outback for Banjo Paterson to recognise its 'Australian' meaning and appreciate the wonderful poetic nature of the expression. Otherwise, like most aspects of early German history in Australia, 'waltzing matilda' may have been lost forever.

Luckily, by the time of World War I, 'Waltzing Matilda' had achieved renown as an Australian song. It is doubtful that the Australian soldiers at Gallipoli and on the Western Front would have sung and marched to 'Waltzing Matilda' with such gusto, pride and ownership if they had known it was a German phrase.

Now, more than a hundred years after 'Waltzing Matilda' was written, we are uncovering the events that surrounded and influenced the writing of our national song. Some aspects regarding the creation of the song will always remain contentious. However, what we do know is that without the volatile and turbulent 1894 shearers' strike, a mysterious love affair and a series of coincidental events, in places as far distant as the lush green countryside of western Victoria and the unforgiving and barren plains of north-western Queensland, there would be no 'Waltzing Matilda'.

The *Bulletin*—the 'Bushman's Bible'—born of a burgeoning nationalistic fervour.
(Christmas edition, 1891, State Library of New South Wales)

2

The Backdrop for
a Song

THE ORIGINAL VERSION of 'Waltzing Matilda' was written by Andrew Barton 'Banjo' Paterson to a tune played to him by Christina Macpherson, during January 1895, at Dagworth Station in western Queensland. The tune Christina played was 'The Craigielee March', which was a variant of the Scottish song 'Thou Bonnie Wood of Craigielea'.

Over the last century many people have alluded to Banjo Paterson's love affair with Christina Macpherson at the time he wrote 'Waltzing Matilda'. But this was not the only factor in the creation of Australia's unofficial national anthem.

'Waltzing Matilda' has two clearly defined parts, a chorus and verses, encompassing two very different stories and emotions. Both parts of the song were a carefree response by Banjo Paterson to much deeper, more complicated events surrounding his life at the time of writing.

And quite simply the chorus is undoubtedly a love song, inspired by Paterson's love affair with Christina Macpherson. Unfortunately for Banjo, his fiancée of eight years, Sarah Riley, Christina's friend, was also staying at Dagworth Station at the time. This affair ended in humiliation and embarrassment for all involved, leading Paterson to distance himself from the writing of 'Waltzing Matilda' and events at Dagworth Station. Perhaps tellingly, eight years after the song was written, the same year Banjo married his new lover, Alice Walker from Tenterfield, he sold the lyrics of 'Waltzing Matilda' for the meagre sum of £5 to the publisher Angus & Robertson. There is now speculation that he did this to hide the true story of the triangular love affair in which he was embroiled when the song was written. This decision further damaged the lives of the two women involved with him at the time, Christina Macpherson and Sarah Riley.

The verses are drawn from specific events that occurred during the 1894 shearers' strike, reflecting the serious conflict between the landowners and union shearers. In fact, without a series of violent and disturbing events that occurred during that particular strike, 'Waltzing Matilda' would never have been written. These events culminated in the alleged suicide of Samuel Hoffmeister (the swagman) beside the Four-Mile Billabong near Kynuna in western Queensland. But did Hoffmeister drown himself in the fabled billabong, or could the death of this Australian icon be one of the biggest cover-ups in Australian history? Does the truth remain with the coolibah trees, standing like sentinels, gently swaying and whispering guarded secrets across the silent waters of a remote billabong?

For more than a hundred years Australians have struggled with the perception that their cultural hero apparently committed suicide. This is at odds with the Australian legend. The legacy of the bushrangers and escaped convicts was an unwritten code—never be taken alive. It was better to die fighting than be captured. Now we have evidence that will cast new light on Paterson's immortal ballad.

With proper examination, the events leading up to and surrounding the writing of 'Waltzing Matilda' are significant to the development of Australia's political, social and cultural characteristics. Their articulation cannot fail to enhance the understanding of modern Australia and will excite the imagination of anyone exposed to them. All great folk songs are written about a significant time in a particular country's history. What would 'John Brown's Body' mean without the American Civil War? Who could appreciate the significance of 'Flower of Scotland' if not for the victory of the Scots, led by Robert the Bruce, over England's Edward II at the Battle of Bannockburn in 1314? The same can be said for 'Waltzing Matilda'; if not for the shearers' strike of 1894, there would be no 'Waltzing Matilda' for Australians to sing. So to fully understand this complex song, we must examine the people and events leading up to and surrounding its creation.

During the 1890s traces of a new Australian culture were emerging, building upon an already developed Australian character. An article in *Australian Essays* written during that time by the English critic Francis Adams noted that:

> In England the average man feels he is an inferior; in America he feels he is a superior; in Australia he feels he is an equal.[1]

While Australia at that time might not have achieved this moral equality, it wasn't a bad thing to try to achieve. Why not aim for the stars, even if you're more likely to hit the chimney pots? It's all about 'having a go', or in the case of 'Waltzing Matilda', 'having a fair go'.

During the second half of the nineteenth century, Australia experienced what might be termed a 'social avalanche', with thousands of people migrating to its shores. Although still predominantly Anglo-Irish in its make-up, Australia saw people from nations around the globe arriving in boats. This immature new country's composite history of compressed cultural and social diversity was really taking root. Australia was showing concern for the dilution of old-world class structures and tolerance for new immigrants.

This was a country extending the hand and offering freedom of speech, freedom to practise one's own religion and freedom to be proud of the country whence they came.

At the same time it was offering the chance to claim a new home, and the exhilarating opportunity to make a contribution to that home.

This did not occur overnight or by accident, and it certainly wasn't achieved without some regrettable mistakes and pain along the way, but disparate groups of people were becoming Australian—those who came here in chains, who were lashed while they worked in convict gangs at Port Arthur; those who like many others were driven by starvation or oppression from their homelands to the shores of this new country, Australia. In general, they decided not to harbour grudges or discontent but rather to look to the future. They embraced this country as their own and said, 'Let's get on with it, this is a new land and this is our home.'

One of the main factors unifying this burgeoning nationalistic fervour during the 1890s was the *Bulletin* newspaper, known as the 'Bushman's Bible'. The country was still clouded by the bank crashes of the early 1890s and crippled by the searing drought out on the western plains of Queensland and New South Wales.

The *Bulletin* achieved huge popularity and circulation. In a way, it was not only the voice of Australians, but was actually written by its own readers. Contributions came from small settlements scattered all over the interior, mining camps and shearing sheds. These were the people who were giving Australian life a distinctive character. In contrast, only a few years earlier the *Bulletin* had been more concerned with the experiences of some fictitious, adventurous, noble Englishman on a stereotypical western station, impressing the squatter's daughter with his manners, sophistication and dazzling feats of daring. Eventually captivated by her natural charm and homeliness, and her skill in horsemanship and kangaroo hunting, he offers his hand in marriage.

The newspaper announced that it stood for a republican type of government; for payment for members of parliament; for one person, one vote; for the complete secularisation of education; for reform of the criminal code and prison system; and for a united Australia and protection against the outside world. Readers were excited by the prospect of dispelling the old-world ills, looking backwards no more, but looking forward to new horizons. The *Bulletin* may not have been responsible for igniting nationalistic fervour, but it can be seen as throwing petrol onto the fire, fanning a hotter, brighter flame that had been burning since Peter Lalor raised the Eureka flag on Bakery Hill in 1854. The miners on the goldfields around Ballarat in central Victoria had united against the government's oppressive licence tax, and although they were defeated, their fight for social reform had been given a public platform:

> We swear by the Southern Cross to stand truly by each other,
> And fight to defend our rights and liberties.
> The bloody licence tax made diggers unite,
> And under one flag the miners did fight.
> Twenty-nine men died on that fateful day,
> While the ashes of the licence tax were blowing away,

Rise up and fight, sons of liberty,
Rise up and fight for this land to be free.[2]

The 'Bushman's Bible' gave the country a reality and unifi-
cation its people had been without, drawing into its pages
all who had something to say about their work or life. They
came from all walks of life—the shearer, the swagman, the
miner, the government official, the engineer—and they were
allowed to speak in their own voices. The paper was their
forum and the nation listened.

Now the nationalistic fervour was being fuelled by poets
like Banjo Paterson, Henry Lawson, Barcroft Boake, Harry
'The Breaker' Morant, John Farrell, Harry Siebell and Alex
Montgomery, to name a few. A lot of stories and poems
from this period were never signed. Some writers signed
only with pen-names. The tradition of oral balladry and
story-telling was still alive. The bush people responded
with enthusiasm to the imaginative renderings of their daily
life. In little bush settlements, in shearing sheds and union
camps, the audience was growing. An army of potential
contributors was emerging.

The oral tradition had done its work, keeping alive the
stories that were quickly put into rhyme and told around
campfires and in the shanties. The noble qualities of the
Australian legend—mateship, courage and loyalty—were
now being recorded in print. The characters in real
Australian life, which everyone knew existed, were now
given much wider circulation.

What better example of our blossoming nationalism than from Australia's greatest military commander, General Sir John Monash? His father, Louis, was of Jewish ancestry and had been forced to leave Prussia (now Poland) in 1853. Louis read of the goldrushes on the other side of the world, somewhere in a distant land called Australia. Like countless other immigrants, he decided to come to Australia for a few years, make his fortune and then return home. But like so many other immigrants, he would never go back. In 1882, as a young boy of seventeen, Louis's Australian-born son John, like so many young Australians, was already feeling a new sense of nationalism. Although Germany had reunited during 1871, John Monash realised that although he was connected culturally to Germany, politically, socially and morally he was an Australian. He wrote in a letter to his cousin Leo Monash:

> To what country and people do I owe most? To that which I have never seen, with which I have no connection, but that it is the home of some of my relatives? Or to that in which and among whom I was born, have grown up, where I have learned all that I know, to which I owe all happiness that I have experienced? Shall I, in return for this, look upon it as a foreign land, to be deserted at the first convenient opportunity? No, it is my native land; and I have contracted from it a heavy debt, and it will ever be to me a prominent object, in some measure to repay that debt.[3]

This sense of nationalism had been growing for some decades now. While Australia was still predominantly British both in its government and property ownership, new immigrants were bringing with them different cultures and new ideas. Pools of new immigrants, mainly from Europe, followed in the wake of the convict system to join the time-expired and ticket-of-leave men as a source of cheap labour. As the 1890s approached, lurking in the background was a new, sinister political and social theory called 'unionism', and it was gaining momentum.

Stories from Pennsylvania, America, of workers going on strike for better wages and conditions struck a chord with many Australian workers suffering appalling conditions. Most shearers, station hands, seamen and drovers were not entitled to vote. The law in Australia required six months' permanent residence before enrolling on the electoral register, which was not possible for the great numbers of itinerant workers, the swagmen, working away from home and continually on the move. Lacking faith in the political system, the bush workers set about trying to establish a voice for themselves through this new type of organisation, called trade unions.

The squatter pastoralists were becoming increasingly anxious and spiteful regarding the development of this relatively new movement. Following the maritime strike of the late 1880s in Britain, which involved not only seamen but also waterside workers, carters and coalminers, they feared such an organised workforce. When the English workers were almost defeated by starvation, the Australian union movement came to the rescue with a gift of £30,000. The spirit of this gesture can only be measured by the fact that less than £50,000 was raised from all other sources worldwide. At the end of the strike, in recognition of the generosity and solidarity of the Australian workers, the Brits held their victory demonstration by marching to London's Hyde Park beneath an Australian flag.

Unionism spread through the Australian outback like a bushfire. The swagmen who walked hundreds of miles in the Australian outback, unable to vote, found comfort and strength in the mateship and loyalty of the union. Confronted by wealthy pastoralists, who were backed by the government and the military, they began the great shearers' strikes of the 1890s. During 1891, battalions of soldiers armed with Gatling guns were dispatched to western Queensland to confront the workers.

The attack on the labour organisations of Queensland in 1891 was but a part of the employers' great scheme to eradicate unionism. The shearers had made no new or unreasonable demands. The squatters had cut wages and were insisting on 'freedom of contract'. Shearers and shed hands had no alternative but to go on strike. Then the worst drought in Australian history set in—small farmers became destitute. The squatters felt their self-assured dignity as well as their profits being threatened by the unionists.

During those years, most of eastern Australia was all but in the grip of a civil insurrection. Photographs taken during that time in western Queensland, of regiments of armed and mounted troopers ferrying non-unionists to the shearing sheds, are a stark reminder of the division between squatters and the shearers, which almost escalated into civil war. This was a vastly different Australia.

This is the world Banjo Paterson found himself in, and like every writer worth his salt in Australia he could not have been unaffected by the oppression of the working class, or the unequal distribution of the nation's wealth, with great proportions of the profit from the wool-clip going back to England. Absentee landlords collected the profits from land they had never seen and sheep they had never shorn.

During 1894, Australia was in the grip of another recession. The squatters moved to maintain their profits in the face of falling overseas wool prices and a prolonged drought. The mechanism was to invoke a new unilateral 'agreement'. This 'agreement' held a most objectionable clause (Clause 8), which placed the sheds under the unequivocal control of the owner or shed boss. Any shearer refusing to shear wet sheep or carry out duties as directed would be in breach of the agreement and would thus be liable to criminal prosecution.

The pastoralists also proposed to cut the machine-shearing rate by 12.5 per cent, and insisted on using non-union labourers. Given the incompetence of most 'scabs', this was a provocation rather than a serious attempt to complete the shearing. The shearers refused to accept the new terms and the pastoralists would not submit their case to arbitration, so a fresh strike developed.

Banjo Paterson was living in Sydney during 1894 and, like many other people in capital cities along the east coast of Australia, may have thought the shearers' strike in the back-country was verging on civil war. Thousands of shearers formed large strike camps at rail-heads and river ports throughout western New South Wales and western Queensland. Sydney newspapers were awash with headlines of violence and arson occurring daily. The strike reached boiling point when events such as the burning of the paddle steamer *Rodney*, the shooting of union shearer Billy McLean, the burning of the Dagworth shearing shed and the death of unionist Samuel Hoffmeister, among numerous other violent occurrences, attracted national attention in city newspapers. It is difficult, in our modern world of 'processed' communications, to understand just how imaginations and emotions throughout the colonies were so stirred by this series of local events.

The union shearers were resolved to gain better conditions and a foothold in parliament, while the squatters were determined to maintain their profits in the face of falling wool prices and a prolonged drought. Into this class war strode Banjo Paterson, Australia's most loved poet. It was against this backdrop of violence and social and political upheaval that Banjo was confronted by the beautiful young

Christina Macpherson, who played for him the wonderful old Scottish tune 'Thou Bonnie Wood of Craigielea'. Banjo was moved, not only by the tune, but also by the player.

Stirred by his feelings for Christina, while his fiancée of eight years, Sarah Riley, was present in the same house, and surrounded by the upheaval of the 1894 shearers' strike, Banjo Paterson wrote 'Waltzing Matilda'.

In 1905, Paterson published *Old Bush Songs*, containing some fifty ballads, most of which would now have been lost but for him.

3

Clancy and the Man from Snowy River

In *THE LEGEND OF THE NINETIES,* Vance Palmer writes about myth-making, arguing that people cannot feel at home in any environment until they have transformed the natural surroundings with myth, creating heroes and sacred places. Myths are an important means of communication, bringing people together. They give isolated communities something in common. Many of the myths and heroes of the Aboriginal world were lost as Indigenous cultures were suppressed and destroyed, and so were never transformed or accepted by Australia's new inhabitants.

Mythology is born from the original urge towards the creation of art, without which the imagination and soul would starve. Myths are usually infused with a supernatural flavour, although this may be too pretentious a description for our early settlers who began to adapt themselves imaginatively to their new country.[1]

During the 1880s, Australia was a disparate bunch of colonies with no unifying hero and no national voice. The colonies' newspapers were also distinct—until the *Bulletin*, which became the first truly national newspaper. These days, it's difficult to imagine a journal's readers thirsting for the next edition to read the latest poems, but such was the lust for local stories and literature. Paterson's literary philosophy to 'take life as a high adventure, even if it risks a broken neck' found a national stage through the pages of the *Bulletin*. He was depicting a truly Australian character that existed in the bush people—the shearers, drovers and the like. Paterson didn't create the legend; he was merely reinforcing it, injecting momentum, taking a provincial ethos and airing it nationally.[2]

In 1889, when the *Bulletin* published Paterson's poem 'Clancy of the Overflow', the first Australian literary hero was born. Apart from the heroes of the Eureka Stockade, the only legendary figure in Australian culture was the famous bushranger Ned Kelly.

Paterson, then a solicitor, was tiring of being cooped up in his dingy little office, where a stingy ray of sunlight struggled feebly down between the houses tall. In place of lowing cattle he could hear the fiendish rattle of trams and buses hurrying down the street. He could hear language uninviting of gutter children fighting, coming fitfully and faintly through the ceaseless tramp of feet.[3] The foetid air was gritty in the dusty dirty city, so Paterson poured his

heart out about wanting to be back in the bush, to the
heroes he'd imagined as a boy.

> In my wild erratic fancy visions come to me of Clancy
> Gone a-droving 'down the Cooper' where the Western
>   drovers go;
> As the stock are slowly stringing, Clancy rides behind
>   them singing,
> For the drover's life has pleasures that the townsfolk
>   never know.
>
> And the bush hath friends to meet him, and their kindly
>   voices greet him
> In the murmur of the breezes and the river on its bars,
> And he sees the vision splendid of the sunlit plains extended,
> And at night the wond'rous glory of the everlasting stars.[4]

Although not truly mythical, Clancy achieved legendary status
almost overnight. He embodied a life that city dwellers could
only aspire to. And Paterson, too, took the fancy that he'd like
to change with Clancy and 'take a turn at droving where the
seasons come and go'. But there was no way Clancy in turn
would swap and live in the city, not 'Clancy of the Overflow'.

So a folk legend was born. Paterson had established the
bushman as a romantic and archetypal figure. Then and
now, Clancy is the nearest thing to a 'noble frontiersman'
that we will ever have. But Banjo wasn't finished. In a
stroke of brilliance, less than six months later he would
give Australia two more legends when he wrote 'The Man
from Snowy River'.

One of the most character-defining moments in Australian history was when Paterson's mostly fictitious hardy little mountain pony reached the mountain summit and the man from Snowy River let him have his head. Even 'Clancy', Australia's first superhero, who had been away droving down the Cooper, couldn't hold the horses down that treacherous mountain descent. Clancy had hurried back to the station when the word had gone around that the colt from old Regret had got away, and all the cracks had gathered to the fray[5]:

> All the tried and noted riders from the stations near and far
> Had mustered at the homestead overnight,
> For the bushmen love hard riding where the wild bush
>   horses are,
> And the stock-horse snuffs the battle with delight.
>
> There was Harrison, who made his pile when Pardon
>   won the cup,
> The old man with his hair as white as snow;
> But few could ride beside him when his blood was fairly up—
> He would go wherever horse and man could go.
> And Clancy of the Overflow came down to lend a hand,
> No better horseman ever held the reins;
> For never horse could throw him while the saddle-girths
>   would stand,
> He learnt to ride while driving on the plains.[6]

Chasing wild bush horses is a dangerous and difficult job. There is no point in a young man on a small, weedy beast wanting to go, no matter how sad and wistful he may be. The 'old man' Harrison knew the horse would never stay, and told the young rider, 'For a long and tiring gallop, lad, you'd better stop away, those hills are far too rough, for such as you!'

But Clancy—considered the best rider—had seen a lot of horsemen in his wanderings, and knew that the Snowy River riders were at home in the mountains. He also knew the horse was tough—the sort that won't say die:

> There was courage in his quick impatient tread;
> And he bore the badge of gameness in his bright and fiery eye,
> And the proud and lofty carriage of his head.

Any horse and rider up by Kosciusko's side, where horses' hooves strike firelight on the flint stones every stride, was good enough for him. Only Clancy could defy the old man, and he confronted him. 'I think we ought to let them come,' he said, 'I reckon they'll be with us if they're needed at the end, for both his horse and he are mountain bred.'

So they went . . .

The wild horses were resting in the bush by a big mimosa clump when they were found, and they raced away towards the mountain's brow. The old man gave his orders to go at them from the jump—no use to try for fancy riding now.

> So Clancy rode to wheel them—he was racing on the wing
> Where the best and boldest riders take their place,
> And he raced his stock-horse past them, and he made the
>   ranges ring

With the stockwhip, as he met them face to face.
Then they halted for a moment, while he swung the
  dreaded lash,
But they saw their well-loved mountain full in view,
And they charged beneath the stockwhip with a sharp and
  sudden dash,
And off into the mountain scrub they flew.

Then fast the horsemen followed, where the gorges deep
  and black
Resounded to the thunder of their tread,
And the stockwhips woke the echoes, and they fiercely
  answered back
From cliffs and crags that beetled overhead.
And upward, ever upward, the wild horses held their way,
Where mountain ash and kurrajong grew wide;
And the old man muttered fiercely, 'We may bid the mob
  good day,
'*No* man can hold them down the other side.'[7]

And there on top of that mountain Clancy reined in his
horse; neither he nor the other crack riders would chase
those wild horses any further. The treacherous mountain
descent was thick with scrub, the ground full of hidden
wombat holes, and any slip would mean death. But the man
from Snowy River let the pony have his head, swung his
stockwhip round and gave a cheer, then raced him down
the mountain and into immortality.

There and then, a defining element was cemented into
the Australian character: a win for the underdog—the

'little bloke' can do it! It was justification for an audience throughout Australia that knew and understood what Paterson was writing about. Two or three generations of Australians had already believed that life in Australia could be made better than anywhere else in the world. This was a new country, an opportunity to forge a new society.

This feeling of empowerment, hope and belief was thrust upon future generations of Australians. Today this belief contributes to Australia's reputation as a sports-mad nation. Performing way above expectations on the world stage has created a distinct national identity. Victorious sports people often become national heroes and some, such as cricketer Donald Bradman, have become revered as Australian icons. Sport gives weight to well-loved national values like 'mateship', 'having a go' and egalitarianism. Australians also revel in the expression of 'fair play' on the sporting field—hence, cheats are often chastised for being 'un-Australian'.

'Hard and tough and wiry—just the sort that won't say die' could well have been written to describe the diggers who fought on the shores of Gallipoli, at the Western Front and Pozières, Ypres, the Somme, Tobruk, El Alamein and Villers-Bretonneux, where still today the slogan above the schoolyard reads, 'Never Forget Australia'.

There, on top of the mountain, our established hero Clancy believed it was impossible for any horse and rider to chase the wild horses down the other side. Not even Clancy himself could. But when the young rider on his mountain pony did just that, 'like a torrent down its bed', they both attained legendary status. In an astonishing piece of writing, Banjo had re-introduced Clancy, and then used his defeat to establish two more Australian legends. Only Clancy could be the one to be defeated by the Man from Snowy River and his hardy mountain pony:

> He sent the flint stones flying, but the pony kept his feet,
> He cleared the fallen timber in his stride,
> And the man from Snowy River never shifted in his seat—
> It was grand to see that mountain horseman ride.
> Through the stringy barks and saplings, on the rough and
>   broken ground,
> Down the hillside at a racing pace he went;
> And he never drew the bridle till he landed safe and sound,
> At the bottom of that terrible descent.
>
> He was right among the horses as they climbed the further hill,
> And the watchers on the mountain standing mute,
> Saw him ply the stockwhip fiercely, he was right among
>   them still,
> As he raced across the clearing in pursuit.
> Then they lost him for a moment, where two mountain
>   gullies met
> In the ranges, but a final glimpse reveals
> On a dim and distant hillside the wild horses racing yet,
> With the man from Snowy River at their heels.
>
> And he ran them single-handed till their sides were white
>   with foam.
> He followed like a bloodhound on their track,

Till they halted cowed and beaten, then he turned their heads
    for home,
And alone and unassisted brought them back.
But his hardy mountain pony he could scarcely raise a trot,
He was blood from hip to shoulder from the spur;
But his pluck was still undaunted, and his courage fiery hot,
For never yet was mountain horse a cur.

And down by Kosciusko, where the pine-clad ridges raise
Their torn and rugged battlements on high,
Where the air is clear as crystal, and the white stars fairly blaze
At midnight in the cold and frosty sky,
And where around the Overflow the reedbeds sweep and sway
To the breezes, and the rolling plains are wide,
The man from Snowy River is a household word to-day,
And the stockmen tell the story of his ride.[8]

Within a few short years, Banjo Paterson would add another
two folk legends to the Australian cultural landscape.
'Waltzing Matilda' would ensure that the squatter and the
swagman would have an eternal place in Australian culture.
Symbolic figures, each represents one of two very different
classes that existed in Australian society.

To voice the sentiment of your country in a song which
then enters into the very psyche of the people is a claim
few writers in history can make. Paterson did more than
that. The three most popular pieces of Australian literature
are 'Waltzing Matilda', 'Clancy of the Overflow' and 'The
Man from Snowy River'. Countless Australians will recall
the names of these three pieces and their author before any

other Australian poem or poet. 'The Man from Snowy River' and 'Clancy of the Overflow' are deeply etched into Australian literary history, but 'Waltzing Matilda' has entered deep into the Australian character and will always remain Paterson's most popular work.

4

There Once Was a Swagman

THE SWAGMAN who inspired the writing of 'Waltzing Matilda' was a striking union shearer whose dead body was found beside a waterhole, but Paterson didn't simply stumble upon an isolated incident on a remote billabong in western Queensland. Paterson was using the term 'swagman' not only to describe an individual, but also to represent a whole class of Australians who were suffering oppression by the ruling squatter class. So, who were these swagmen who went 'waltzing matilda'?

The word 'swagman' is not found in the *Shorter Oxford English Dictionary on Historical Principles*, and the earliest recording of the word 'swag', in 1660, meant 'to move unsteadily with a swaying or lurching movement', to 'sway' or to 'swagger'. However by 1864, the English dictionary

recorded a different *Australian* meaning for the word 'swag'—
'The bundle of personal belongings carried by a traveller
in the bush, a tramp, or a miner'.[1] The *Australian Concise
Oxford Dictionary* is a little more precise and describes the
'swag' as 'the collection of possessions and daily necessaries
carried by one travelling, usually on foot, in the bush'. Also
in the Australian dictionary we find the word 'swagman',
with its short and concise meaning—'a person who carries
a swag, especially an itinerant worker'.[2] Swagman is an
Australian word. In Henry Lawson's article 'The Romance
of the Swag' he asserted that the Australian swag was the
easiest way in the world to carry a load, and later reflected
on the plight of some swagmen:

> The Australian swag was born of Australia and no other
> country—of the great lone land of magnificent distances
> and bright heat; the land of self reliance, and never-give-
> in, and help your mate . . . The land where a man out of
> employment might shoulder his swag in Adelaide and take
> the track, and years later walk into a hut on the Gulf,
> or never be heard of anymore, or a body be found in the
> bush and buried by the mounted police, or never found
> and never buried—what does it matter?[3]

Over the years the term 'swagman' (or tramp) became
synonymous with travelling bums, mostly because of the
depression in the 1930s, but during the 1890s it was simply
the name for the workers in the outback—men who walked
hundreds of miles through the bush looking for work.

A great many of our traditional songs sprang from this army of 'swaggies'; the shearing industry in particular contributed not only songs, but also much of the humour, wit and slang that is now so much a part of our Australian identity. *The Springtime It Brings on the Shearing* is a reflection of these itinerant workers travelling through the country when the shearing season begins, and, like clockwork, leaving at the same time every year.

> Oh, the springtime it brings on the shearing,
> And it's then you will see them in droves,
> To the west country stations all steering,
> A-seeking a job off the coves.
>
> With a ragged old swag on my shoulder,
> And a billy quart pot in my hand,
> I tell you we'll astonish the new chums,
> To see how we travel the land . . .
>
> Oh, and after the shearing is over
> And the wool season's all at an end,
> It is then you will see the flash shearers
> Making johnny-cakes round in the bend.[4]

These swagmen or bushmen, as a group, were recognised as 'practical men', not easily given to abstract speculation. Ideas they held in common were practical rules of conduct, with habitual modes of thought and action, springing directly from the conditions of their life and from traditions already formed as a response to their environment. This intangible bond among the bushmen, swagmen and itinerant workers, although not comparable to any traditional religion in any serious philosophical sense, would eventually be described as 'mateship'.[5]

Much has been written about Australian 'mateship', but what is it and where did it come from? What are some of its characteristics and attitudes to life, which seem to be uniquely Australian? While the peculiar mix of solidarity, disrespect for authority and laconic humour appeared at Gallipoli and on the battlefields of World War I, the Anzacs were merely enforcing an aspect of Australian culture that was already strongly felt throughout the nation.

The history of European Australians started from terrible beginnings. The first unhappy compulsory migrants were landed at Sydney Cove in 1788, where the Tank Stream meandered through the bush near what is now Bennelong Point, surrounded by strange bushland and animals. Many of them petty criminals, they were taken from the crowded, insane streets of London and deposited in a wilderness on the other side of the world. Most of them knew they would never see their homeland again.

From the beginning their entire existence was terrible and the discipline and punishment they suffered were awful. The first hanging was carried out just one month after they staggered ashore, when a convict named Thomas Barrett was executed for stealing food. Two days later, two other convicts were condemned to death; one, a man named Freeman, gained a reprieve at the foot of the gallows by agreeing to become the public flogger and executioner.

The colony was close to starvation by the time the Second Fleet arrived, in June 1790. Of the 983 male convicts that embarked from England, 273 died on the voyage out, while 244 landed sick, many of them dying soon afterwards. In a letter home to England, the Reverend Richard Johnson wrote:

> The landing of these people was truly affecting and shocking; great numbers not able to walk nor move hand or foot; such were slung over the ship side in the same manner as they would sling a cask, a box, or anything of that nature. Upon their being brought up to the open, some fainted, some died upon deck and others in the boat before they reached shore. When come on shore many were not able to walk, to stand or to stir themselves in the least, hence some were led by others. Some creeped upon their hands and knees and some were carried upon the backs of others.[6]

Those that made it ashore were crammed four to a tent, with one blanket to each tent, to lie upon the bare earth. The Reverend Johnson continued:

> When any of them were near dying and had something given them such as bread or any other necessaries the person next to him would snatch the bread etc. out of his hands and with an oath say he was going to die and therefore it would be of no service to him. No sooner would the breath be out of their bodies than others would strip them entirely naked. Instead of alleviating the distresses of each other, the weakest were sure to go to the wall.[7]

It is difficult to imagine that in appalling conditions, where humans were reduced to animals, eventually these people and their descendants would develop an ethic called mateship. One of the contributing factors was that many of the convicts were political prisoners, removed from their homelands for rebelling against the conditions under which they were made to live. Rather than seeking personal gain, they were concerned with social change and protesting against injustices within their communities. In this new country they continued their fight for freedom.

The first Scottish martyrs transported to New South Wales in 1794 were five men who supported the ideals of the French Revolution—liberty, equality and fraternity. Then, in 1797, there was a mutiny in several British naval bases. The mutineers rebelled against the sailors' poor food, poor pay and poor conditions, whereby they could be flogged for even minor offences. Some of the mutineers were hanged and fifteen of them were transported to New South Wales.

A group of sixty Welsh Chartists were transported from Monmouthshire to Van Diemen's Land in 1842. They had lobbied for a universal vote by ballot, a parliament that sat every year, and pay for their members of parliament. They drew up a charter of the changes they wanted to see in their political system. Their demands, which today would seem unexceptional, were considered revolutionary and dangerous by those who held a monopoly over power.

During the convict era, there were several rebellions in Ireland, especially in 1798, 1803, 1848 and 1867. The people of Ireland were agitating for political separation from Britain, and large numbers of political rebels were transported to Australia.

Perhaps the most marked of all convict traits among these people was a strong egalitarian sentiment of group solidarity and loyalty.[8] This was also the prime distinguishing mark of the swagman long before Henry Lawson and Banjo Paterson wrote about mateship in the 1890s.

This solidarity was born of the oral bond between convict groups. Oaths, especially secret oaths, were a form of binding contract during the nineteenth century. There could be no written contract for a secret society and no signatures for a secret oath. Sworn oaths were binding, not only between man and man, but also between man and God.

The Tolpuddle Martyrs were six men from the village of Tolpuddle in Dorset who were transported to Australia on the *Surrey* in 1834. They were sentenced for unlawfully administering oaths of loyalty to the Friendly Society of Agricultural Labourers, which they had established to fight the continuing reduction of their wages. This marked the beginning of trade unionism in England.

In Australia, this spirit of group solidarity can be seen in the Castle Hill rebellion, which was led by the United Irish Rebels of the 1798 revolt in Ireland. The rebels' catchcry was 'Death or liberty'. On 4 March 1804, soldiers were called in to crush the uprising of 300 Irish convicts at Castle Hill to the north of Parramatta in New South Wales. Fifteen Irishmen were killed and nine of the leaders were later hanged.

Before the Castle Hill uprising, a young Irish convict by
the name of Patrick Galvin was flogged to make him reveal
where the pikes for the rebellion were hidden. Protecting
his mates from hanging, his beautifully metaphorical
response to his brutal torture was: 'You may hang me
now, for you'll get no music out of my mouth to make
others dance on air!'[9]

Many other rebels, usually also members of secret
societies opposed to agrarian laws, were transported to
Australia. On the convict ship *Eliza*, which arrived in
Sydney in September 1832, there were twenty-six men
transported as 'Whiteboys'. Ten of these had been convicted
for taking 'unlawful oaths'. Also transported on the *Eliza*
was Francis MacNamara, who came to be known as 'Frank
the Poet'. MacNamara would write *A Convict's Tour to Hell*
on 23 October 1839:

> You prisoners of New South Wales,
> Who frequent watchhouses and gaols
> A story to you I will tell
> 'Tis of a convict's tour to hell. [10]

William Astley, who wrote under the name of Price
Warung, in *Tales of the Old Regime* describes an 'under-
ground' brotherhood, whose organisation centred around
the 'convict oath':

> The five agreed . . . and . . . took the Convict Oath. They
> chanted the eight verses, which began:

Hand to Hand,
On Earth, in Hell,
Sick or Well,
On Sea, on Land,
On the Square, Ever.

And ended—the intervening verses dare not be quoted—

Stiff or in Breath,
Lag or Free,
You and Me,
In Life, in Death,
On the Cross, Never.

They chanted them with crossed and re-crossed hands, and the foot of each pressed to the foot of another . . . The convict oath was a terrible thing; it was never broken without occasioning death to someone . . .[11]

The convict gangs and ticket-of-leave men developed their own internal rules to enhance their chances of survival. They had seen unscrupulous men from their own convict ranks recruited to become overseers, floggers and police. Men who were prepared to stand over their former mates were despised. So the gangs and ticket-of-leave men closed ranks against the outside world and developed their own secret laws and code of behaviour. These were ruthless and binding, because the greater majority supported them and were prepared to use violence against those of their fellows who infringed the code. They were hard and merciless men, made so by the system that chained them.

In one month alone in 1833 in New South Wales, which had a convict population of 28,000 men, some 2000 were convicted and given a total of 9000 lashes. The same month in Tasmania, where there were 15,000 convicts, 1250 convictions were made and 4250 lashes given.

It is small wonder that these men were ruthless themselves, and relentless in pursuit of their fellows who broke the unwritten, but generally understood, code that evolved among them. Their sole hope of survival lay in presenting a united front against a society that exploited their labour.

When these convicts had served their allotted time and gained their freedom, their former suffering could never be forgotten. They harboured a deep resentment and distrust of authority, especially uniformed authority, attitudes that they passed on to their children. The following transportation ballad, 'Jim Jones of Botany Bay', is typical of the lingering bitterness.

> Where night and day the irons clang, and like poor
>   galley-slaves,
> We toil and moil, and when we die we fill dishonoured
>   graves;
> But later on I'll break my chains, into the bush I'll go,
> And join the bold bushrangers there—Jack Donahue and Co.
>
> And some dark night when all around is quiet in the town,
> I'll kill the tyrants one and all, and shoot the floggers down.
> I'll give the law a little shock, remember what I say.
> They'll yet regret they sent Jim Jones in chains to
>   Botany Bay.[12]

There is little doubt this was the early manifestation of the solidarity that would surface upon the goldfields and, later, in the early days of trade unionism. It showed stubborn persever-ance, with a united front against force and a determined will for freedom. Little wonder that incidents like the stockade at Eureka and the burning of woolsheds and paddle steamers would unfold as the century progressed. The diggers at Eureka swore an oath to be true to the Southern Cross flag and to each other, as Victor Daley, another of the *Bulletin* poets of the 1890s, wrote in his powerful poem 'Eureka':

> On Bakery Hill the Banner,
> Of the Southern Cross flew free;
> Then up rose Peter Lalor;
> And with lifted hand spake he:
> We swear by God above us,
> While we live to work and fight,
> For Freedom and for Justice,
> For our Manhood and our Right.
>
> Then on the bare-earth kneeling,
> As on a chapel-floor,
> Beneath the sacred Banner,
> One and all, that oath we swore;
> And some of those who swore it,
> Were like straws upon a flood,
> But there were men who swore it,
> And who sealed it with their blood.[13]

Some took the oath casually, but not the Irish. Ireland was still an oath-bound society. Many of the Irish diggers died underneath the flag in a hopeless stand against armed police. Among the diggers at the Eureka stockade were members of the secret Whiteboy society. In Ireland the Whiteboys shaped a popular culture of protest, which evolved modes of organisation, techniques of direct action and, most importantly, a communal ambivalence towards the law and civil authority. The styles of protest action in Ireland that stretched from the 1798 uprising into the first half of the nineteenth century originated with the Whiteboys in Tipperary in 1761. The name derived from their practice of wearing coarse white linen over-shirts, and the movement grew out of local resistance to the enclosure of common land. Between 1761 and 1765, Whiteboys were active in the counties of Cork, Limerick, Tipperary, Kilkenny and Waterford, where five of them were hanged in 1762. The scale of the outbreak is indicated by the introduction of the Whiteboy Act in 1765. The key provision of the act made the administration of oaths by threat of violence a capital offence. This went to the heart of the problem. Oaths binding members to secrecy were the defining characteristic of Whiteboyism.

·

During the middle of the nineteenth century, this convict creed 'went bush' as numerous itinerant workers tramped around the outback looking for work. Initially, shearers were usually of convict origin and it is safe to say that a large proportion of the moving population was of the same class. For most of the year, large outback stations required only a minimum of workers to run the place. But at shearing time, large numbers of men were needed. This erratic demand for skilled workers was fulfilled by a strange breed of men. They developed various skills, living mostly off the land and becoming accomplished bushmen. They were nomadic, reticent and made their own entertainment everywhere they went.

Russel Ward in *The Australian Legend* describes the pride of the 'old hands', with their newly acquired mastery of the outback and the basic elements of their outlook, which later came to be thought of as typically Australian: 'a comradely independence based on group solidarity and relative economic plenty, a rough and ready capacity for "stringybark and greenhide" improvisation, a light-hearted intolerance of respectable and conventional manners, a reckless improvidence, and a conviction that the working bushman was the "true Australian"'. It was an ethos that sprang mainly from convict, working-class, Irish and native-born Australians.[14]

A century later, in 1959, Sidney Baker, a philologist and internationally recognised expert in linguistic psychology, attempted to define qualities of a distinctive Australian character. Many of these traits retain their validity today—as they did in the first sixty years of European occupation. They include:

1. A resentment against authority of all kinds, a dislike of regimentation and a tendency to lawlessness that is rarely violent.

2. A strong egalitarianism, primarily based on the loyalties of one man to another rather than of a man to an organization; as a direct corollary of this a totally unforgiving attitude toward 'rats', 'scabs' and betrayers in general.
3. An outlook that is largely unsentimental and not greatly given to self-pity.
4. Practicability, an imaginative flair for improvisation, willingness to work extremely hard and to co-operate in any undertaking provided the co-operator can thereby retain his independent self-respect.
5. A well-developed capacity to withstand hardship.
6. A bitter dislike for affectations, especially affectations of accent, since the Australian entirely rejects any idea that refinement of speech implies intellectual stature.
7. A great willingness to take a chance—to gamble.
8. Strong resistance to any type of social hysteria, especially verbal hysteria; a determination to make up his own mind.
9. A distrust of extravagant claims by advertisers or political parties.[15]

Mateship among shearers was not just an idea but often a necessity. 'Pen mates', two shearers who would have to catch sheep from the same pen, were required to work together; even if the men were hostile towards each other, their mateship was compulsory. In the blade-shearing days, the 'keeping' (or sharpening) of shears was vital for the shearers' work. It was necessary to have a mate turn the grindstone. Each pair turned for one another—they were 'grinding mates'. 'Travelling mates' were those who, thrown together by chance, went the same way together, camped together and when tucker was scarce, 'cadged' together. Begging was a distasteful task but often had to be done. Some travellers shirked their share but were quite willing to partake of the results when a more hardened mate had done the cadging for them—but they would soon learn.

The life of a shepherd was particularly arduous. Shepherds habitually lived alone for months or even years, the only company being that of their dog and the occasional visit from the supply wagon. To prevent scurvy, they added the local weeds and grasses to the meals they cooked. Shepherds lived in a bark or slab hut, tended their sheep during the day, penned them each night and protected the flock from marauding dingoes and Aboriginal hunters.

Shearing was a nomadic occupation. For much of the year these swagmen were away from their families and lived in spartan conditions in earth-floored huts with minimal sanitation, and on monotonous subsistence rations. They were at the whim of the station owner. Some rations could be purchased from the station store at inflated prices. Conditions were sometimes so overcrowded and insanitary as to be almost unlivable. W. G. Spence, of the Australian Workers' Union, wrote:

> The accommodation for the workers at shearing was something quite awful. Mostly it was unfit to put human beings into, and consisted of long, draughty buildings

without windows, the timber often being so open that you could put your arm through. Two and often three tiers of bunks, one above the other, would be ranged all round the walls of a narrow hut. The table at which the men ate their meals ran down the centre. The cooking was done in a huge fireplace at one end, with the oven at its side. When the cook wanted to grill chops he spread coals on the earthen floor in front of the fireplace and laid his gridiron—a frame about three feet square—on the coals, the smell of burning fat filling the hut where men had to dress and undress, eat and sleep, all in one room. They were only a bare six feet in length overall, and as Australians are mostly tall men . . . the closeness of your neighbour's feet to your nose can be pictured.[16]

The shearers were a large, migratory workforce and walked from station to station. This 'nomadic tribe', enshrined in the literature of the time, embodied the distinctive characteristics of the Australian—drinking, swearing, hard-working and resourceful mates. 'To get the sack', a term commonly used today for termination of employment, meant that work had finished and the worker was given a sack of provisions to put in his swag, containing a roll of corned beef and some flour to get him to the next shearing shed.

The outer coating of the swag was usually a blue blanket, hence the term 'humpin' bluey'. Inside were the odds and ends the swagman required. It was rolled lengthways and folded over in a horse-collar shape, and the ends were tied with rope or greenhide. This was then looped over the head and one arm, with the weight of the 'matilda' or 'bluey' taken on the shoulder. The swaggie's waterbag often dangled from the swag's end, giving rise to the term 'leading a waterbag'. The swaggie with his blanket roll and billy became a familiar figure tramping in the Australian outback.

> Picture to yourself a muscular, low-set man walking along at a moderate pace. In one hand he holds a tin 'billy', black with constant boiling of tea; in the other, the water-bag full of precious fluid, while across the back of his shoulders, soldiers'-knapsack-fashion, is strapped a neat but apparently heavy bundle of round, oblong shape, showing only a white calico covering outside. This is the tent; and inside rolled up in a pair of blankets, red or blue, are—what he will most likely tell you with a grim smile—his 'forty years' gatherings', consisting of, perhaps, a couple of shirts, ditto trousers, comb, soap and towel, a small bag containing flour, and two yet smaller for tea and sugar. A broad-leaved straw hat, shading a face tanned and weather beaten, cotton shirt open at the throat and breast, and round the neck a loosely knotted handkerchief. His trousers are tied tightly between knee and ankle with a broad piece of calico.[17]

Most stations would have several permanent workers who would muster the sheep from outlying paddocks, bringing them close to the shearing shed. The sheep were washed in elaborate pools and made ready for shearing. The shearer would throw the sheep on its back and first remove the belly wool, then attempt to take the remainder in one piece. Harry 'Duke' Tritton wrote *Shearing in the Bar* one Saturday afternoon in 1905, when thirty or forty shearers were in the Tarcoon pub boasting about how good they were at shearing:

> I shore away the belly wool,
> then trimmed the crutch and hocks,
> Opened up along the neck,
> While the broomie swept the locks;
> Then smartly swung the sheep around,
> And dumped him on his rear;
> Two blows to clip away the wig—
> I also took an ear.
> Then down around the shoulder
> and the blades were opened wide,
> As I drove 'em on the long blow
> and down the whipping side.
> And when the fleece fell on the board,
> He was nearly black with tar,
> But this is never mentioned
> When I'm shearing in a bar.[18]

If a sheep was cut, the wound would be painted with tar to stop the bleeding. Serious wounds were sewn up with a large needle and thread. Using hand shears, shearers could shear about eighty sheep a day, although tallies of more than 200 have been recorded. When machine-shearing was introduced in 1888, the average rose to about 120 per day.

The life of a shearer's wife on their small settlement was no better. Australia owes a great debt to these women on the land in early days of settlement, who often battled alone in times of fire, flood or drought, depending only upon their own quick brain and steady hand. Each day for a bush wife was a busy one, churning, baking, melting beeswax to mould candles, changing the brine on the 'salt junk' (meat), rubbing the bacon with saltpetre and sugar, smoking fish, gathering eggs and scaring the crows and hawks from the chickens, cooking the dinner, and doing the ordinary housework. There are no statues erected to honour these women, nor will we find their portraits gracing the walls of our national galleries. Many memorials have been raised for people who deserved them far less than these women of the bush.

One song that comes down to us from those times is a theme popular since the days of minstrels. A devoted maiden vows to cut all her hair, dress as a boy and follow her knight to war. In our bush version it is the dialogue between a shearer and the girl he is leaving behind, as he speaks to her:

> Oh, hark the dogs are barking
> I can no longer stay.
> The men are all out mustering
> And it is nearly day;
> So I must off by the morning light
> Before the sun doth shine
> To meet the Queensland shearers
> On the banks of the Condamine.

To which she gives her reply:

> Oh, Willie, dearest Willie,
> I'll go along with you,
> I'll cut off all my auburn fringe
> And be a shearer too.
> I'll cook and count your tally, love,
> While ringer-o you shine
> And I'll wash your greasy moleskins
> On the banks of the Condamine.[19]

The convicts, ticket-of-leave men and poor immigrants had little hope of ever escaping from this country, so they learned to adapt to it. The heat and monotony of flies were mixed with flood, droughts and fire, and the wide brown land was harsh, remote and unforgiving. With humility, hardship and anguish, these people began to esteem the land, see colour where once they saw drabness and extract satisfaction from its endless challenges. Abandoning pretence and affectation, they realised they would have to draw together to survive. They learned to think laterally, improvise endlessly and always be wary of authority. They were hard-headed people, guarded in their emotions and enthusiasm, forever wary of disaster, yet wryly ironical in their humorous restraint. As a group of people, they were developing a character that would become so different to that of the British, yet never so arrogant that they were unwilling to learn or so undiscriminating that unbalanced comment could command devoted attention.

These were the swagmen who developed their own Australian codes of behaviour and ways of life. Banjo Paterson would draw on these characteristics to write about the most famous swagman of all, who in a way represents the working people of the nation as a whole.

On the wallaby track—itinerant workers waltzing their matildas.
(National Library of Australia)

5

Up Rode the Squatter

While 'Waltzing Matilda' is a song about a fair go and resisting the excessive use of authority, it also celebrates the squatter, not necessarily as a tyrannical ruler, but as he was—someone who had power, property, style and the full support of the law. The squatter in Paterson's song was Robert Macpherson, but like the swagman, he was symbolic of a whole class of Australians.

From early days in Australia, a split-level society was being established. Separate to the class of Australians who were driven by their convict code, another group of people arose with diverging customs and attitudes. They deplored the convict class. The feeling was mutual; neither tolerated the other, and a line was drawn.

As soon as Governor Macquarie's convict gangs built roads across the forbidding Blue Mountains, out onto the Bathurst Plains, to Goulburn and the Argyle country, a pastoral frontier society began to develop. Grants of land were made by successive governors, mostly to retired naval and military officers. Along with their free emigrant counterparts in Sydney society, they began to form a closed clique, to the ranks of which no ordinary person could aspire. The 'pure merinos', later termed the 'squattocracy', the landholders and wealthy entrepreneurs from the city, formed their own exclusive society; anyone else, save for those they considered their social equals, need not apply. Those who stood on top of the ladder as they saw it, believed that:

> to have been a convict or be a sixteenth removed from it, is an indelible stain which no power on earth can wash away. There was no country in the known world where different grades of Society were so strictly marked as here, therefore those who have just got within the pale of the better Circles are afraid to be seen taking any notice of a Stranger until he becomes known within the walls of Government house.[1]

This split-level society also created two levels of art and literature in Australian culture, which the poet Robert Fitzgerald referred to as 'the stockyard and the common-room'. Down-to-earth natural Australian writers such as Shaw Nielsen, Henry Lawson and of course Banjo Paterson can be set against the more polished, and perhaps more derivative, educated writers. In later years, the squatting class, devoid of any realist Australian writing of their own, would attempt to claim Banjo Paterson as one of themselves.

Although there existed a fair proportion of overseas landlords who scarcely knew what a sheep looked like, most squatters worked as hard as the men they employed. The image of the squatter riding around on his thoroughbred watching his workers toil is one that some squatters, wanting to be thought of as English gentry, might like to have had believed of them, but anyone wanting to verify it would only have to look at their hands.[2]

In the old countries, a master would never be seen working beside his employees. It was beneath him. It never happened. Not only that, but in most cases a worker was not allowed to even speak with his master.

In Australia it was different. The first landholders were resolute in their attempts to establish the old-world system of master and servant. But as the years passed, as Geoffrey Dutton writes in *The Squatters*, the Australian graziers developed a different relationship with the land and the men who worked for them. The acceptance of hands dirty with dust, greasy dags of wool and the blood of cattle was the fundamental difference between the landed gentry and the squatters. The boss was the boss, certainly, but if he was any good, he never made a worker do what he couldn't do himself. Whether it be working in the sheep-yards, lamb-marking, cutting out cattle or bringing in a mob of sheep, he would do it. There was nothing in action or appearance (or in his use of the judicious, helpful oath) between an owner and a station hand. After work, the owner might retire to the main house, but at work everyone was together.[3]

One reason most squatters could do every job on the station was that in many cases they had no choice, because labour was short. Some would say, rightly, that this did as much as anything else to change the boss-and-worker relationship in Australia. It's a suggestion that will never grace the pages of any socialist manifesto. Although history will recall that they oppressed their fellow Australians, this staunch and often ruthless group of people still have a heroism and story of their own.

The word 'squatter' in the early 1800s—broadly meaning 'a settler having no normal or legal title to the land occupied by him'[4]—originally referred to ex-convicts, ticket-of-leave men who squatted on government land and stole other people's stock. The first recorded use of the term 'squatting' was in 1828, when Lieutenant-Governor George Arthur issued an order about unauthorised occupation of property in Van Diemen's Land. It was, he said:

> the means of keeping up a system of depredation upon the Flocks of respectable Settlers. The practise of squatting as it is denominated in the Colony, has been followed for the most part by freed Convicts possessing sheep, probably acquired by the most exceptional means; and the huts of these people (some ostensibly pursuing the occupation of Sawyers or Splitters) have been the constant resort of runaway Convicts and others whose characters are of the most vicious stamp, and the area of

their Sheep Runs has formed a most convenient depot for stolen sheep.[5]

Interestingly, and ironically, at that time settlers were the respectable class and the squatters were the villains, but by the 1860s this would reverse, with the term 'squatter' gaining an aura of power and respectability. As a group, squatters occupied vast areas of the best land in the country. With the aid of their city interests and class brothers, they established a base for their future political power in the legislative councils of the colonies.

During the 1860s, squatters entrenched themselves firmly on their runs and stations. The pastoral industry was again entering a boom period, and once more Australia would ride on the sheep's back. In less than thirty years the number of sheep would explode, from approximately 20 million to about 100 million by 1891. In the southern states of Victoria and Tasmania, where all of the good land was already occupied, numbers remained mostly unchanged. The largest expansion took place in western New South Wales, through the Riverina and the Darling Basin (the back of Bourke), as pastoralists pushed inland from the coastal belt, into drier, more inhospitable land.[6]

After Queensland separated from New South Wales in 1859, western Queensland became a frontier where men could take up unsettled tracts of land, as the earliest pioneers had done in the southern states. From her home at Mount

Abundance in the Manaroa district of New South Wales, Mrs Mary McManus described the rush for land:

> Our house was crowded with visitors. I have seen our dining table covered with maps and compasses. Many a time I have made . . . ten beds on the table and some under it. I have often seen as many as twenty riding-pack saddles and other . . . gear, tents and pack bags lying on the verandah.[7]

She would later see her husband drive 10,000 sheep by himself from Maitland to Tyrconnel Downs Station, in south-west Queensland, using two horses a day and galloping all the time, because he could get no labour to assist him.

•

Some squatters who rushed to take up land in Queensland would prosper, while others, heavily mortgaged to the banks, would eventually walk off the land with nothing. The boom of the 1860s would be over by the 1890s, and by 1894 the plight of the land-owners struggling to keep their stations profitable, while confronting the union shearers in Queensland, prompted the writing of 'Waltzing Matilda'.

Historian Geoffrey Dutton comments on the contribution this class of people made to the Australian character:

> The ingrained Australian attitude of disrespect for authority is usually held to stem from the convicts in their slow journey from bondage to emancipation. Australians are the most democratic people on earth and they like to

romanticise democracy, to believe that energy and attitudes of enterprise and independence have always flowed from the workers. In a general way there is a lot of truth in this, but in fact a taste of illegality, an ability to make swift decisions and an iron capacity to carry them out in circumstances of extreme individualism usually came from the squatters.[8]

No matter how history records the contribution of Australia's earliest landowners, as a class they were men of stubborn fortitude, often choosing hardship in the hope of future fortune. Today we may judge these people, who led the way in frontier settlement, as selfish, but rightly or wrongly, the men and women who finally succeeded had pursued their ideals with a tenacity that deserves admiration. Their success was stoically earnt, never accidental. In some seasons they were favoured by fortune, but these God-fearing men of capital were ruthless, courageous and single-minded. Many more would fail than would succeed, and even the most intelligent and enduring families would be tested in the depression of the late 1880s and early 1890s.

The early landholders were assigned free labour direct from the convict ships as soon as they landed in Australia. These men, pickpockets and political prisoners, many of them city-dwellers who had never known any sort of farm life, were sent into the bush and flogged if they misbehaved. Obviously, the great advantage for the squatters in employing convict labour was that they didn't have to pay them. Free men received £10 a year plus keep.

Under the regulations set by Governor Bourke in 1835, a squatter was allowed one convict servant for every 160 acres he grazed and one extra servant for every forty acres under cultivation. However, the governor provoked violent protests from landholders when he limited to seventy the number of free servants that any one squatter could have. Until then large landholders had been allocated up to 150 free convict servants. The requirement for landowners was to provide the convict with twelve pounds of wheat and seven pounds of meat per week, and a few issues a year of what were referred to as 'slop clothes'.[9]

If the convict misbehaved, he would be sent to the nearest magistrate, usually a neighbouring squatter, and flogged. The floggers, or 'scourgers', as they were called, would be flogged themselves if they did not make the cat-o'-nine-tails lay bare the flesh and draw the blood of the convict. The House of Commons Committee for Transportation, in 1838, was told that the system was nothing but slavery. The report on flogging for the previous year recorded an average of forty-five lashes for each convict, with a total of 304,000 lashes being meted out for the year.

Some believe that the attitude of squatters in accepting this slavery fuelled the violence that would occur between them and the union shearers more than fifty years later in the shearing strikes of the 1890s.

During 1847, wanting an alternative to the ex-convict workers being made available from the penal colonies of New South Wales and Tasmania, a number of influential squatters formed 'The Port Phillip Immigration Society'. Its purpose was to arrange the migration of workers from the British Isles to Melbourne. For each worker, a sum of ten shillings was paid to cover the cost of selection and arranging passage to Melbourne, which was recouped by the squatter when the immigrant started working for him. This ensured an adequate supply of cheap labour, as they were engaged for a set period at low wages.[10]

The corporate spirit of the 'old hands', or ex-convicts, had made them increasingly difficult to manage. Masters and free immigrants were treated with contempt by the ticket-of-leave men, and every attempt was made to discomfit them. Even though free immigrants soon outnumbered the 'old hands', the ex-convicts had a distinct influence on the whole attitude and approach of the new labour force. It wasn't long before the immigrant 'new chums' conformed to the colonial custom of making a squatter's life a burden to him. The hapless squatter was hopelessly outnumbered. The 1841 census revealed that eighty-nine per cent of the classified population (which included assigned convicts, wives and children) were servants of various descriptions. Only eight per cent were land-owners, proprietors, bankers, merchants, professional men or other employers.[11]

The actual conditions for convict servants in the early settlement of Australia can only be imagined. The convicts themselves left little literature behind; most could not write, and it is doubtful that any landowner would bother to document the daily life of the convicts and ex-convicts in his employ. Some perception can be gained from Julian Stuart's *Part of the Glory*[12] in which he reminisces about his early childhood in the New England area of New South Wales.

Stuart's father, Donald, had bought a riverside estate from an Anglo-Indian army officer who had been transferred from Bengal to look after convicts at Botany Bay. He left the services and settled on the rich soil of the Hunter Valley, building up his fortune, like many early Australian land-holders, with cheap convict labour and ticket-of-leave men.

Transportation had finished before Donald bought the property, but the taint of the old days lingered. Grim mementos were often unearthed. Among some broken bullock chains and hay-bands, the young Julian found some leg-irons, shackles and manacles, a gruesome reminder of the convict days.

A time-expired convict known simply as 'Old Jacob' had finished his sentence on the property before it was purchased by Julian's father, Donald Stuart. Like many other convicts with no family or friends in Australia, Old Jacob had nothing better to do, so he stayed around the place. He told Julian how, more than once, he had been 'strung up' to the ironbark flogging post that stood in the garden opposite the dining room window, to get twenty-five strokes of the cat-o'-nine-tails. The floggings were carried out at breakfast time so the Colonel could watch them while he ate; it saved time!

Also living on the property was 'Dummy', the 'idiot son' of a convict woman. Old Jacob cared for Dummy, and together they made quite an odd couple; Jacob almost ninety years old and Dummy almost half his age but with the simple mind of a five-year-old. Jacob may have known his history but no-one else did. Between two fields was a plot of unused land, upon which grew prickly crab-apples, deadly nightshades and poison berries. The previous owners had, for reasons which Julian guessed later, left the unsightly plot uncultivated for almost twenty-five years. To bring the wasteland into line with the vineyard, the plot was cleared and trenched. When digging out some loose stones, they came across a skeleton, which had evidently been there for a quarter of a century or more. The rusted leg-irons and loop chains still around the bones showed it to be a convict. There was nothing to show how he had met his death.

Dummy was greatly distressed at the discovery. He got a tub and after shaking the bones free of clay, placed them tenderly in it. The whole time he made pitiful and unavailing efforts to be understood, while at the same time stamping on the chains and kicking them savagely. It was evident that in his afflicted mind something, a memory perhaps, had stirred but what it was no-one could tell. Julian, old Jacob and Dummy fashioned a rough coffin so the bones of the unfortunate convict could have a more dignified burial. When the grave had been filled in, they planted an oleander tree at the head of it. From that day on, Julian's mind associated oleanders with the voiceless human being and the tragedy that had no words.

Another example of the treatment workers suffered during the 1830s was that doled out by Richard Rouse, who had taken up Guntawang Station near Gulgong in New South Wales. For many years it was worked by convicts. Rouse was said to be a very harsh man and flogging was an everyday event. Being a magistrate, Rouse could make his own laws for the convicts in his employ. The 'punishment post' was set up in front of the main door of the convict barracks; an ironbark post eight feet high, with shackles for hands and feet. Here a man would be trussed up, helpless and screaming as the cat-o'-nine-tails cut his back to pieces.

Rouse was also famous for the horses he bred; horses wearing his brand, the Crooked R, were prized all over the state. Banjo Paterson used Rouse's Crooked R brand in his anti-squatter poem, 'The Bushman's Song'.

> This old black horse I'm riding—if you'll notice what's
>   his brand,
> He wears the crooked R, you see—none better in the land.
> He takes a lot of beatin', and the other day we tried,
> For a bit of a joke, with a racing bloke, for twenty
>   pound a side.[12]

•

While some squatters and settlers treated the Aboriginal people with some degree of respect, history will forever record that the Indigenous peoples of Australia were decimated by European settlement.

The new inhabitants often poisoned the Aboriginal tribes to rid their runs of the 'vermin', in some cases 'mixing a quantity of the corrosive sublimate used into compounding sheepwash into a damper, and giving it to the most troublesome of the tribe'.[14] They died writhing and convulsing. Apart from deliberate killings, by far the worst horror inflicted upon the Aboriginals was disease. Influenza, pneumonia and smallpox devastated many tribes, while the other main cause of death was sexually transmitted disease.

Some squatters kept harems of 'black gins', who were abandoned when the squatter and his men fell ill from such diseases. Of course, it was assumed the Aboriginal women were responsible for infecting the men; they did not know (and probably didn't care) that the disease did not exist before the arrival of the white man. Niel Black, a squatter who owned a run near Noorat in the western district of Victoria that destroyed a sacred Aboriginal meeting place, recorded in his journal:

> several of the men are now very ill with the Native pox which shows how they acted with the Blacks. Notwithstanding the bad name the Aboriginals had here, I am told it is not an uncommon thing for these rascals to sleep all night with a Lubra and if she poxes him or in any way offend him, perhaps shoot her before 12 next day— I am certain it is a thing that has frequently occurred.[15]

While it is difficult to know how many thousands of Aboriginals were living in the clans of western Victoria before European settlement, within forty years, by 1876, the number had been drastically reduced to about 600. The tribe around Geelong, which numbered about 173 in 1840, had dwindled thirteen years later to a miserly thirty-four.[16] The most marked decrease was in Queensland, where numbers had dropped from approximately 100,000 to only 5,137 in 1901. In Tasmania, all 2,500 were exterminated.[17]

In 1923, the prolific Australian poet John Keith McDougall—who was born in 1867, three years after Banjo Paterson, and wrote five volumes of poetry—published his poem 'The Old Squatter's Soliloquy'. McDougall, who was the sitting federal Labor member for Wannon in western Victoria from 1906 to 1913, referred to certain squatters as 'land grabbers and slayers of Aboriginals'. Written in the classic Australian 'horse-chase' tradition, like Adam Lindsay Gordon's 'From the Wreck' and Paterson's 'The Man from Snowy River', McDougall takes us on a ride few Australian poets or writers were prepared to acknowledge. The atrocities in the poem were by no means unique in the early years of settlement in western Victoria and this is a rare example of Australian literature about what is referred to as 'the forgotten war'.

> The blacks I slew when I settled here, not far away are sleeping,
> And the big gums, o'er their gloomy graves, a sullen watch
>   are keeping.
> True, they were victims of British greed and they rot where
>   the ferns are growing,
> In the shadow of the lonely hills—by a river ever flowing.

Fierce, wild men of the woods were they and content with
    their mode of living,
They fought their battles as fierce men do—unforgiven and
    unforgiving; . . .

But I am Lord of their country now, though a convict here I
    landed,
Clad in a suit of Government clothes and shackled and
    shaved and branded;
And my youngsters carry their noses high and brag of their
    father's merit,
Though they won't proclaim how I got the land, which they
    will of course inherit . . .

But the blacks imagined my land was theirs and they pestered
    me—parson said rightly—
By spearing my cattle or stealing my sheep or laming my
    horses nightly;
At last, grown tired of their frequent thefts and their deeds of
    native daring,
I rode, one day, with my shearers armed, to kill them or give
    them a scaring.

There were ten of us there, who had all been lagged and
    feared neither man nor devil,
And we rode to murder that tribe of blacks as we'd ride to a
    dance or revel;
I can still remember our wild hurrahs and our blood-hounds'
    savage baying,
As we galloped abreast in sight of the camp, where the young
    of the thieves were playing . . .

Our hot blood leaped and our hearts beat high and we stayed
   at our headlong riding,
Till we neared a creek where we plainly saw the blacks
   through the bushes gliding;
And laughed aloud at their frantic looks and their fleet
   uncertain running,
For we feared their spears and their boomerangs far less than
   we feared their cunning.

We penned them like sheep in a rocky gorge—there must
   have been full fifty—
And we shot them and stabbed them as fast as we could for
   the law was lax and shifty;
And our bloodhounds fought in the fierce melee and assisted
   to kill and ravage,
Each fixing his fangs with a desperate grip, in the throat of a
   wounded savage.

A lubra fled with her screaming child, through the line of
   pitiless rifles,
And I galloped away to kill the two, for the lives to me were
   trifles;
As my horse strode after the dusky pair, like beasts, I could
   hear them panting,
But I shot them both as they fell fatigued, beneath a
   lightwood gently slanting.

Then back to my comrades I rode through the bush, in the
   light, like a phantom rider,
And I saw that the work of blood was done, as the vista got
   shorter and wider;
Where I checked my steed they were busy enough in a ring of
   sable corpses,

Wiping the blood from their gleaming knives and the sweat
from their heated horses.

We dug a trench in the golden sand, where the wattles skirted
the river,
And we buried the slaughtered side by side and left them to
rest forever;
And those were the blacks who had speared my sheep and
maimed and destroyed my cattle,
And I reckon we slew them as fair that day as soldiers are
slain in battle.

But . . . in tortured dreams when I fall asleep, I can hear the
lubras weeping,
And spectral blacks through spectral woods are always
towards me creeping;
And ever and ever they beckon me on to strange and
mysterious places,
Where, in fancy, I see their comrades lie with blood on their
ghastly faces.

Like the miserly men who oppress their kind to make heavier
still their purses,
I walk through life a detested thing and the mark for a
thousand curses;
And, although I feast on ambrosial fare and imbibe my winey
nectars,
I'll be hunted down to my grave at last, by horrible shapes and
spectres.[18]

•

Since the beginning of settlement in Australia the wealth of many graziers has often been overrated. Many squatters were extremely wealthy, while other landowners, although appearing to be rich in terms of gross assets, often had large debts and, at times, relatively poor income. Still today, graziers have very little real say in the setting of prices for their produce. To this uncertainty must be added droughts, rabbit problems, floods, fires and insect plagues.

The sheep graziers also had to combat many diseases, which could spread throughout a whole flock in no time at all, destroying much of their livelihood.

'Scab' was a fungal infection affecting the skin, causing the poor animals to scratch and tear at themselves. If it wasn't treated immediately, scabby patches would spread and the unfortunate sheep would die a slow and lingering death. Initially it was treated with a corrosive sublimate solution, which burnt the men's hands and sometimes killed the sheep. But it was believed this substance was the best cure. The workers had to catch the sheep, tie their legs, dip them into a big tub of this solution, and lift them out onto an iron grate. Then to allow the solution to penetrate the skin, the sheep were cut, or scarified, along their backs with knives, to a depth of almost half an inch, with the cuts no more than half an inch apart. For three months the men dressed the affected sheep every few days. The men fared little better than the sheep; their fingernails fell out and their hands turned black and were covered with sores. Their eyes became sore and full of pus, and they had stomach cramps for days on end.

It was a terrible disease. Eventually, after a lot of trial and error, it was realised tobacco mixed with sulphur was a better treatment. Most landholders grew their own tobacco. The plants would be hung out to dry, then mulched into a thick sticky paste and mixed with equal amounts of sulphur. One pound of the tobacco–sulphur mixture would be added to five gallons of boiling water. The sheep would then be dipped into the mixture, as hot as the sheep or the workers could bear without being scalded. This was done three times with an interval of two weeks between each dipping. It was bloody hard work; sometimes thousands of sheep would have to be treated at the same time.

Another common disease was foot-rot. This is when the hoof gets inflamed, swells with infection and eventually falls off. The sheep then dies of starvation or fever, as it can't forage for food.

The worst disease of all was catarrh, otherwise known as pneumonia in sheep. It had no known cure and it was not unusual to find 500 dead sheep in the yards after a single night.

Although disputes over land boundaries were common among early squatters, externally these men became a tightly knit group, united by common interest. Before 1888, there was no cohesive organisation representing the pastoralists and graziers of Victoria and New South Wales. On their regular visits to town, the influential squatters would meet at the

Melbourne Club, where the Crown Lands Commissioners were also members. When the local Magistrates' Benches were established, they consisted entirely of district squatters and the Commissioner of Crown Lands who was in charge of the area. This quasi-regional government needed little other union. However, after the huge influx of people during the goldrush period, voting rights were extended to ordinary people (permanent residents) and the squatting interests were deprived of much of their power.

In 1862, the populist cry of 'Unlock the lands' resulted in the Charles Gavan Duffy Land Act. Duffy was an activist in the cause of Irish freedom. He had been tried for treason and imprisoned in Newgate prison in Dublin. He arrived in Melbourne as a free settler in 1856. He had been one of the fifty Irish members of the House of Commons, but had decided he might be able to do more for his countrymen abroad than in Ireland. In Australia he was given a rousing welcome, and soon after arriving was elected to the first Victorian Legislative Assembly. He introduced a new land act, with the intention of opening up land for small selectors.

The next few years brought many anxious times for entrenched landowners as they were threatened with the disappearance of their former leaseholds. The squatting class had to formally secure the land they currently leased for a pittance. To ensure the selection and purchase of their own runs they employed bogus selectors, a practice known as 'dummying'.

Approximately a quarter of a million acres in the Ararat–Willaura district of Victoria had been made available for selection. The names of a few permanent settlers appeared in the list of selectors, but the majority had been merely dummying for the squatters. Farmers and small selectors had no chance with thirty or forty dummies against them. Men were seen applying for land at the Ararat office with arms full of applications. One squatter waited with seventeen of his employees for the Land Office to open, each servant ready with £350 to take up his block of 640 acres. Such was the arrogance of some squatters that they even took up selections in the names of working bullocks. One stubborn bullocky, knowing that the name of one of his bullocks had been used in this way, stuck his own survey poles on the land and defied the squatter. The transaction was deemed illegal and the bullocky won the selection.[19]

Margaret Leurs, in her biography of John Keith McDougall, *Laureate of Labour*, describes how the land was distributed. Monday 5 June 1865 was the busiest day that Ararat, in the western district of Victoria, had experienced since the 1855 goldrush. It marked the beginning of the 'land sales' of the mid-sixties. Would-be farmers, hired dummies and certificate holders jostled around the temporary Land Office in the Market Square. Each was given a ticket by one of the clerks sitting behind a long table, which was dropped into a lottery box. A hush fell on the impatient crowd as the district surveyor whirled the ballot box around and drew out the first ticket. The lucky ticket-holder then came forward, inspected the map, made his selection of 640 acres and paid a deposit. This went on for hour after hour. A selector known to be genuine was greeted with applause, but a 'squatter's dummy' made his selection to the accompaniment of jeers and a running character assessment of him and his family, while a group of squatters stood by, discussing the scramble for land on which their flocks had grazed freely for more than twenty years. One of them had forty dummies ready to select for him. On this occasion twelve of them were drawn in the ballot and between them selected nearly 4000 acres for their boss.[20]

Within two years, about two-thirds of the one million acres sold throughout Victoria under the Duffy Act had fallen into the hands of around a hundred men. Most of these owned land in western Victoria.[21]

John Keith McDougall described the western district of Victoria as 'the landlords' paradise' and commented in a pamphlet headed 'Landlordism and Land Trusts':

No-one can beat the average squatter in the devious quips and twists of bush-lawyerly diplomacy. He can look as simple as Cuddie Headrigg and yet be as subtle as Machiavelli.[22] The landlord is the same in all countries and in all ages. Holy writ reeks with the denunciation of him. The dry rot of his greed destroyed the Roman Empire. He bribed and bossed the crowbar brigade of Ireland. He burned by the hundreds the cottages of Highland crofters in Scotland. He evicted tenants at Willaura. He has been tears to childhood, disappointment to love, and misery to old age from the dawn of civilisation to the present day.[23]

By the 1880s many of these problems for the landowners had been overcome, particularly in the western district of Victoria. Many financially strong, astute and resilient squatters had not only survived but had flourished. Now owning large freehold estates, they built impressive stone homesteads, woolsheds and outbuildings. They were stocked with large numbers of high-quality and very productive sheep and cattle. Many of these squatters had been so successful that they extended their interests and took up large runs in western Queensland or left their stations in the care of managers and went to live in mansions in Toorak and other fashionable parts of Melbourne. A few made their homes back in the old country, Britain.

The squatter had now risen to prominence; a symbol of power and status. The itinerant workers, through unification, were on the rise as well, cementing a class divide in the Australian bush. They were two of the main players in a burgeoning new society that Paterson would exploit with 'Waltzing Matilda'.

Teamsters stopping for a meal break and cup of tea—men like these fascinated the young Barty Paterson with their songs and stories. (National Library of Australia)

6

'The Banjo'

ANDREW BARTON 'BANJO' PATERSON (1864–1941) was born at Narrambla, near Orange in New South Wales, on 17 February 1864. He was the eldest child, eventually having five sisters and one brother. His early education took place at home under a governess. As a young boy, he was always referred to as 'Barty'. By his own admission, he was a lonely child, being twelve years older than his only brother.[1]

The first years of his life were spent on Buckinbah Station. His father was eventually driven into bankruptcy, forced to sell up to buy a smaller property. When Barty was seven, his parents, Andrew Bogle Paterson and Rose Isabella Paterson, moved to Illalong Station in the Yass district. Years later Banjo would lament his father's plight and treatment by the banks in his poem 'On Kiley's Run':

> But droughts and losses came apace
> To Kiley's Run
> Till ruin stared him in the face;
> He toiled and toiled while lived the light,
> He dreamed of overdrafts at night.
> At length, because he could not pay,
> His bankers took the stock away.
> To Kiley's Run.[2]

Moving to Illalong was the genesis of his great and abiding love of the bush. Like many lonely bush children, he took constant pleasure from the sights, sounds and stillness around him. The memories lingered and in 1933, over sixty years later, he would vividly describe them in *The Animals Noah Forgot*:

> A land of sombre, silent hills where mountain cattle go
> By twisted tracks, on sidelings steep, where giant
>   gumtrees grow.
> And the wind replies, in the river oaks, to the song of the
>   stream below.
> A land, as far as the eye can see, where the waving
>   grasses grow
> Or the plains are blackened and burnt and bare, where the false
>   mirages go
> Like shifting symbols of hope deferred—land where you
>   never know.

There was no end of horsemen, bullock teams, drovers and Cobb & Co. coaches passing along the road, stirring the imaginations of a young boy. He was fascinated by the bush characters, more so the bullockies than anyone—compassionate people often travelling with their families, dogs and sometimes their chooks, which hopped down from the wagons as soon as camp was made, to scratch for food.

The bullockies would come down the track through the valley. In the summer, amid the dust, the load would appear, a blob of cargo moving silently along, the dust slowly revealing the bullocks. No noise, just these magnificent animals, slowly but surely trudging along in the distance. The bullocks would gradually grow clearer and beside these strong beasts would be the bullock driver, greenhide whip coiled in readiness, walking along, totally in control. He'd sit on the fence and watch 'em come up through the valley; a four-wheeled dray, eight bullocks yoked to it in pairs, and then he could be heard half-shouting and half-caressing the team. Calling 'em all by their own names—'Careful there now, Dusty. Come on, Star. Pull your weight, you lazy good for nothing bastard!'—sooling them on towards the water. The poor buggers travelled for three days, about sixty miles between water holes. A lot of Australia's main roads were originally old bullock trails; that's why so many country towns are roughly sixty miles apart. Anyway, they'd come in; the teamster would give away his cussing and swearing and start singing. The whole team just lumbered in and pulled to a halt. 'The Great Northern Line' is one of a few collected traditional songs reflecting on a bullock driver's life:

When he swings his green-hide whip, he raises skin and hair,
His bullocks all have shrivelled horns, for Lordy he can swear,
He signals with his bullock whip as he comes through the vines,
With his little team of bullocks, on the Great Northern Line.[3]

Barty's parents were always scolding him for talking to the old teamsters, and said all sorts of things about them being horse-stealers, but they never did him any harm, not one of them. They'd stand there in smelly old moleskin trousers, held up by a piece of greenhide around the waist, dirty blue serge shirt with a rotten handkerchief knotted around their neck, peering out from underneath an old hat of dried cabbage leaves. They would usually never talk until the bullocks had had a good drink and been settled down for the night. A lot of them were Irishmen, content in their mode of living, happy to have their freedom. It was a tough, lonely road they travelled, but they were free. Ex-convicts or ticket-of-leave men, most of the old blokes could not read or write, yet they all had yarns to tell. The young Barty was enthralled by their stories and old songs you don't hear these days, like 'The Old Bullock Dray', and 'The Broken-Down Squatter'—and just about every teamster had a different version of 'The Wild Colonial Boy'. But unfortunately, a lot of good songs went to the grave with the old teamsters.

Years later, when these old blokes were dying off, Paterson realised the value of their songs, so made it his purpose to go out and collect as many as he could. In 1905, he published *Old Bush Songs*, containing some fifty ballads, most of which would now have been lost but for him. Not only is this highly important publication an intimate reflection of early colonial life, it is testament to the genius of a man who realised the worth of such social literature—the first Australian folklore collector, whose patience and persistence preserved these songs for generations to come. Even though he was by then a famous poet himself, he had the insight and social conscience to realise a full canvas of Australian stories was more important than individual success.

Paterson's thorough understanding of the value of this collection can be gauged by his own introduction:

So far as materials for ballads go, the first sixty or seventy years of our history are equal to about three hundred years of the life of an old and settled nation. The population of the country comprised a most curious medley. Among the early settlers were some of the most refined and educated, and some of the most ignorant, people on the face of the earth. Among the assisted immigrants and currency lads [those born in Australia] of the earlier days, education was not a strong point; and such newspapers as there were could not be obtained by one-half of the population, and could not be read by a very large percentage of the other half. It is no wonder, then, that the making of ballads flourished in Australia just as it did in England, Scotland and Ireland in the days before printing was in common use. And it was not only in the abundance of matter that the circumstances of the infant Colony were favourable to ballad-making. The curious upheavals of Australian life had set the Oxford graduate carrying his swag, and cadging for food at the prosperous homestead of one who could scarcely write his name; the digger, peeping out of his hole—like a rabbit out of his burrow—at the license hunters, had, perhaps, in another clime charmed cultivated audiences by his singing and improvisation; the bush was full of ne'er-do-wells—singers and professional entertainers and so on—who had 'Come to grief' and had to take to hard work to earn a crust to carry them on until they could 'strike a new patch'. No wonder that, with all this talent to hand, songs and ballads of a rough sort were plentiful enough.[4]

Illalong was on the main route from Melbourne to Sydney, a trip of about 600 miles. Cobb & Co. was at its peak efficiency, and the journey would take about five days. They'd urge the teams along at breathtaking speeds of up to ten miles an hour. In the morning, before the coach arrived, a fresh team of horses would be fed and watered for the change-over, ready for the next leg of the journey. As the coach's arrival time approached the expectant horses would get excited. The horses of the arriving coach would gallop into town with a 'Whoa there!' from the driver as the team pulled up outside the stable. The coachman would jump down, open the door for the passengers, and then disappear into the stable for a break.

The gentlemen passengers would often wander up and down the road, pipe hanging from their mouth, silently puffing away, while the ladies would scuttle into the rest-room, which was nothing more than a little bush dunny out the back.

The team would be unhitched and led into the stable, and the watered and rested horses taken out and hitched to the coach. The hot and sweating horses would be sponged down with water—magnificent powerful creatures, veins bristling, blood-red nostrils, fire in their eyes and pounding hearts pulsating through every part of their bodies. This would all take about ten minutes, but it seemed like a few seconds, with all the colour, movement, smells, noises, chatter, sweat, flies, dust and excitement. The coach-driver would reappear from the stable as though nothing had happened.

'Right! All aboard.' He'd swing up into the driver's seat, and with one flick of his whip, 'Come on now! Giddy-up there,' he'd yell. And they were gone!

But Banjo was not the only poet whose imagination was captured by the lights of Cobb & Co. In December 1889, his contemporary Henry Lawson would write in 'The Roaring Days':

> Oft when the camps were dreaming,
> And fires began to pale,
> Through rugged ranges gleaming
> Would come the Royal Mail.
> Behind six foaming horses,
> And lit by flashing lamps,
> Old 'Cobb & Co's', in royal state,
> Went dashing past the camps.[5]

The gold diggings at Lambing Flat (now Young) were only a day's ride away from Illalong. At least twice a week, the gold escort, on its way to the Sydney banks, would race by the front gate, with armed troopers, rifles at the ready, one riding along in front and another sitting with the coachman. Years earlier Barty had gone to a little bush school in the 'two-pub town' of Binalong, which was famous because the bushranger Gilbert was buried in the police paddock. In the little school he sat alongside boys and girls who were directly related to the famous bushranger. The typical daydreaming young boy, fascinated with bushranger stories, Barty used to hope that the escort would be 'stuck up' outside Illalong so that he 'might see something worthwhile, but what with the new settlers and the scores of bullock teams taking loads out to the back country, no bushranger stood half a chance of getting away unseen . . .'[6]

Filled with sentimentality and nostalgic memories of his days at the little bush school, years later Paterson penned a pro-bushranger poem, written in his best literary ballad style and called 'How Gilbert Died'.

> Then he dropped the piece with a bitter oath,
> And he turned to his comrade Dunn,
> 'We are sold,' he said 'we are dead men both!—
> Still, there may be a chance for one;
> I'll stop and I'll fight with the pistol here,
> You take to your heels and run.'
>
> So Dunn crept out on his hands and knees
> In the dim, half dawning light,
> And he made his way to a patch of trees,
> And was lost in the black of night;

And the hunters hunted his tracks all day,
But they never could trace his flight.

But Gilbert walked from the open door
In a confident style and rash;
He heard at his side the rifles roar,
And he heard the bullets crash.
But he laughed as he lifted his pistol hand,
And he fired at the rifle flash.

Then out of the shadows the troopers aimed
At his voice and the pistol sound.
With rifle flashes and darkness flamed—
He staggered and spun around,
And they riddled his body with rifle balls
As it lay on the blood-soaked ground.

There's never a stone at the sleeper's head,
There's never a fence beside,
And the wandering stock on the grave may tread
Unnoticed and undenied;
But the smallest child on the Watershed
Can tell you how Gilbert died.[7]

Also, there were events like the time a rouseabout from a nearby station took Barty to the Bogolong picnic races. (Bogolong is now Bookham, on the Hume Highway between Sydney and Melbourne.) He wouldn't have been any older than eight, and rode over on his little pony. It wasn't a real racetrack, no grandstand or anything of the kind, just a rough track laid out through the stringybark scrub. There were horses tied up to trees all over the place.

Among the accomplished riders were the Murrumbidgee horsemen, Aborigines, half-castes and the men from Snowy River.[8] This was probably the first time Paterson had seen these men.

Before the main race one of them removed the saddle from Barty's pony. Barty ran over but was too scared to say anything. The mountain man looked down at Banjo and smiled, saying, 'Don't worry, laddie, this saddle is much lighter than mine, you'll have it back after the race; if I win there'll be something in it for you.' The name of his horse was Pardon. Around the back of the track the horses would disappear from vision, but every time Barty got a glimpse of the runners, Pardon was sitting about third in the field of nine, the mountain man calmly astride, holding a tight rein. As the field came around the last bend, the track dipped a little, down behind the scrub. One can only imagine the little boy's excitement—when they came into sight at the top of the straight, Pardon was a length in front, with the mountain man riding for his life. When he came back after the race, he thanked the young Barty for his saddle and invited him to come and have a drink with his mates.

When the Murrumbidgee horseman assured him, as he gave him a ginger beer—bitter, lukewarm stuff with hops in it—that Pardon could not have won without his saddle, Barty's joy was complete. He stood, sipping his ginger beer, among some of the greatest horsemen in the country—no, the world—as they talked about their horses and the race.

Years later, in December 1888, he wrote 'Old Pardon, the Son of Reprieve':

> Then loud rose the war-cry for Pardon;
> He swept like the wind down the dip,
> And over the rise by the garden
> The jockey was done with the whip.
> The field was sixes and sevens—
> The pace at the first had been fast—
> And hope seemed to drop from the heavens,
> For Pardon was coming at last.
>
> And how he did come! It was splendid;
> He gained on them yards every bound,
> Stretching out like a greyhound extended,
> His girth laid right to the ground.
> A shimmer of silk in the cedars,
> As into the running they wheeled,
> And out flashed the whips on the leaders,
> For Pardon had collared the field.[9]

From a very young age, Barty would ride bareback four miles to school every morning and back each night. He had to, or he wouldn't have been able to get to school, and that was the first and most important part of his education. From this young age he was developing a love for horses and horsemanship. Mostly he rode alone, imagining he was anyone he wanted to be. Sometimes he would be a bushranger, being chased by the troopers, or a lone trooper, chasing the bushranging gang of Ben Hall, Dunn and Gilbert. He was always on his horse.

As he galloped along, the pounding hooves would beat out a rhythm to the wild and abounding imagery in the young boy's head. From this young age, quite without his awareness, stories set to rhythm and meter were being planted in his subconscious, to emerge years later in his poetical works—first as a trickle, then as a flood. This love of horses also saw him on many racetracks, winning both flat and jumps races. Although it would be some years before Paterson would write about his childhood experience, the visions and stories stayed with him all his life. Those types of characters had great effect, and later on helped him create fictitious characters like Salt Bush and Mulga Bill:

> 'Twas Mulga Bill, from Eaglehawk, that caught the
>   cycling craze;
> He turned away the good old horse that served him
>   many days;
> He dressed himself in cycling clothes, resplendent to be seen;
> He hurried off to town and bought a shining new machine;
> And as he wheeled it through the door, with air of lordly pride,
> The grinning shop assistant said, 'Excuse me, can you ride?'[10]

But Barty's bush schooldays were all too soon ended. How he would have liked a few more years of that curious freedom. But it wasn't to be; his parents were adamant he'd have an education. Even when he was living in the bush, with his father struggling to make ends meet on his modest farm, books were a priority—Scott and Dickens and the like—so off to Sydney he was sent. Barty's parents decided he should go to Sydney Grammar as a day-boy at the innocent age of eleven years. The first few months were spent attending a private preparatory school—'where all the young gentleman,' he drily recalled, 'had to wear good clothes instead of hob-nailed boots and moleskins in which his late schoolmates invariably appeared'. Gone were the days of wearing spurs and getting off school to be sent after 'the 'orses'. To add to his horror, the bush-bred boy had to learn dancing as well.[11]

He lived with his grandmother Emily Barton at Gladesville, in outer Sydney. Emily would have a huge influence on his writing in later years. A talented writer herself, she spent thirty years living as a pioneer's wife on a station called Boree Nyrang near Orange. An area bounded by the towns of Orange, Molong, Dubbo and Wellington would become known as Banjo Paterson country, having provided idyllic homestead settings for his ballads and novels—not because he ever really lived there, but because of the descriptions he had from his grandmother and read in her letters.[12] There is no doubt these years of formal education during Banjo's adolescence moulded him into a more cultured and educated young man, but they cut his childhood short.

As a bush boy of eleven he was not ready for the traffic and the people in bustling Sydney Town. In the bush there was a natural progression of life, plenty of time to understand the changes, a certain reality and understanding of the natural order of things. Money was a means to an end; it always seemed elusive to his father, who seldom had enough, though he worked very hard, but this never overshadowed the importance of life in general. Everyone in Sydney was in such a rush, self-important. Crowded into the city's narrow streets, lined with tall buildings on either side, were rattling steam trams towing their upper-decked passenger cars, and every imaginable type of horse-drawn vehicle, weaving in and out of the shoppers up and down George and Pitt streets. Groups or 'pushes', larrikins congregating on corner streets, ladies with umbrellas and hawkers shouting out their cheap wares; street markets, itinerant musicians and barrel organists made all sorts of din from underneath street verandahs, which were supporting all manner of cheaply painted, and often bawdy, advertising banners. That was Sydney. Something that would not escape Banjo's attention when he wrote 'Clancy of the Overflow' in 1889:

> And in place of lowing cattle, I can hear the fiendish rattle
> Of the tramways and the 'buses making hurry down the
>   street,
> And the language uninviting of the gutter children fighting,
> Comes fitfully and faintly through the ceaseless tramp of feet.
>
> And the hurrying people daunt me, and their pallid faces
>   haunt me
> As they shoulder one another in their rush and nervous haste,
> With their eager eyes and greedy, and their stunted forms
>   and weedy,
> For townsfolk have no time to grow, they have no time
>   to waste.'[13]

Emily was extremely fond of literature and introduced him to the classics, as well as teaching him to speak some French and giving him an appreciation for Carlyle, Ruskin and Swinburne. Sitting in the kitchen late into the night, with candlelight flickering around the walls, he revelled in her stories of the old days in the bush, before he was born, back in the 1840s and 50s, stories of the old bark hut she lived in with a resident snake, who went about his business of keeping down the mice and rats. The snake lived under the tank-stand and never harmed anyone. When they had visitors, the concertina and banjo would come out for a good old sing-song and a few tunes, and the snake would be known to peep his head around the bottom of the door to see what was going on. The ceiling was made of hessian and every night the possums would race across it as Emily and her sister would try to poke them with a stick. Her characters were so descriptive Barty thought they could walk into the room at any moment. Years later, he would include 'The Old Bark Hut' in his edition of *Old Bush Songs*:

The bucket you wash your feet in, is to boil your meat in too,
They think that you are mighty flash if you should ask
    for two,
I've a billy and a pint pot and a broken handled cup,
And they all adorn the table in the old bark hut.

My table it's not made of wood as many you have seen,
If it was only half as good I'd think myself serene,

It's just an old dry piece of bark, God knows when it was cut,
It blew down off the rafters of the old bark hut.

I've seen the rain come in this place just like a perfect flood,
Especially through the great big hole where once me table
      stood,
There's not a flamin spot me boys where you could lay
      your nut,
For the rain it's sure to find you in the old bark hut.[14]

As the years progressed, the young Barty came to enjoy life at Gladesville, especially the activity on the nearby Parramatta River. Always wanting to get outdoors whenever he could, after school he'd watch the wooden sailboats laden with wood and fruit sailing along the river towards Sydney, with the westerly wind behind them. He went to school each day on the steam ferry and in the first few years wished he was working on one of those wooden boats, instead of spending his days cooped up in a hot stuffy classroom studying behind a wooden desk. He had a great affection for life and years later would write nostalgically in a script for the ABC titled *On the River*:

If the wind died away and the boats were left in the doldrums; well, they didn't worry. They anchored and caught themselves a feed of fish, which they cooked on their little galley fires, the scent of frying red-bream mixing not unhappily with the aroma of guavas, grapes and the big hautboy strawberries, which now seem to have gone out of fashion. Then, when the tide turned, they would up with the anchor and drift down till they opened up upon the harbour, where there was always some sort of breeze. They would strike Sydney some time or other, and would deliver their cargo into horse-drawn carts and would then point the boat's nose up the river again, back to the gardens and the splitting of firewood with wedges and American axes . . .[15]

Eventually, Barty and a couple of mates pooled their pocket money and bought an old boat, working on it every night after school, sanding, caulking up the holes and eventually painting it, till it was shipshape enough to take out onto the river. With great pride he would come home to Grandma and announce the evening's catch, laying them all out, freshly cleaned or alive and flapping on the kitchen table.

For the first few years, he would get back home to the bush at Illalong every school holidays, but by the time he was fourteen, Barty was quite happy to spend holidays in Sydney fishing with his mates. Around that time he took up competitive rowing, which was quite the rage then. The Sydney Rowing Club's headquarters were across the river at Abbotsford. At sunrise on any given morning it would be nothing to see twenty or so scullers out on the Parramatta River, gliding through the mist along the championship stretch of water. These times were awash with visiting rowing teams for the regattas from all over Australia and abroad.

Gladesville had numerous inns and accommodation houses to give rest to the drivers and passengers of teams, coaches and travelling horsemen. A ferry service had also been built at Gladesville as part of the Great Northern Road to Maitland connecting up with Wiseman's Ferry. So there were always plenty of characters wandering around the place amid the frenetic comings and goings of all sorts of traffic.

Emily was quite well known and connected. There never seemed to be any end to the visitors arriving up the river from Sydney to spend a few days with her. Barty didn't take much interest in all these people in the early days, but many of them were from very well-connected families in Sydney. Barty had been introduced to Teddy Betts, who was a champion jockey at the time. Teddy had heard, through family, about Barty's love of horses and came to meet him. He took Barty under his wing. His full name was Edward Marsden Betts, and his grandfather was the Reverend Samuel Marsden, otherwise known as the 'Flogging Parson'.

Teddy was a member of the Australian Jockey Club and had won races right throughout the country. He was very well respected, not only for his horsemanship but also as a successful businessman. Barty was almost sixteen years of age, and with Teddy attended agricultural shows and many horse-racing events. They were constantly around horses and Teddy kept a watchful eye on his riding, commenting on his rough-riding, up-country style. During these years, Barty competed in, and won, many amateur races at Randwick and Rosehill. Flat races or steeplechases, he loved them all. Later some of the characters from the racetrack would surface in Paterson's prolific racing poems such as 'The Amateur Rider':

> 'Him! Going to ride for us! Him!—with the pants and the
>   eyeglass and all,
> Amateur! Don't he just look it—it's twenty to one on a fall,
> Boss must be gone off his head, to be sending our
>   steeplechase crack,
> Out over fences like these, with an object like that
>   on his back.'[16]

•

Barty's schooling was cut short when, only days before his examination to qualify for university, there was a typhoid outbreak in Sydney. Barty contracted severe fever and for days hovered between life and death. There is no record that he ever passed his matriculation exam, and in 1939 he wrote in the *Sydney Morning Herald*, 'Leaving school, I had a try for a bursary at the University but missed it by about a mile and a half, so I had to go into a lawyer's office.' His attitude to his schooling is further summed up with another laconic and characteristic comment: 'If I had paid as much attention to my lessons as to fish and rabbits, I too, might have been a Judge on the High Court. There is a lot of luck in these things.'[17]

With the assistance of his father he found a job as an articled clerk for a Sydney firm of solicitors, Spain and Salway. Banjo was employed at various law firms, and eventually became a managing clerk for a firm that handled the dealings of several banks. He clearly disliked the task of chasing after debts and pursuing debtors, many of whom were never going to be able to pay. Here, he became familiar with the plight of small landholders, as his father had been, and wondered why the banks were continuing to screw money out of people who didn't have it. These bush people made no distinction between one bank and another. They looked upon all banks as public enemies, like bailiffs and book-canvassers.

One day a lady came into his office. She was a widow towing two children behind her. She arrived in the office, somewhat breathless with the unaccustomed exercise of toiling up the stairs, and she started to explain her errand before she had quite recovered her wind; consequently she gasped a little in her speech.

'Are you the—ah—solicitor?' she enquired.

I admitted I was a lawyer; perhaps not the lawyer of the century—

'Well,' she said, 'my 'usban' died a' Friday week and Fitzpatrick said to come an' see you an' see what we ought to do about sellin' the land.'

'Oh,' I said, 'what did your husband's estate consist of?'

'Estate,' she said, wonderingly, 'he hadn't no estate. Just a free selection up on Kuryong Creek was all he had. It was on Kiley's Run, you know. We thought Kiley'd buy us out when we selected, but after me 'usband finished his time, old Kiley went broke—got busted in the drought—and now the bank has the station.'[18]

At twenty-two years of age, in 1886, he was admitted as a solicitor of the Supreme Court of New South Wales. It wasn't long before he started to lose interest in the daily grind of soliciting duties. He was highly critical of some aspects of the legal profession, mainly solicitors not being able to appear in court, but having to brief counsel instead, and later satirised the practice in a poem titled 'The Hypnotist', published in the *Bulletin* on 19 July 1890:

> I am a barrister, wigged and gowned;
> Of stately presence and look profound . . .
> When courts are sitting and work is flush
> I hurry about in a frantic rush.
> I take your brief and I look to see,
> That the same is marked with a thumping fee;
> But just as your case is drawing near,
> I bob serenely and disappear.
> And away in another court I lurk,
> While a junior barrister does your work;
> And I ask my fee with a courtly grace,
> Although I never came near the case,
> But the loss means ruin to you, maybe,
> But nevertheless I must have my fee!
> For the lawyer laughs in his cruel sport,
> While his clients march to the Bankrupt Court.[19]

During 1886 Banjo had his first poem published in the *Bulletin,* titled 'The Bushfire', an allegorical poem supporting Irish home rule against English repression. His next piece of verse, in the ballad style of Adam Lindsay

Gordon, was titled 'A Dream of the Melbourne Cup' and appeared in the *Bulletin* on 30 October 1886. He was paid seven shillings and sixpence. The *Bulletin*'s editor, J. F. Archibald, described the poem as 'humorous enough doggerel' and sent for Paterson to meet him.

Archibald inquired, 'D'you know anything about the bush?' Paterson replied, 'Well, I've been reared there.'

'Right, have a go at the bush,' answered Archibald. 'Have a go at anything—if it strikes you. Don't write anything like other people . . . Let's see what you can do.'[20]

Paterson found his writing necessary relief from the boredom of his legal office. None of his colleagues or clients would have known he was a poet. His first published poems were under the simple pseudonym of 'B'. Eventually he was persuaded to choose a pen-name. He could think of no better name than one of his favourite childhood horses called 'Banjo'. No-one but his family knew who 'The Banjo' was.

His career and popularity were soon to change. He wrote a standard legal letter to a gentleman in the bush who had not paid his debts. To his delight, he got an answer from the bushman's friend, who scribbled the exact words, 'Clancy's gone to Queensland droving and we don't know where he are.' So there it was—the idea, the suggestion of the drover's life, the meter, the exact words for a couple of lines of verse, all delivered by Her Majesty's Mail at a cost of a postage stamp. Banjo made the most of it, and in

December 1889 his writing career skyrocketed when 'Clancy of the Overflow' was published in the *Bulletin*.[21]

Within months, he had written his most famous ballad, 'The Man from Snowy River'. In December 1892, what is generally regarded as his most humorous ballad, 'The Man from Ironbark', appeared with an entire front page of illustrations by Lionel Lindsay.

The identity of 'the modest young man from Sydney' was becoming increasingly intriguing; more and more readers eagerly looked forward to the latest poem from the mysterious man they only knew as 'The Banjo'.

Union shearers at Brookong Station, Lockhart, New South Wales, on strike in the 1890s. (National Library of Australia)

7

The Old Billy Boiling

LONG BEFORE THE BALLAD WRITERS like Paterson and Henry Lawson came along in the 1890s, the tradition of oral legend had nourished the imaginations of Australian audiences. The ground had been tilled and fertilised for the perfect crop. Now, in the face of the written word, oral legendry and myth-making were being fragmented and largely forgotten. It is little wonder that when Banjo Paterson wrote 'The Man from Snowy River' and Lawson wrote about 'Joe Wilson', they achieved immediate success. They had an audience who intimately knew the characters they were creating.

Later in a retrospective essay for the *Sydney Mail* in December 1938, Banjo Paterson spoke of his verse and that of his friend and contemporary Henry Lawson:

> Our 'ruined rhymes' are not likely to last long, but if there is any hope at all of survival it comes from the fact that

such writers as Lawson and myself had the advantage of writing in a new country. In all museums throughout the world one may see plaster casts of the footprints of weird animals, footprints preserved for posterity, not because the animals were particularly good of their sort, but because they had the luck to walk on the lava while it was cooling. There is just a faint hope that something of the same sort may happen to us.[1]

They were speaking directly to the Australian people, enriching the development of the Australian legend or national mystique—a specifically Australian outlook that grew up first and most clearly among the bush workers. When C. E. W. Bean wrote *The Dreadnought of the Darling* he described the outback thus:

> The Australian, one hundred to two hundred years hence, will still live with the consciousness that, if he only goes far enough back over the hills and across the plains, he comes in the end to the mysterious half-desert country where men have to live the lives of strong men. And the life of that mysterious country will affect Australian imagination much as the life of the sea has affected that of the English. It will always be there to help the Australian to form his ideals . . .[2]

Paterson, with his deep love of the outback, probably more than any other writer understood this as a permanent and universal reality of our national consciousness. Even though the majority of people were living in cities along the coastline, this smaller group of pastoral workers influenced the attitudes of the whole Australian community. Norman Lindsay recalled that this was fundamental in Paterson's beliefs and 'that isolation in the bush makes individuals out of men whereas city life tends to make them into types and masses'.[3] The cities were crammed with the unemployed; with almost no manufacturing industries and no access to land, they had very little hope. There were no unifying factors in the city. A huge gulf existed between the residents of Potts Point and Surry Hills or Toorak and Williamstown; they were different classes with varying aspirations. This was not an environment to produce a unique Australian spirit.

Since European settlement and long before, the most important influence on the Australian character was the country itself. It was a strange land, with exacting demands on those who attempted to master it, gradually imposing a loyalty and respect from those who were born to it. This loyalty expressed itself in a casual stoicism, a 'she'll be right, mate' attitude, a capacity to take a hard knock without whingeing.

It was a barren wilderness where men walked, looking for work, carrying only the minimum requirements to keep themselves alive until the next job, and maybe stealing the odd jumbuck along the way. The nomadic workforce seemed to be on an endless, timeless journey and Duke Tritton described what it was like to tramp in the heat:

We were plodding along, fighting a ceaseless battle with the flies, too tired to even think. Throats were dry and even though our water bags were full, we had to resist the urge to drink, and contented ourselves with occasional sips, having learnt the value of water and the need for conserving it on those dry tracks. The heat was terrific as though coming from a bush fire. The silence was oppressive and there was no movement in the air. Birds had disappeared; even the crows which always seemed to be with us as though hoping to dine on a couple of tasty young swagmen, had gone; even the rabbits had gone down their burrows . . .[4]

Walking, being on the tramp, allows the mind to witness hawks picking the eyes out of injured helpless animals and drought-stricken or diseased stock slowly dying, their forlorn cries for help extending across the never-ending plain, falling on the ears of no-one.

The walking mind also witnesses the beginning and end of each day, one's own oil painting transforming before one's eyes. Is it those rich colours that only belong to the sunrise and sunset of the Australian outback, deep in blues and reds, like being in the middle of an enormous Pro Hart oil painting, or do the colours just seem so rich compared to the blinding, vertical white light of the day? Through this world the swagman would walk, recording as they went, not by paintbrush or by pen, to be recorded and recorded and carried again. But recorded in verse and recorded in song, tramped out in meter the whole day long. Taken to bed and kept in their head, repeated around campfires at night, sometimes noted but often misquoted, often learnt wrong and rarely learnt right. In 1893, Henry Lawson would describe his own experience of tramping from shed to shed in his poem 'Out Back':

> For time means tucker, and tramp you must,
>   where the scrubs and plains are wide,
> With seldom a track that a man can trust,
>   or a mountain peak to guide;
> All day long in the dust and heat—when summer
>   is on the track—
> With stinted stomachs and blistered feet,
>   they carry their swags Out Back.[5]

Many outback stations issued rations as a way of ensuring a supply of casual labour. Station owners who were plentiful with hand-outs always had men to choose from, but tight ones were avoided by any self-respecting worker. Many squatters did not stick to the bare issue laid down by the Pastoralists' Union, which was ten pounds of flour, ten of meat, two of sugar and a quarter pound of tea, but would add a tin of jam or baking powder or, in the case of a sick man, some of the rough medicines of the period.[6]

Whether travelling alone or with a mate, swagmen would spend their nights poking the coals of a fire while the billy was on the boil. Many a lonely swagman would pass the time yarning with his billy, the most used utensil in the bush, cheap, light, handy and a burden to no man.

The derivation of the word 'billy' is probably from the Scottish word 'bally', meaning 'a milk pail'. It travels with every swagman, it figures in comedy and tragedy, and it has been the repository of the last words of many a perished soul. Often it was found with a grim message scratched on the bottom—beside the dead owner.

Billy is famous. Story-writers and poets have immortalised him; he figures proudly in hundreds of songs and poems, and in 'Billy of Tea', tradition claims there is no better drink:

> You can talk of your whiskey, you can talk of your beer,
> There's something much nicer that's waitin' you here.
> It sits on the fire beneath a gum tree,
> There's nothing much nicer than a billy of tea.

While the romanticising of the bush was bolstered by countless poets to a point where it is now legendary stuff, the truth is, it wasn't always like that. The swagman 'camped in the billabong' immortalised in Paterson's folk song was union shearer Samuel Hoffmeister, whose body was found beside the Four-Mile Billabong on 2 September 1894. On the previous night, Hoffmeister and a gang of union shearers attacked and burnt down the Dagworth shearing shed in a violent gun battle with more than forty shots being fired. Hoffmeister, thought to be of German origin, had the nickname of 'Frenchy', and was probably from the Alsace-Lorraine region in France, which was taken over in the early 1870s by Germany. There is even a possibility that, like many other French–Germans, Hoffmeister had left Europe to escape the conflict and was, in a sense, *auf der Walz* in Australia.

Hoffmeister was just one of thousands of union shearers who had gone on strike during 1894 for better wages and conditions and compulsory arbitration. Unionism was still a relatively new movement in Australia, especially for the outback. When this nomadic tribe of bush workers were convinced to organise themselves into a relatively new movement called unionism, as the miners and waterside workers had done, they more than anyone else paved the way for the political and social reforms that modern-day Australia now takes for granted. It has been said that the whole of middle-class Australia owes its existence to the shearing strikes of the 1890s.

During the 1890s a man possessing property in various districts might have had a dozen votes; a nomadic worker had none. This resulted in working men ignoring politics and throwing all of their energy into the organisation of their own labour—their union.

During 1885, attempts to form unions in the eastern states failed. The organisers, though earnest, could not overcome the great distances that resulted in lack of unity. The guidelines they drafted were crude and incomplete. During the next decade, William Spence would take on the job of organising the bush workers. He would become known as the 'father of Australian unionism' and he wrote:

Unionism came to the Australian bushman as a religion. It came bringing salvation from years of tyranny. It had in it that feeling of mateship which he understood already, and which always characterised the action of one 'whiteman' to another. Unionism extended the idea, so a man's character was gauged, by whether he stood true to union rules or 'scabbed it' on his fellows. The man who never went back on the Union is honored to-day as no other is honoured or respected. The man who fell once may be forgiven, but he is not fully trusted. The lowest term of reproach is to call a man a 'scab'.[7]

William Spence became General Secretary of the Australian Miners' Union in 1882, after a mining accident in which twenty-two men were drowned. He was to remain in the post for fifteen years. He was successful. Every miner in the district joined the association. Creswick became known as 'the holy ground of unionism'. When he left the mining organisation there were 23,000 members in the federal body. Spence was a superb negotiator, always organising. Unionism for him was in the manner of a religion. Spence said:

Discontent properly directed is one of the essentials of progress. A feeling of injustice will bring about discontent in a man's mind. The man who, in press or pulpit, renounces injustice is noble, but nobler by far is the man who goes out and fights it. To defend oneself and family is good, but to suffer in unselfish defence of others is to my mind, the highest pinnacle man can attain.[8]

During this time Spence approached the greatest challenge of his life—the organisation of the bush workers. It had been one thing to organise the miners; but it would be another entirely to get the concept of political organisation from the goldfields to the outback. The men he was to get the message to were strung out in more than 2000 isolated shearing sheds across a land so vast that some of it had not been settled.

It required some unusual attack in the shape of additional infringements upon shearers' rights to bring the crucial psychological moment. The catalyst that changed this situation so dramatically was an advertisement in *The Australian* newspaper on 2 April 1886. The Pastoralists' Association declared that the shearing rate was to be cut to seventeen shillings and sixpence (from the long-standing traditional one pound per hundred). It was this cut of two shillings and sixpence that was to change employer–employee relationships forever for Australian workers.

After being prompted by David Temple, a shearer, Spence wrote a letter to the *Ballarat Courier* on 29 May, urging unification and offering assistance to the shearers. On 14 June the first general meeting was held. Spence was elected President and David Temple Secretary. The Australian Shearers' Union (ASU) had started and was the beginning of what we know today as the Australian Workers' Union (AWU). Folklore suggests this mighty union began when Mrs Temple was in her kitchen cooking a meal for her two boys who had returned from a season of shearing. On learning of the condition and wages:

> Mrs. Temple said, 'David, it just doesn't make sense,
> Get on down to Creswick and have a talk with Mister
> Spence,
> He organised the miners back in 1882,
> Tell him, that you shearers want some organising too.'
>
> William Spence was working six years after he was born,
> He saw the miners assemble upon Eureka morn,
> He was there when twenty-two men drowned in the
> Creswick mine,
> He said, 'It's time we formed a union, it's time by God
> it's time.'[9]

They took up office at 30 Armstrong Street, North Ballarat, and advertised this fact. Other branches of the union sprang up almost immediately. Wagga Wagga and Bourke branches started a few months later in October. Moree and Cobar soon followed, then Young in 1888 and Adelaide, Port Augusta and Casterton in 1889. By 1890 the Australian Shearers' Union had eleven branches.

•

World wool prices had started falling in 1886, but Australia as a whole didn't heed the warning of the approaching economic collapse. During the mid-1880s the seasons were extremely good and so much wool was produced that it didn't seem to matter about lower prices. The landowners were still making a lot of money and there was much extra borrowing from the banks, which by and large was overseas money, for more land and more stock. During the early 1890s, wool prices continued to drop, causing a financial crisis. British investors starting withdrawing large sums of money they had placed in Australian banks, when higher interest rates were on offer in Argentina. Cracks appeared in the whole economy.

With the Amalgamated Shearers' Union becoming a powerful and well-organised body during the second half of the 1880s, the pastoralists of New South Wales and Queensland were forced to form an association. Now that an arbitration system was established, it was vital for the graziers to speak with a united voice when presenting their case, so Pastoralists' Associations were formed in 1888–1889.[10]

For the new trade union movement led by William G. Spence, the ideology had been fairly uncomplicated. By acting together the workers would surely obtain gradual improvements in pay and conditions. But the task of organising the pastoralists' union, 'the men of wide vision', was not so clear-cut and easily managed. The early minute books of the Pastoralists' Association are littered with 'petty jealousies and instances of wounded vanity, coupled with much obdurate determination to resist co-operation with fellow sheep-owners'.[11]

In 1890 the Australian Labour Federation was formed and joined the Queensland Shearers' Union and Labourers' Union to confront the pastoralists in various sheds. This

confrontation came to a head when Jondaryan Station on
the Darling Downs employed non-union labour. Unions
throughout Queensland united to stop the wool getting to
Brisbane. Members of the Teamsters and Carriers' Union
refused to transport the wool. Eventually Jondaryan organised
their own workers to transport the wool to Brisbane docks.

The British–India boat, the *Jumna*, was ready to sail in
order to catch the opening wool sales in London. When
at last the wool reached the wharf and was within thirty
feet of the hold, the waterside workers said it would stay
there until the 'Day of Judgement'—and a day or two after,
unless the owners of Jondaryan gave an undertaking to grant
Queensland Shearers' Union rates and conditions.

They succeeded, but trouble was only temporarily staved
off, with the squatters becoming more organised than before.
The Employers' Federation organised all sections of the
pastoralists into one united federal body. The Pastoralists'
Union took on the fight for 'freedom of contract' to crush the
union movement, and like all other sections of employers,
declined a conference unless that was first conceded.

During December 1890, the Shearers' Union decided
not to be ignored. Knowing that the forces of the state
were being aligned against them in the squatters' cause,
they remained optimistic of the outcome, bearing in mind
that they had by now achieved 90 per cent membership in
the industry.

The squatters became increasingly eager to break the
strike and transported non-unionists to their stations,

but much of the scab labour recruited was of little use and unable to carry out the task of the more experienced 'bladesmen' of the outback.

To ensure that the shearing would proceed in the 150 large holdings in Queensland, the Premier, Sir Samuel Griffiths, deployed armed police and troops to provide escorts and protect the non-union labour at rail-heads and stations. The main strike centre was at Clermont–Barcaldine, where 400 armed police, together with a detachment of artillery and mounted infantry, machine-guns and even a field piece (cannon), were stationed.

The union established committee rooms in Barcaldine and called for volunteers to reinforce the Clermont strike camp, as it seemed Clermont would be the centre of importance in the coming struggle. There was no shortage of volunteers, as some 250 men with laden pack-horses raced across the country; those without horses went by train. It was now February 1891, and the strike camp was established at Sandy Creek, some three miles out of Clermont.

With the blue flag of the bushman's Australia flying over the camp, the unionists were bolstered by the knowledge they were supported morally and financially by the coastal and inland unions. People of the small towns also supported the strike camps by giving them 'cuts' on prices and organising concerts and games. The camp bolstered a fine fighting spirit and strong democratic attitude. A butchery was set up to handle the cattle that were needed to feed the men and bulk-buying of commodities was quickly instituted, with the camp being conducted in orderly fashion and on sound economic lines.

The first sign of a strike camp was thin strands of blue smoke rising gently above distant coolibah trees. The canvas tents and lean-tos were like another world. Most of the tents were constructed of two saplings or branches, seven or eight feet long and forked at one end, driven into the ground, fork upright, in line with one another. A third sapling of like length was fixed horizontally between the two forks to form a ridgepole. Canvas was thrown across the ridgepole and arranged so both sides were even, then fastened to the ground by means of ropes and pegs at the corners, or by being nailed to heavy logs placed along either side of the tent. Strips of leftover canvas were used to secure the tent-flaps at either end. The dirt floor was picked clean of most of its stones, leaving a flat space to lay out your swag. Outside the tents was a smouldering fire, with an old black billy gently simmering. Hanging over a tent might be a hand-painted sign declaring it to be the SHEARERS' UNION STRIKE COMMITTEE.

The government issued a proclamation to the men in the camps to 'lay down their arms and disperse'. The unionists replied that their arms were for kangaroo shooting, an acknowledged occupation, and that living in camps was not unlawful as it was the custom for shearers to gather in camps prior to a shed or district commencing shearing. That was what they were doing now . . . waiting for the season to start . . . on their terms!

As the weeks passed, the squatters battled to get their wool 'tommy-hawked' off with men who had never handled a shear-blade before. If their wool cheques were to be safely deposited in the banks at the end of the season, the unionists must be brought to heel faster. Gaolings were stepped up, and dozens of union organisers were arrested and prosecuted for the most trivial—and often trumped-up—charges. As they were led away, new office bearers were elected.

On 7 March news reached the Sandy Creek strike camp that four members of the Pastoralists' Association, 'pure merinos' who were responsible for the co-ordination and movement of non-union labour 'scabs', were arriving by train. At once more than 200 men galloped and ran from the strike camp to meet the train. Jeers greeted the four pastoralists as they alighted from the train. The angry mob of shearers formed a tight circle around the eight policemen and the four-in-hand buggy required to take the unwanted visitors to their hotel. As the head of the procession became jammed at a narrow bridge leading into town, the driver of the buggy began to use his whip to strike at the mounted unionists. The men on foot then surged forward, increasing the congestion and confusion. No-one was injured, except for the police sergeant, whose head was scratched by the badge from his own helmet. However the damage was done and as a result of the Clermont disturbance warrants were issued for the arrest of seven of the principal 'rioters'.

Following this, on 24 March a gathering of some one hundred unionists attempted to persuade some sixty free labourers on a heavily guarded train not to continue their journey to Peak Downs Station, where they were engaged to shear. The station was owned by George Fairbairn, a member of the Pastoralists' Association executive, who called for special action against those who had hooted, groaned at the police and infantry and tried to persuade his band of free labourers to join the union. Eleven men were arrested and charged with riot.

The leaders of the Sandy Creek strike camp were then arrested. The chairman, Julian Stuart, and union delegate, George Taylor, were both charged with conspiracy and later convicted for 'conspiring, combining, confederating and agreeing together to force and endeavour to force certain of Her Majesty's well beloved subjects to alter the mode or method of conducting their business, thus imperilling the peace of our sovereign lady the Queen, her crown and dignity'. This law was an English statute of 1824, repealed in England not many years afterwards. When the defence pleaded this fact, the magistrate replied: 'It is in force here.'[12]

The efforts of the government's squatter-invoked attack on the striking workers were increased. Hundreds of arrests were made. At Barcaldine, one hundred and twenty mounted infantry were marched into town and lined up in front of the union office, while infantry with fixed bayonets were stationed at the police offices. Nine armed policemen entered the building, made five arrests, searched the offices and confiscated the union's files.

James Martin, or 'Shearblade' as he became known, was next to be arrested for making a seditious speech. Martin had called on his fellow bushmen to take up arms and fight by attaching their shear-blades to the sticks, making a weapon resembling the Irish pike.

Against this background the hearing of the charge against the 'Peak Downs rioters' was conducted at the beginning of April. Stuart and five other prisoners were handcuffed to a heavy chain, charged with conspiracy and remanded to Barcaldine on a closely guarded train. Two companies of mounted infantry met the train outside the town, hoping to avoid any demonstration at the station, but a crowd of over a thousand soon gathered at the spot, cheering wildly as the prisoners descended from the train, still handcuffed to the heavy iron chain and escorted by eight police armed with rifles and sword bayonets. An escort of mounted infantry formed around the prisoners and marched them into town at a slow pace. Scenes of wild excitement greeted the procession, the boisterous crowd cheering and clapping the unionists as they passed.

The hearing of the conspiracy charges against the union leaders resulted in them being committed for trial at Rockhampton; bail was refused. At the same time James 'Shearblade' Martin was convicted of sedition and conspiracy, and sentenced to three years with hard labour.

Transcripts from the Rockhampton trial indicate that Justice Harding was determined to make an example of the union leaders. When evidence was being submitted about the Peak Downs riot, Justice Harding inquired as to how many troopers were present. To the reply of 'four' he commented, 'Let me see, they all had a six shooter, four sixes are twenty-four—there would not have been many who *boohooed* the second time.' The defence counsel pointed out that men could not be shot for disorderly conduct, but Justice Harding replied, 'Very probably they [the police] could have found justification.' At the end of the trial Justice Harding summed up for seven hours. He was determined to do the will of the establishment and set an example to all.

All thirteen were sentenced up to three years' gaol on twenty counts—those arraigned were somewhat relieved when Justice Harding paused and muttered, 'to be served concurrently'. The prisoners were led away in chains, including Julian Stuart, who later wrote, 'We went to penal servitude for three years, and if I remember rightly, the Judge was dead before we came back. We had no regrets . . . worth mentioning . . . on his account!'

With support for the union prisoners being publicly displayed, the authorities were nervous about keeping them at Rockhampton. They were rushed directly to St Helena prison, in Moreton Bay. With almost one hundred police to escort them, the prisoners were chained together and marched out of prison to the cheers of all the other inmates. A crowd had also gathered on the wharf to cheer and applaud the convicted men.

The squatters and government spent a massive £90,000— in today's terms twenty million dollars—to crush the strike.

The gaoling of the union leaders, lack of finance, and hardship for the shearers and their families led to the strike being called off and an agreement to allow 'free contract' to be imposed. That is, the employer was free to employ and the shearer free to accept employment, whether belonging to shearers' or other unions or not, without favour, molestation or intimidation on either side.

The gains of a previous decade were swept away. It was a bitter moment for the workers' movement—William Spence warned prophetically that at no distant date the tables would assuredly be turned, and justice and truth would prevail.

Randolf Bedford records this scathing summary of the shearers' plight:

> Here was pastoral Australia made into armed camps; Nordenfeldts and Gatlings [machine guns] and nine pounders [cannons]; melodramatic magistrates reading the riot act to unarmed men. Shearers' camps are unlawful assemblies and crimes, under the atrocious laws; these laws, archaic except in convict times, could not get themselves buried and forgotten. The great sheep pastures of the States—held under mortgage to banks and financial companies. With Australian names and overseas shareholders, battening on Australia; the State governments merely mouthpieces for the banks and finance companies that held the best of the State lands—one hundred and thirty-one million acres in Queensland alone. The full force of Government, of the money power, of police and military, and of the kept presses, directed against

these Australians, who asked in return for good service, a living wage and conditions of food and lodging better than that afforded by . . . an overcrowded slum area in an old world city. Labor was opposed by government, by the money power, by the armed forces and the public opinion of the cities manufactured by hireling newspapers to defeat it . . .[13]

As a response to the 1891 shearers' strike and jailing of the union leaders, Henry Lawson wrote his poem 'Freedom on the Wallaby', which is probably the only Australian poem to have been debated in a house of parliament. In a bitter attack by some speakers in the Queensland Parliament, striking unionists were called 'the scum of the country'. Some verses of 'Freedom on the Wallaby' were then quoted. It was claimed Lawson's writing was one of the influences at work among the unionists, 'fomenting in their minds feelings of hatred and distrust as well as envy'. Lawson was branded a dangerous subversive.

Australia's a big country
An' Freedom's humping bluey,
An' Freedom's on the wallaby
Oh! don't you hear 'er cooey?
She's just begun to boomerang,
She'll knock the tyrants silly,
She's goin' to light another fire
And boil another billy . . .

So we must fly a rebel flag,
As others did before us,

And we must sing a rebel song
And join in rebel chorus.
We'll make the tyrants feel the sting
O' those that they would throttle;
They needn't say the fault is ours
If blood should stain the wattle![14]

There are some comparisons to be drawn between Lawson's poem, which was influenced by the 1891 strike, and the writing of Paterson's 'Waltzing Matilda', which would be influenced by the 1894 strike.

In the first verse Lawson refers to 'freedom's humpin' bluey', and 'freedom's on the wallaby', obviously Lawson is using the word 'freedom' to describe the bush workers— that is, the 'swagmen humpin' bluey' and 'swagmen on the wallaby'. He then wrote that 'freedom' is going to boomerang and knock the tyrants (bankers) silly. Lawson was telling us that even though the union had lost the fight, they, like the boomerang, would return for another strike, which he refers to as 'light[ing] another fire and boil[ing] another billy'. Lawson was right and in a few short years another major strike and conflict would occur; the billy would boil again. Immediately after the 1894 strike Paterson would write 'Waltzing Matilda'. Was it a coincidence or just damn good writing that in his first verse Paterson would refer to the 'swagmen boiling a billy' and 'waltzing Matilda'? Which, of course, is another term for 'humpin' bluey' or being 'on the wallaby'.

The following themes and sentiments in the verses of 'Waltzing Matilda' differ little from Lawson's poem: the excessive use of authority and the steely resolve not to be controlled by the system. During the next few years Paterson and Lawson would be involved in a much-publicised literary stoush in the *Bulletin*. Is it possible 'Waltzing Matilda' was a continuation of that rivalry and a response by Paterson to Lawson's 'Freedom on the Wallaby'?

8

Warrnambool to Winton

DURING THE EARLY 1870s the pastoral districts of north-west Queensland in the Winton region were declared open for settlement. Some years earlier, the explorer Major Thomas Mitchell returned from Queensland with news he had discovered the best grazing lands in Australia. The Mitchell grass, as it became known, was up to his stirrups as he rode through on his horse.

The land was opened up to anyone who wanted it. Many Victorian families went. Virtually the only requirement needed to claim and lease the land was the ability to stock the run within a year. Many of the wealthy 'men of influence' who presided over great tracts of land in the western district of Victoria wasted no time in securing their leases. Prominent family names like Manifold, Chirnside,

Fairbairn, Fisher, Riley, Bostock, Bell and Tozer took up the land and began the huge task of driving their stock north.

Another factor contributing to the exodus of Victorians to Queensland was the new land tax being introduced upon the landholdings of Victorian squatters, as Niel Black wrote at the time:

> Our little world is shrouded in gloom . . . All is gloom . . . I only state true facts, facts universally amongst us here . . . the change of the value of property of all kinds is incredible in one short year's time. The fact is we have no standard value in anything. Land is almost unsaleable, no one has the courage to invest in Victoria.[1]

But the horse had long bolted; capital had been pouring out of Victoria into Queensland for several years, not only because of the land tax, but also due to a recession during the 1870s. On 4 November 1885, the *Argus* commented on the period: 'Queensland is keeping half Toorak.' Within a few short years the process would be completely reversed . . . 'Toorak and Melbourne generally were keeping half Queensland.'[2]

The first few years were excellent, not only in Queensland, but also in Victoria, and they did extremely well. But money had to be saved from the good seasons to get through the bad seasons. In those days, it was said, 'you needed a very long purse to run a property in Queensland'.

The idea in the beginning was to raise the cattle on the vast Queensland holdings and send them south, to fatten up for the Melbourne markets. The sheep they would raise and shear in Queensland. However it wasn't long before they learnt about the Queensland climate, with its long, hot, dry spells.

These days, while travelling in the air-conditioned comfort of planes and cars, it is easy to forget the awesome task that the squatters undertook when overlanding their stock from Victoria to Queensland. They drove the beasts some four thousand miles on horseback, through virtually unmapped territory. Several of these families were part of a very small social circle, directly or indirectly connected with the writing of 'Waltzing Matilda', and this exodus was the beginning of a relationship between Warrnambool, where Christina heard the tune for 'Waltzing Matilda', and the Winton area of western Queensland where she played it for Banjo Paterson. During the time that Paterson was in the Winton district and wrote 'Waltzing Matilda' he observed the opulence of these families. When writing about the bore water in Queensland in 'Golden Water' he commented:

> The districts around Longreach and Winton were inhabited by squatter kings who made royal progresses to each other's stations, driving four horses in harness, with four spare horses, driven loose by a black boy, following up to be used as a change halfway through the journey.
>
> There was a lot of Melbourne money in those parts. Chirnside and Riley were at Vindex, Knox at Evesham, the Ramsays at Oondooroo, Bells, Fairbairns, *et hoc genus omne* at other places.[3]

On the surface, in 1894, it seems unusual for Christina Macpherson to be at the Warrnambool races in south-west Victoria and then, only months later, thousands of miles away in north-west Queensland. But Christina, like many Victorians, had relatives who first settled western Queensland. She was visiting her sister in western Victoria when she attended the races at Warrnambool, and later that year, after the death of her mother, travelled to Queensland to be with her immediate family. Many western Victorian families were making similar journeys.

Warrnambool Downs, which is not far from Winton, is one of many stations in Queensland that bears the name of a south-west Victorian locality. A cattle trek starting from Tower Hill (near Warrnambool) in 1872 to the channel country of Queensland was responsible for the name given to Warrnambool Downs, and still appears on the Queensland map today. Warrnambool Downs was taken up in the 1870s by William Pitt-Tozer and two brothers, Frederick and Thomas Archer.

While Pitt-Tozer and Frederick Archer went on with converting barren land into a station, Tom Archer rode four thousand miles, on horseback, three times to Victoria and back, and brought up mobs of heifers, bulls and horses. It was a tough business, with cattle continually on the move for six months, crossing swollen rivers and swamps.

On the station, there was a large shallow watercourse that had an important bearing on the management of the run. It was dangerous for sheep in flood times, but carried a heavy body of good feed following a flood. The watercourse was known to the Aborigines as 'Warrnambool'. It seems the word 'Warrnambool' was also used by Aborigines in other parts of Queensland to denote similar watercourses. The Aboriginal meaning for the name of the town Warrnambool, in south-west Victoria, has a similar meaning, 'a meeting place between two rivers'.

Thomas Joseph Ryan, who was Premier of Queensland from 1915 to 1919, was born the son of an illiterate Irishman near Port Fairy, eighteen miles from Warrnambool in Victoria. One of the founders of QANTAS in Winton was Paul McGuiness, who was from Framlingham near Warrnambool, and in the centenary records of Winton, published in 1975, there are at least three prominent Warrnambool names well known among the pioneers of the Winton district: Bostock, Bell and Manifold.

Bostock was a steward for the Winton Racing Club, and in 1887 was a foundation councillor of the Winton Shire. Ten years earlier in 1877, Bostock had been a Warrnambool councillor and was also Treasurer of the Warrnambool Racing Club in 1879.[4]

Another western Victorian family closely associated with 'Waltzing Matilda' was the McArthurs of Menningort near Camperdown, which is where Christina Macpherson would stay with her sister Margaret on her way to the Warrnambool races during 1894.

The McArthurs, along with the Manifolds, were among the first people to take up land on the rich volcanic soil in the western district of Victoria, around what is known today as Camperdown. By 1837, the British convict settlement at the end of the earth, in Australia, was being publicised as a place where men with a little capital might succeed. Originally known as the Port Phillip district, the village (now Melbourne) was home to some 500 inhabitants and approximately 100,000 sheep. When Melbourne was founded with its shallow port of Hobson's Bay, many settlers from Van Diemen's Land transported their sheep across to the Port Phillip district in the hope of securing new land.

Others like the McArthurs travelled from Scotland and arrived in the port of Melbourne during 1837. While on the boat Peter McArthur met Nick Cole. Being from a farming background, they had always intended to take up land as soon as possible. They worked at whatever they could, eventually saving the money for a mob of sheep and a few horses. By this time, land had been taken up between Melbourne and Geelong. There was almost no-one settled further out than fifty miles from Melbourne. Most of the settlers were afraid of the blacks. A surveyor by the name of Gellibrand had been through the western district and reported lush pastures and plenty of natural water. He went out on another trip in the Otway Ranges and was never heard of again.

McArthur and Cole rode on horseback with their first mob of sheep into the western district. Having travelled together they took up their first holding in joint names. It was simple; there were no survey lines, so basically they took what they liked, amounting to 30,000 acres. They were the first Europeans there; there was no-one else except the Aboriginals. After the first two seasons the two men decided that while they were good friends, they would be better off in the long run to go their own ways. They had plenty of land so decided to divide their holding.

Not knowing their own boundaries, they drew a map in the dirt of what they believed was the shape of their land. Then they drew straws. Whoever drew the longest straw would mark what he believed to be a fair line bisecting the property, offering each man an equal holding. The other then had the first choice of which holding he wanted. The McArthurs and Coles have lived on the same land as neighbours for more than 170 years.

The Manifold name would not only have a close association with 'Waltzing Matilda', Warrnambool and Winton, but would become synonymous with thoroughbred racing throughout Australia, with the Sir Edward Manifold stakes being run in Victoria every year. Walter Manifold was educated in Europe in the 1850s before graduating in law from the University of Melbourne. He was vice-president of the Winton Racing Club in 1879 and was a squatter in north Queensland from 1876 until 1884. He returned to the Warrnambool district where he purchased the Wollaston estate and became president of the Warrnambool Racing Club.[5]

The Manifolds were among the very first settlers in the western district of Victoria. The original run taken up by Thomas Manifold was more than 100,000 acres. The Manifolds became extremely wealthy during the goldrushes of the 1850s. Running between 8000 and 10,000 head of cattle on their property, they made their fortune almost overnight when livestock prices skyrocketed. During those years squatting stations, on average, quadrupled in value.[6]

Thomas Manifold possessed the ability to think into the future, running sustainable properties and businesses; not overstocking, but growing quality stock. During the years of the Duffy Land Act, he had managed to buy back his entire leaseholding of 100,000 acres at 30 shillings an acre.[7] The Manifolds also managed Oondooroo Station, near Dagworth (where 'Waltzing Matilda' was written), and were good friends and neighbours with the Macphersons.

Bob Macpherson was a native Australian, born in Victoria in 1855. His father was born in Scotland in 1821 and married Margaret Rutherford in 1845. Together with their three sons, Gideon, John and Angus, they migrated to Victoria in 1855 shortly before Robert (Bob) was born. Other children followed: Jane Elizabeth (Jean) in 1859, John (Jack) in 1862, Christina in 1864, Ewen Cluny in 1867 and Margaret Rutherford in 1869.

The Macphersons were Highlanders from Sutherland-shire, in the north-east of mainland Scotland, where in the early 1800s more than 1000 families were removed from their homes and ancestral lands. Five hundred years of history were made irrelevant, not unlike seventy years earlier, when the farmers of rural England were driven from their homes, making way for larger, more economic farms.

Thus were born the Scottish crofters, who either worked for a wage or received no wage in lieu of rent. The old clan system, in which the clan chief was not a landlord but more like a father, was ended by the Highland clearances. Sheep-raising spread to the Highlands, where it largely displaced cattle.

The Macphersons were typical of the first class of Scottish emigrants who migrated to preserve a threatened way of life, leaving a crumbling social order in the hope of establishing a self-contained, family-based and communal agricultural settlement.[8] At first the family took up land in the remote Victorian bush, fifty kilometres from Melbourne at Goonawarra, now the city of Sunbury. Following that, they moved to Peechelba Station near Wangaratta, in northern Victoria, fifteen kilometres south of the Murray River. Ewan Macpherson bought Dagworth Station, near Kynuna on the Diamantina River in Queensland, in 1883. It was mortgaged to The Trust and Agency Company of Australia Ltd. Robert (Bob) Macpherson was sent to manage the station with the assistance of his brothers Gideon and Jack. The name 'Dagworth' was that of a horse that ran third in the Melbourne Cup on 7 November 1872.[9]

Unlike other Victorian squatting families, such as the Manifolds, who could finance their Queensland stations with 'old money', the Macphersons sank all of their money into Dagworth Station. Attempting to establish themselves in outback Queensland, they borrowed heavily from the banks, against the huge revenues expected from the wool-clip. Twenty years later they would walk off the land with what they could fit on the back of a dray, and apparently there was plenty of spare room. The property was taken over by mortgagors and Bob Macpherson became a pastoral inspector. Many years later in 1930, he attended a ball at Kynuna, renewing many old friendships. The next morning, while leaving his hotel, he collapsed and died. His body was taken to Dagworth Station where he was buried.[10]

•

While it would be some years before Bob Macpherson would achieve legendary status in Australian culture as 'the squatter', his sister had already entered the history books.

Christina Macpherson's role in 'Waltzing Matilda' is now entrenched in Australian history and folklore. Less known is the part she played in the capture of the notorious bushranger 'Mad' Dan Morgan in 1865, at Peechelba Station, where she was born on 18 June 1864. Christina was only a few months younger than Banjo Paterson, with whom she would years later have an affair. She was less than one year old when she was credited with assisting in the capture of Morgan.

Born in 1830, Daniel Morgan won the respect of nobody at a time when some outlaws, like Frank Gardiner and

Ben Hall, were referred to as 'gentlemen bushrangers' and accorded some respect, as shown in the traditional ballad 'The Death of Ben Hall':

> Come all Australian sons to me,
> A hero has been slain.
> Butchered by cowards in his sleep,
> Along the Lachlan plain.
> So do not stay your seemly grief,
> But let your teardrops fall.
> For all Australians mourn today,
> The gallant bold Ben Hall.

'Mad' Dan Morgan was despised by everyone. He was ruthless and gunned down anyone who stood in his way. During April 1865, Mad Dan left New South Wales and crossed the border into Victoria. Apparently, he wanted to even the score with two squatters he harboured grudges against, but also to defy the Victorian police, who warned him he would never live for more than a week if he rode south and crossed the Murray. Morgan first held up a station on the Ovens River and then rode towards the Macpherson property at Peechelba Station.

Entertaining visitors from Melbourne, the Macphersons were enjoying dinner around 8 pm when footsteps were heard on the verandah. Gideon, the eldest boy, went to the door and was confronted by Morgan, who put a gun to his head and threatened him with his life. Ewan Macpherson sprang to the aid of his son, but he too was held at gunpoint and shoved back into the dining room, where Morgan imprisoned everyone, the ladies fearing for their lives.

Mad Dan, wanting to enjoy some of the finer things of life, asked for whiskey and demanded to know who was playing the piano he had heard while approaching the homestead. When told it was one of the Macpherson girls he said, 'She had better give us some music.' Miss Jean Macpherson, as her younger sister Christina would do for Banjo Paterson thirty years later, composedly seated herself at the piano and played several marvellous tunes. During the recital, baby Christina was heard to be crying in another room, so the nursemaid, Alice McDonald, immediately moved to attend the infant, but was ordered at gunpoint not to leave the room. Eventually, Morgan relented and allowed Alice to soothe the persistent crying of baby Christina. Alice managed to alert a station hand, John Quinlan, that Morgan had bailed up the household, and he in turn ran to tell the Rutherfords, living nearby.

John Rutherford acted without delay, rounding up horses and arming men. He sent word to the Wangaratta police. By daybreak, the Peechelba homestead was secretly surrounded by more than forty armed police and volunteers. Meanwhile, Mad Dan continued to party all night. In the morning he left the house to choose one of Macpherson's best horses from the nearby yard. Within forty yards of the house, the notorious bushranger was shot by John Quinlan through the throat, tearing out his windpipe. He died within hours.[11]

Edward Harrington would later recount the death in his poem 'Morgan':

> Day broke upon the Murray, the morning mists were gone,
> The magpies sang their matins, the river murmured on.
> When Morgan left the homestead and neared the
>   stockyard gate
> He heard the boobook's warning, and turned but
>   turned too late—
> For Quinlan pressed the trigger as Morgan swung around,
> And sent the grim bushranger blaspheming to the ground.
>
> So fell the dread Dan Morgan in Eighteen sixty-five,
> In death as much unpitied as hated when alive.
> He lived by blood and plunder, an outlaw to the end;
> In life he showed no mercy, in death he left no friend.
> And all who seek to follow in Morgan's evil track
> Should heed the boobook's warning: 'Go back, go back,
>   go back!'

Morgan's body was taken to Wangaratta where it was propped up on bags and exhibited to the public. The eyes were opened and one of his Colt revolvers was placed in his right hand. Dr Henry of Benalla, using his pocket-knife, cut away his beard, declaring he would have a tobacco pouch made from the hair. The head was nearly bald by the time the police called a halt to the macabre goings-on. Next, the head was removed and placed on the chest of the torso. Later it was shaved, soaked in brine, wrapped in hessian and sent to Melbourne University for examination.

John Quinlan collected a reward of £1000 for shooting Morgan and would later move to Dagworth Station with Bob Macpherson.

As the Victorian pioneers had driven their cattle across our great vast land, carrying their belongings with them, so would Christina travel the same distance, carrying in her head the tune called 'Craigielea'. She wouldn't know the importance of the tune or that it would be the beginning of a song the whole world would come to identify as Australian. Through her actions we can trace and credit the birth of 'Waltzing Matilda' to two places on the Australian map; the town of Warrnambool in the western district of Victoria and the Winton–Kynuna district in north-west Queensland.

Previous page: Andrew Barton 'Banjo' Paterson in 1890, the year his famous poem 'The Man from Snowy River' was published. Within a few short years, Paterson would add another two folk legends to the Australian cultural landscape—the squatter and the swagman. (National Library of Australia)

Top right: The squatter in Paterson's song was Robert 'Bob' Macpherson of Dagworth Station in outback Queensland, but, like the swagman, he was symbolic of a whole class of Australians. The squatter was someone who had power, property, style and the full support of the law. (State Library of Queensland)

Middle right: Sarah Riley was Paterson's fiancée of eight years before he met her best friend, Christina Macpherson. The Rileys were good friends and neighbours of the Macphersons, with pastoralist interests in and around the Winton area. (O'Keeffe collection)

Bottom right: Henry Lawson in Bourke in 1892. Lawson and Paterson were involved in a much-publicised literary stoush in the *Bulletin*. 'Waltzing Matilda' may have been a continuation of that rivalry, and a response by Paterson to Lawson's poem 'Freedom on the Wallaby'. (State Library of Victoria)

Left: Christina Macpherson was taken by a 'new' march tune she heard at the races in Warrnambool; she later played it by ear for Paterson at Dagworth, and together they wrote 'Waltzing Matilda'. This photograph was taken in 1900, five years after their ill-fated relationship had ended. (National Library of Australia)

Local Aboriginal people arrive at Dagworth Station in western Queensland in 1878 with flags of truce and encounter the new 'owners' of the land. (State Library of Victoria)

Wilmot Abraham (Corwhorong) was a well-known identity in the Warrnambool area, popularly, if not necessarily correctly, referred to as 'the last of his tribe'. (State Library of Victoria)

A settler's cottage: a vertical slab hut with a slab roof. (State Library of Victoria)

A squatter's residence: the Chirnside family's Werribee Park Mansion. (State Library of Victoria)

Click go the shears, boys, click, click, click: the blade shearers of the 1870s.
(State Library of South Australia)

Shearing at Vindex Station (previously part-owned by Sarah Riley's family), near
Winton in 1895. A line of blade shearers on the left, shed hands and wool-classers on
the right, with the 'boss of the board' in the middle. (State Library of Queensland)

Striking union shearers parade through the main street of Charleville, Queensland, during the strike. (State Library of Queensland)

Non-union shearers being ferried to the sheds in western Queensland under police protection, 1891. (National Library of Australia.)

Within the image: *Unionist Camp*, *Shearers coming in*, *Searching Train for Non Unionists*, *Wool Teams Escorted by Police*.

The Shearers' Strike in Queensland (wood engraving), 1 April 1891.
(State Library of Victoria)

In 1891, Queensland seemed on the brink of civil war, with armed union shearers forming large strike camps outside many western towns. Mounted and regular infantry were sent out from Townsville to take on the shearers near Hughenden. (State Library of Queensland)

'Freedom Without Dishonor': the thirteen union leaders jailed for sedition and conspiracy during the 1891 shearers' strike, posing for a photograph on their release in November 1893. Within six months the shearers would be on strike again across the eastern states of Australia. (State Library of Queensland)

Special police at Longreach in western Queensland during the strike of 1894. (State Library of Queensland)

The Paddle Steamer 'Florence Annie' on the Darling River under police protection during the 1894 shearers' strike. (State Library of South Australia)

The new grandstand at the Warrnambool Racecourse, 1882. (State Library of Victoria)

The fashions and betting ring at the Warrnambool Races, 1894. (Warrnambool Racing Club)

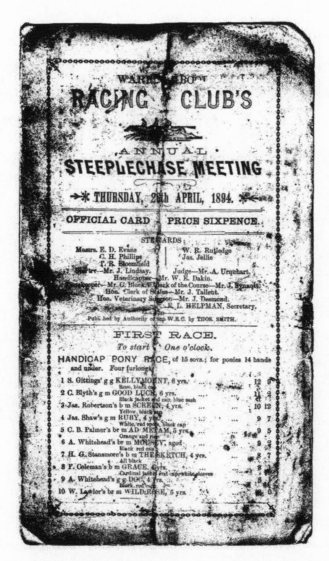

The card for the Grand Annual Steeplechase on the day Christina Macpherson heard 'The Craigielee March'. (Warrnambool Racing Club)

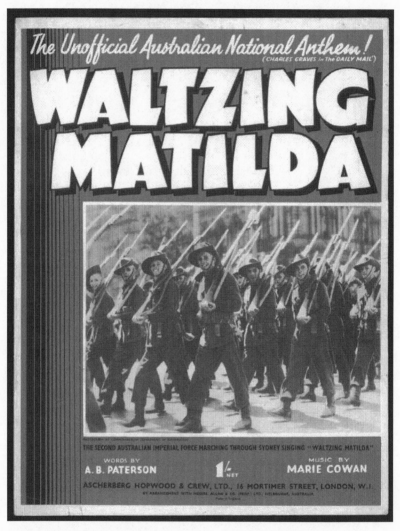

In 1940, when Australia's national anthem was 'God Save the Queen', Australian diggers were marching to 'Waltzing Matilda'—the unofficial Australian national anthem. (National Library of Australia.)

A happy group of ex-prisoners of war singing 'Waltzing Matilda', Japan, 1945.
(Australian War Memorial)

Two soldiers painting a mural to illustrate our iconic swagmen 'camped
by a billabong', Vietnam, 1966. (Australian War Memorial)

Dennis O'Keeffe and Richard Magoffin perform 'Waltzing Matilda' on 2 September 1994 at the Blue Heeler hotel in Kynuna, western Queensland, to commemorate the centenary of the death of the swagman, Samuel Hoffmeister. (O'Keeffe collection)

9

Australia for the Australians

Flocks die, friends die,
You yourself die likewise;
But if one has won an honoured name,
Then that can never die.[1]

Maybe the only thing Banjo Paterson was not famous for was playing the banjo! Such was the man with many varied talents, himself a legend; he will never die. Authors describing his illustrious life rightfully tell us he was Australia's most famous poet, a war correspondent, champion horseman and a major in World War I. Few commentators on his life will mention he was also a womaniser, destroying Sarah Riley's life and leaving Christina Macpherson broken-hearted— 'Barty has so many lady friends . . . including a divorcee whose name went round the family in whispers.'[2]

Although Paterson left us with culturally defining literary works, it would seem few people ever really got to know him personally. Paterson was an enigma—secretive. He was described by Norman Lindsay, who was the cartoonist and illustrator for the *Bulletin* when Banjo was at the peak of his popularity, as a 'sardonic aristocrat'. This, perhaps, is not how we want to imagine our most popular poet.

His personality and literary talent were influenced and shaped by a combination of family background and personal circumstance.

Paterson wrote of his fabled homestead:

> I see the old bush homestead now
> On Kiley's Run,
> Just nestled down beneath the brow
> Of one small ridge above the sweep
> Of river-flat, where willows weep
> And jasmine flowers and roses bloom,
> The air was laden with perfume
> On Kiley's Run.

'On Kiley's Run' is a lament for Paterson's loss of his inheritance, as well as an elegy of his father's failure. Further lines depict ruin wrought by drought, overdrafts and the forced selling of stock to satisfy bankers, all reflecting his father's plight on Illalong Station.

The Patersons had over-reached themselves, something Barty would never admit. His father was not a robust man, with his mother constantly referring to her husband's delicate health. He suffered from lumbago and some other mysterious ailment that no amount of doctoring seemed capable of diagnosing. When suddenly he collapsed and died in 1889, at the age of fifty-six, the coronial finding read, 'overdose of opium, the weak state of the septum being accelerated by heavy drinking'. Banjo, then twenty-five and in practice as a solicitor for three years, wore the personal tragedy of his father's failed life, an early lesson in 'keeping the blind well down'.[3]

The idyllic memories of his boyhood and dreams of life in the bush had ended. Later, when accounting for his entry into the legal profession, he wrote:

> I soon saw there wasn't a livelihood to be gained in the bush. Everyone who goes in for farming right out, comes to grief sooner or later. At the best it is only a continual struggle. My idea was always to have enough to live on comfortably, so that if I wanted a thing that didn't cost too much I could get it. And station life didn't seem to me to promise that in any way at all. So though I was in the thick of the bush, I didn't let it get such a hold on me that I couldn't leave it. As a profession the law seemed about the best thing for a man to take on.[4]

At twenty-five years of age, Paterson had a real concern for his own and Australia's future. He was bitter with the government about his father losing his land and launched himself into his own private study of history and economics, writing a political pamphlet, published at his own expense, dealing with land reform from a Protectionist point of view, titled *Australia for the Australians.*

The pamphlet received very little attention; in Paterson's own words, it fell 'as flat as a pancake'. By his own admission, he was in a Hamlet mood and felt himself called on to set society right on the land law. He contrasted the settlers in the interior, 'striving day to day on their little properties, with no comforts, no leisure and no aspirations', with property owners in Sydney, 'living luxuriously, travelling between this colony and England, drawing large rentals, or spending large values which they never did a hand's turn to earn or deserve'.[5]

The pamphlet did, however, show that Paterson, between the years of 1886 and 1890, was in the same camp as Henry Lawson and did much to prove he was a rebel against the established order and believed in the value of personal labour. He was venting his social conscience and raging nationalism.

He attacked the system for not working, saying there should be much greater wealth among Australians than presently existed. He attacked the English system called 'fee simple tenure', which was the system under which land was given away when the first Europeans arrived. That is to say, the grantees took the land from the Crown, to hold it forever and ever, for themselves, their heirs, and whoever they assigned it to, free of any rent or payment to anyone. He argued that the present system was enabling some people to falsely obtain huge benefits from the community, and holding valuable land idle, which discouraged industry and prevented production.

To illustrate his thoughts he described a freehold estate owned by one family, which was now valued in many millions. This land was almost the entire area between Williamstown and Geelong, and was still in the same state as when Batman first settled Melbourne, carrying sheep and nothing else. And in Sydney on the North Shore was a vast block of pristine waterfrontage land, still in exactly the same bold, rugged state as when Captain Cook sailed past in the *Endeavour*.

> It is now worth hundreds of thousands of pounds. What has given these properties their value? Clearly not the labour and trouble of their owners, as they are unimproved. They have steadily increased in value ever since the settlements were founded, because as a country gets more and more settled, the demand for such land near the capital cities becomes greater and greater. When the community parted with these lands they got a few pounds only, which was all they were worth. Then the people set to work to transform the howling bush into a wealthy city; they worked and worked, building houses, making railways and wharves, extending the suburbs; they added to the value of all the lands about there. Meanwhile the owners of these lands stood by and looked on. 'We can wait', they said. They were paying no rent for the land, and they saw that it was gradually going up in value, and that they would in time make a handsome profit, not out of their own exertions, but those of the community.[6]

He believed the wealth of the community was being created by labour and the community as a whole should benefit, blaming the rotten, absurd system that was making such things possible. Paterson warned against the poverty that might come from the land system if it was not changed, citing the bitter hatred between tenants and their landlords in Ireland, Scotland, England and Wales: 'and then the fun will begin . . . plenty of good landlord shooting then.'

Having proffered his opinion on the distribution of land, he attacked the burgeoning capitalism and profiteers in Sydney, suggesting that those who doubted him might take a nightly stroll around the poorer quarters of our larger colonial cities, as he had done himself:

> They will see poor people herding in wretched little shanties, the tiny stuffy rooms fairly reeking like ovens with the heat of our tropical summer. I, the writer of this book, at one time proposed, in search of novelty, to go and live for a space in one of the lower class lodging houses in Sydney, to see what life was like under that aspect. I had 'roughed it' in the bush a good deal. I had camped out with very little shelter and very little food. I had lived with the stockmen in their huts, on their fare, so I was not likely to be dainty; but after one night's experience of that lodging I dare not try a second.[7]

Although he conceded that some of this might be the fault of the people themselves his sense of nationalism and social conscience drove him on:

Do you, reader, believe that it is an inevitable law that in a wealthy country like this we must have so much poverty? Do you not think there must be something wrong somewhere? Of course people are much worse in the older countries. God grant that we never will reach the awful state in which the poorer classes of England and the Continent now are. Are we not going in the same direction? That is the question, which we have to consider. The same trouble is showing itself here, which has come up everywhere. The improvement in productive power has been like the speed of a racehorse, while the improvement of the people who ought to be benefited thereby, has been like the speed of the mud turtle—if indeed any progress has been made at all.[8]

In later years, Paterson claimed to be somewhat embarrassed by his 'first literary effort'; this seems strange, since both he and his father had suffered as a result of the system he had attacked. In fact, Paterson himself had even participated in the bogus system of settlers 'dummying' for station owners, which obviously irritated his conscience so much that even at the age of seventy-four he was still moved to write:

I am old enough to have seen the transition from cattle to sheep and to have seen a station of 80,000 acres all taken up in 640-acre blocks with their attendant conditional leases. Some of these blocks were take up by bona fide settlers and others by dummies acting in the interests of station-owners. At the age of seventeen I held one of these dummy blocks and duly transferred it when the time came. The bona fide settlers were referred to in speeches as 'the sturdy yeomanry, the country's pride', but in course of time almost all of these bona fide settlers sold their blocks to the station owners and moved on to fresh fields and pastures new, leaving things exactly where they were when they started—except that the station had become a vast freehold instead of a vast leasehold . . .[9]

One can sense Paterson harboured an amount of jealousy for the squattocracy during this period of his life. In verse and prose, he had scant regard for the large property owners and was heavily on the side of the station hands, drovers and the like. When the article was written there would have been many who would have agreed with him, including most leading poets of the day, many of whom knew the shortcomings of the existing land-grant system, with bush workers and small selectors struggling on marginal selections.

A growing conservatism later in his life prompted some to believe that Paterson was an upholder of the established order, as opposed to Henry Lawson, who gave the image of a reforming socialist. The impression that he was a spokesperson for the squattocracy and station owners was certainly not true of Paterson in his early years of writing. True, he grew more conservative among his associates in the Australian Club as the years passed, but along with that his writing declined and would never again reach the levels of his heyday of writing about the underdogs and characters of the bush; 'the strongest emotion felt by this vigorous young man in his twenties was a nostalgic hankering for the way of life he had known in his youth'.[10]

The political pamphlet was testament to Paterson's strong sense of nationalism, which he himself fuelled in the pages of the *Bulletin*. Many of the social and democratic principles he challenged were to manifest themselves in the next few years when Australian workers began to form trade unions and demand reasonable wages: a nationalist fervour which would find stronger voice during the fast-approaching shearers' strikes of the 1890s.

While his popularity as one of the *Bulletin*'s favourite poets was on the rise, his personal life was in turmoil. His father had died a failure and his mother and sisters were forced to leave Illalong Station and move to Rockend. The thread of life at Illalong and regular trips back to the bush had come to an end. Life in Sydney was now almost compulsory, much to Grandma Barton's delight. Emily Barton constantly entertained guests from well-respected families in Sydney while Banjo was living with her. She always had designs for bumping him up the social ladder; Banjo, her grandson, with a noticeable 'gammy' arm he had broken several times in his youth and no inheritance. The sort of social clap-trap he had written about in *Australia for the Australians* was not the sort of stuff to impress the class of people she had in mind for him. He was undermining inflated egos and exalted positions.

Bolstered by his 'old school tie' and Grandma's social connections, Paterson went into partnership with John

William Street and through this family connection, he would become engaged to John Street's cousin, Sarah Riley. Banjo's engagement—and this partnership—took him into the network of friendships that were destined to make legal history in New South Wales, with the Street family producing no fewer than three High Court judges. Sarah Ann Riley was born in 1863 (a year before Paterson), the second daughter of James Riley of Geelong. Sarah came from a very distinguished background, a family regarded highly in social circles, with pastoralist interests in and around the Winton area.

However, Banjo's grandmother Emily often wondered whether he might have been out of his depth when on 18 October 1888 she wrote in a letter:

> Barty's fiancée, Sarah Riley, has been staying with us, and does credit to his taste: she is an exceptionally nice girl, well connected and educated. I sometimes wonder that she should not have look'd higher, but his talent goes a long way, and also makes his worldly prospects pretty secure. He is in partnership with a son of our old neighbour John Street, who is a cousin of hers.[11]

As usual, Grandma was right, but it would be eight years before Sarah would realise and terminate the engagement with her flirtatious boyfriend, rightly thinking that if in eight years he had not come up to scratch, there was not much hope that he ever would.

Banjo continued on with his business partnership with John Street as the turbulent 1890s approached. However his real love was poetry and with his popularity continuing to grow, preparation was made for him to release his first book of poems, *The Man from Snowy River and Other Verses*. Paterson's poems had been published in the *Bulletin* for several years and 'Banjo', as he was now known, was fast becoming a household name.

Another poet who, like Paterson, will always be identified with the surge of nationalism that affected many aspects of Australian life during the upheaval of the 1890s, politically, socially and culturally, was Henry Lawson. Previously an unknown house painter, Lawson had his first story published in the 1888 Christmas issue of the *Bulletin*. Like Paterson he achieved huge acclaim, gathering his own hungry readers. Together they were referred to as 'the twin deities of Australian literature'.[12] Paterson had the utmost respect for Lawson's work and a jealous admiration for his singular approach to life. He was often so warm and engaging and at other times contemplative and remote. Writers like Paterson and Lawson were sort of cult figures, celebrities of the day, very much a part of popular culture.

Bulletin editor J. F. Archibald knew a lot of readers were choosing sides between his two most popular writers, who were perceived as rivals. Lawson was seen to champion the worker, the underdog and the union man, amid the natural disadvantages of the outback. Banjo, the bush dilettante, was more optimistic and resolute in his approach to the bush folk. Although this perception has remained for some writers, it is a long way from the truth, since

Paterson was just as concerned with the rights of the bush worker and with the principles of mateship and unionism. His early radicalism was just as deep seated as Lawson's, though more intellectual and less emotional.[13] Back then, it wasn't unusual for poets to answer, sometimes critically, a poem published by one of their contemporaries. It was sport, a literary stoush—damn good fun; or in Lawson's own words, 'The Height of Fashion'. Australia's two most popular poets slanging away at each other were bound to sell a few papers, so they decided to 'have a go' at each other as a means for advertising themselves. Anyway, Lawson needed the money, so that was that.

But Lawson and Paterson took it a little too far. Their rhyming match left people with misconceptions about their relationship, thinking the *Bulletin*'s two chief bards were on the edge of hostility. This was simply not the case. In fact, Paterson acted for Lawson in negotiating his *Bulletin* contract, was a good friend of Henry and his family and often took suggestions about his poetry from Lawson. Regrettably, they left many readers with the impression they were not friends.

> Henry Lawson was a man of remarkable insight in some things and of extraordinary simplicity in others. We were both looking for the same reef, if you get what I mean; but I had done my prospecting on horseback with my meals cooked for me, while Lawson had done his prospecting on foot and had to cook for himself. Nobody realised this better than Lawson; and one day he suggested that we

should write against each other, he putting the bush from his point of view, and I putting it from mine.

'We ought to do pretty well out of it,' he said, 'we ought to be able to get in three or four sets of verse before they stop us.'

This suited me all right, for we were working on space, and the pay was very small . . . so we slam-banged away at each other for weeks and weeks; not until they stopped us, but until we ran out of material.[14]

Lawson kicked off on 9 July 1892 with a poem titled 'Up the Country', containing a few laconic satirical lines aimed at armchair historians and poets comfortably ensconced in Sydney:

> I am back from up the country—very sorry that I went,
> Seeking out the Southern poets' land, whereon to pitch
> my tent;
> I have lost a lot of idols, which were broken on the track
> Burnt a lot of fancy verses, and I'm glad that I am back.
> Farther out may be the pleasant scenes, of which our
> poets boast,
> But I think the country's rather more inviting round the coast,
> Anyway, I'll stay at present at a boarding house in town,
> Drinking beer and lemon squashes, taking baths and
> cooling down.[15]

So a couple of weeks later, on 23 July, Banjo responded with a poem titled 'In Defence of the Bush'. The first round probably went to Lawson because Paterson directed his verse at him personally and not his poetry:

So you're back from up the country, Mister Lawson,
    where you went,
And you're cursing all the business in a bitter discontent;
Well, we grieve to disappoint you, and it makes us sad to hear
That it wasn't cool and shady—and there wasn't plenty beer,
And the lonely bullock snorted when you first came into view,
Well, you know it's not so often that he sees a swell like you . . .[16]

A few weeks later, on 6 August, came the reply. Lawson
was sharpening the pencil, his attack more personal:

It was pleasant up the country, Mr. Banjo, where you went,
For you sought the greener patches and you travelled like
    a gent., . . .
Did you ever guard the cattle when the night was inky-black,
And it rained, and icy water trickled gently down your back
Till your saddle-weary backbone fell a-aching to the roots
And you almost felt the croaking of the bull-frog in your
    boots—[17]

Before Paterson could answer, Lawson sharpened his pencil
further and cleverly re-wrote Paterson's famous poem
'Clancy of the Overflow'. He changed the title to 'The
Overflow of Clancy':

And the pub. hath friends to meet him, and between the acts
    they treat him
While he's swapping 'fairy twisters' with the 'girls behind
    their bars',
And he sees a vista splendid when the ballet is extended,
And at night he's in his glory with the comic-op'ra stars.

I am sitting, very weary, on a log before a dreary
Little fire that's feebly hissing 'neath a heavy fall of rain,
And the wind is cold and nipping, and I curse the ceaseless
    dripping
As I slosh around for wood to start the embers up again . . .[18]

While the twin deities were hurling bolts at each other, numerous poets had started taking sides and submitting their own verse attacking or defending both of them. Paterson concluded on 10 October with 'An Answer to Various Bards', which brought the contrived controversy to an end and is considered to be the strongest poem of the series:

Well, I've waited mighty patient while they all came
    rolling in,
Mister Lawson, Mister Dyson, and the others of their kin,
With their dreadful, dismal stories of the Overlander's camp,
How his fire is always smoky, and his boots are always damp;
And they paint it so terrific it would fill one's soul with
    gloom—
But you know they're fond of writing about 'corpses' and
    'the tomb'.
So, before they curse the bushland, they should let their
    fancy range,
And take something for their livers, and be cheerful for
    a change . . .
So that ends it Mister Lawson, and it's time to say good-bye,
So we must agree to differ in all friendship, you and I.
Yes, we'll work out our salvation with the stoutest of
    hearts we may,
And if fortune only favors us, we will take the road some day,

And go droving down the river 'neath the sunshine and
the stars,
And then return to Sydney and vermilionize the bars.[19]

Paterson summed up the events by saying, 'So that was
that, I think Lawson put his case better than I did, but I
had the better case, so the honours (or dishonours) were
fairly equal. An undignified affair in the end, but it was a
case of "root hog or die"'.[20]

By the time the last volley was fired Lawson was in the far-
western New South Wales town of Bourke, leaving Paterson
in Sydney, cooped up in his solicitor's office. Lawson had
gone to experience the 'outback' they had been writing about.

Lawson didn't go of his own volition. It was certainly no
secret to anyone that Lawson was drinking heavily, so the
owner of the Bulletin, J. F. Archibald, sent him outback in
search of copy, a few real stories from the interior. He gave
the twenty-five-year-old Lawson five quid and a one-way
ticket from Sydney to Bourke. Lawson boarded the train at
Redfern Station, which was then the terminus for the city
rail-line. Not sure that Lawson would actually go, Archibald
sent a few Bulletin workers to see him off. Along with his
pen and note-pad, Henry packed a few old paintbrushes in
the hope of getting some casual work painting houses. One
of the Bulletin's editors wrote: 'Here was this unfortunate
towny, deaf and shy and brooding, sent with a railway
ticket and a few spare shillings to carry his swag through
the unknown where he knew nobody.'

As the train crossed the Blue Mountains into the hilly country Lawson was familiar with while growing up, he became excited and longed for the bush of his childhood. But it wasn't long before the excitement drained away, as he entered the vast empty landscape of the interior. He had never been this far out before. He scribbled as the train continued on:

> Draw a wire fence and a few ragged gums, and add some scattered sheep running from the train . . . then . . . the railway towns consist of a public house and a general store, with a square tank and a school-house on piles in the nearer distance. The tank stands at the end of the school and is not many times smaller than the building itself. It's safe to call the pub 'The Railway Hotel', and the store 'The Railway Stores', with an 's'. A couple of patient, un-groomed hacks are probably standing outside the pub, while their masters are inside having a drink—several drinks. Also, it's safe to draw a sundowner sitting listlessly on a bench on the verandah, reading the *Bulletin*.[21]

The train reached Bourke in the late afternoon. A long shimmering line of camels, reminiscent of the great inland exploring expeditions, snaked its way along the horizon. The scorching sun reflected brightly from the galvanised-iron roofs of the town. Bourke was a river port on the Darling River with a population of around 3000. It was the largest town in that central area of Australia, some 400 miles from the nearest point of the coast. Even back then, the most-used phrase to describe venturing into the vast outback was 'going to the back of Bourke'.

Lawson found accommodation at the union-patronised pub, the Great Western Hotel, owned by a strong supporter of the Labour League. After a short stroll around the town he sat down and wrote a brief letter to his aunt in North Sydney, Mrs Emma Brooks, on 21 September 1892. Interestingly, the stoush in the *Bulletin* was still firmly in his mind, as he wrote, 'the bush between here and Bathurst is horrible. I was right, and Banjo wrong.'[22]

•

Over the next few months, while Banjo was revelling in the exploits of the Geebung Polo Club, Lawson tramped and tramped in what he described as 'the awful desolation'. Lawson's mate Jim Gordon, from western Victoria, in his poem 'The Old Tin Trunk', would reflect on his time spent tramping with Henry:

'Twas deep in an old tin trunk we found them,
Things stacked away when our blood was red.
(No silken ribbon it was that bound them,
But a twisted double of woolpack thread).
Old droving records and stock-route sketches;
The tanks were marked with a star beside;
Broad arrows pointed the long dry stretches
Where the unfenced pastures were wild and wide.[23]

So, armed with newly acquired union tickets, Lawson and Gordon rolled up their swags, filled their waterbags and tucker bags and left Bourke, 'the great metropolis of the scrub'. This was the beginning of their downriver trek. They were going to become part of the hundreds of seasonal workers who descended on Toorale Station at that time every year for the shearing season: shearers, shed hands (rouseabouts), stockyard men, musterers and cooks. They had jobs waiting for them as shed hands, pre-arranged by Lawson's recently acquired union mates. They tramped in the heat for more than sixty miles until they eventually arrived. Toorale Station was one million acres in size, and usually shore a quarter of a million sheep. It was the largest holding in the Bourke district and was owned by the renowned pastoralist Samuel McCaughey, who also owned the adjoining run, Dunlop Station. With these holdings, McCaughey owned more land in New South Wales than any other person in living history. He never at any time lived on either property, but at his mansion at Yanco in the Riverina, a town which gained a mention in the popular traditional song 'Lazy Harry's':

> Well we reached the Murrumbidgee near Yanco in a week,
> We passed through old Narrandera, and crossed the
>   Burnett Creek,
> But we never stopped at Wagga for we'd Sydney in our eye,
> And we camped at Lazy Harry's on the road to Gundagai.

The two trekkers enrolled at the shearing shed as rouse-abouts. Their new job consisted of picking up the fleece, stacking it into bins and keeping the shed floor in some sort of order. Here, for the first time Lawson experienced life in a western shed with the tough characters of the back-country, saw sheep being shorn on a huge scale, witnessed the chaotic harmony and rhythm of a large shearing shed.

It stimulated his senses, and he spent countless hours taking notes and jotting ideas for further writing. In bush terminology Lawson was a traveller, an itinerant worker, a swagman. He found work in shearing sheds, 'picking up', but even Lawson himself admitted he never had the guts to try his hand at the more skilled and better paid work of shearing. He marvelled at those men. The work was hard and the men honest, and he would write of their journey in his poem 'Out Back':

> The old year went, and the new returned,
>   in the withering weeks of drought,
> The cheque was spent that the shearer earned,
>   and the sheds were all cut out;
> The publican's words were short and few,
>   and the publican's looks were black—
> And the time had come, as the shearer knew,
>   to carry his swag Out Back.[24]

By the end of the year he finished 'shouldering his matilda' and was back in Bourke for Christmas, more easily employed at his old trade of house painting. By this time Lawson had befriended the leading delegates of the local union branch. He was writing poems for the *Western Herald*, but not signing his name. Anonymity was something he treasured. He was enjoying drinking with the locals and barmaids alike, but was the young Lawson questioning the effect of his own drinking? 'Sweeney' is one of the poems he wrote while in Bourke:

> Then a wise expression struggled with the bruises on his face,
> Though his argument had scarcely any bearing on the case:
> 'What's the good o' keepin' sober? Fellers rise and fellers fall;
> What I might have been and wasn't doesn't trouble me
>   at all.'[25]

•

Paterson envied Lawson's restless, gypsy spirit and sojourn into the real outback. The poems he was submitting had a new conviction. Banjo was restless; the acclaimed Australian writer, still cooped up in his dingy little solicitor's office, was constantly juggling daily legal duties with his wish to further his career in writing. His legal job was exactly that—a job. Paterson was quite aware of his station in life, position in society, and the regard the readers of his literary work held him in. But still he was restless. The union strikes of the past years were still very much in everyone's minds. Everyone—especially a writer and social commentator—knew, or felt, that the past troubles caused by the workers had not finished.

He was still engaged to Sarah Riley. He was reluctant to commit to the trappings of a comfortable lifestyle and to the prospect of marriage into a respectable family. He was consumed with an excited passion to immerse himself in his writing and experience first hand the events occurring in the back-country, as Lawson had done. Within the year he would get his wish, and spend time in western Queensland. In the midst of the volatile 1894 shearer's strike, he would accompany his fiancée, Sarah Riley, out to Winton to visit her brother Frederick and his new wife, Marie, who were being married on 12 August 1894.

A few years before, Sarah had attended Madam Pfund's finishing school in St Kilda. While there, she had made a good friend in Christina Macpherson, a lass from the western district of Victoria. Christina's brothers lived at Dagworth Station in western Queensland, near the town of Winton. Sarah's family lived in Winton and had also managed a property, Vindex Station, in the district. Sarah was anxious to be in Winton at the same time as Christina, both to visit her own relatives but more importantly, to catch up with her old school friend.

10

The Fight Begins

THE ITINERANT WORKERS, shearers in particular, would become the most loved and written-about Australians for decades to come. Poems by Paterson, Lawson and many others, along with paintings by artists such as Tom Roberts, elevated this drifting workforce to the stuff of legends. There was a perception of them being fun loving, knockabout blokes, much like Flash Jack from Gundagai in 'All Among the Wool':

> All among the wool, boys, all among the wool,
> Keep your blades full, boys, keep your blades full.
> I can do a respectable tally myself whenever I like to try
> And they know me round the backblocks as Flash Jack
> from Gundagai[11]

This bunch of Australian larrikins were not often associated with militant unionism, organised arson and gunfights. Yet it was these swagmen who confronted more violence than any other workers. In addition to resisting the might of the squatter, the newspapers, the police, militia and judiciary, the shearers also had to contend with the scabs.

As well as *Bulletin* poets during the 1890s, there were many unsung poets who captured the intense feeling of the times and the attitude towards 'free labourers'. The following anonymous ballad was referred to as a 'bush toast' or the 'hymn' of the Queensland shearers:

> A scabby form lay rotting,
> Upon a filthy bed,
> It smelt a damned sight nicer,
> For the weeks it had been dead.
>
> There's no maggots on his carcass,
> There's no worms to crawl and feast,
> The blow-flies turn their noses up,
> They will not blow this beast.
>
> So what's the use of scabbing,
> He cannot go to hell,
> The maggots and the blow-flies
> Will blacken him as well.[1]

•

To fully understand the problems in Queensland, we must look at some important factors the unions were competing with. From as early as the 1860s the Queensland Government legislated to enable Kanakas (Pacific Islanders) to be brought into the colony to work the cane fields. At that time, there was a widely accepted belief that white people were physically unsuited to working in the tropics, but the decision proved controversial in Queensland and throughout the colonies. An entrenched dislike for cheap 'coloured' labour was an important part of the Australian outlook, and led to considerable dissatisfaction. The corruption and cruelty that accompanied the 'blackbirding' and plantation work provided opponents of the scheme with plenty of ammunition. The desire of some southern Queenslanders to ban the trade in labourers led to serious divisions which resulted in an attempt, on the part of the north, to secede. The situation did not resolve itself until the turn of the century when the new Commonwealth Government banned Kanaka labour.[2]

Leading up to the eventual banning of this slave labour, no single issue aroused such bitterness throughout the outback during the 1890s—it was of the greatest concern to the bush workers. There was a closing of ranks against foreigners which saw the beginnings of the White Australia policy. Chinese and Kanaka labour meant a reduction in wages and living standards. Clause 62 of the rules of the Amalgamated Shearers' Union of Australia specifically stipulated that 'no Chinese or South Sea Islanders shall be enrolled as members of the A.S.U. of Australia'.[3]

Though publicly and officially declaring it was against their policy to employ Asiatic labour, the Pastoralists' Association understood that such doings would be secretly 'winked at'. The South Sea Islanders were enticed by such methods as blackbirding, where 'black-gins' were used to offer sexual favours to them, and the islanders were then supplied with free rum until drunk. Once under the influence, they were chained below deck and transported to Queensland, where they were contracted for £20 per year for three years.

Even Banjo Paterson, looking from the window of his secure solicitor's office in Sydney, knew conditions had to change. The union strike of early 1891 was still very much in everyone's minds. The past troubles caused by the workers were far from over. In December 1892 Paterson was moved to champion the union's cause in 'A Bushman's Song'. He left no doubt as to his feelings. He attacked the wealthy landholders, and he referred to the scabs and Chinese workers as 'the leprosy'. He wrote:

> I asked a cove for shearin' once along the Marthaguy;
> 'We shear non-union here,' says he. 'I'll call it scab,' says I.
> I looked along the shearin' floor before I turned to go—
> There were eight or ten dashed Chinamen a-shearin' in a row.
>
> It was shift, boys, shift, for there wasn't the slightest doubt
> It was time to make a shift with the leprosy about.
> So I saddled up me horses and I whistled up me dog,
> And I left the scabby station at the old jig-jog.
>
> I went to Illawarra, where my brother's got a farm;
> He has to ask his landlord's leave before he lifts his arm;
> The landlord owns the country-side—man, woman,
>   dog and cat,

They haven't the cheek to dare to speak without they touch
    their hat.

It was shift, boys, shift, for there wasn't the slightest doubt
Their little landlord god and I would soon have fallen out,
Was I to touch my hat to him?—was I his bloomin' dog?
So I makes for up the country at the old jig-jog.[4]

There was talk of unification of the colonies into one
Federation. The Australian workers wanted to be part of
the process, to have a say in the decision-making. They
were tired of the old-world wrongs, of injustice and greed.

The magnitude of the struggle for shearers to achieve
adequate parliamentary representation, especially in
Queensland, can be further understood by some brief
analysis of the parliamentary make-up, and who owned
the land. Unlike New South Wales where there existed
many small holdings,

> in Queensland with its huge holdings there were only
> 150 sheds, most of which began shearing later in the
> year and thus had ample time to import non-union
> labour from the south. The Queensland Premier, Sir
> Samuel Griffith, a radical of the right, was unlikely to
> offer sympathy, nor indeed the Legislative Assembly
> with seventeen squatter-members, five mine owners and
> many other industrialists. (Only two members expressed
> support for the shearers' cause.) Most of the big sheep runs
> were owned and controlled by the banks and mortgage
> companies.[5]

Indeed, there existed a wealth qualification to be elected to the Legislative Council.

Squatters occupied a vast area of the best land in the continent, and in association with city interests had established a base for their political power in the legislative councils of the colonies. The squatter was 'the lord of the manor'. Few in the district questioned his decisions. Any workers who did would find themselves on the road looking for food. There were two prices for shearing, with the squatter, arbitrarily and often, setting the lesser price as it pleased him. The most primitive conditions were endured, seldom with fresh water or adequate sanitation:

> There was a time when the water supply of the shearers was the daily bath of every cow, pig and mangy dog on the premises. There was a time when shearers slept on boards, and a score of them performed their ablutions in an old nail can full of dried paint. There was a time when the curly horned stag of six summers was dished up for the shearers in melted tallow fat at morning, noon and night.[6]

Before the shearers' unions were formed, shearers, under the Masters and Servants Act of 1846, were like prisoners until their work was done. Rebellion meant fines, imprisonment and confiscation of wages with the squatter as magistrate. As a crowning injustice, rations had to be bought from the squatter at what were described as 'goldrush prices'. It is little wonder that the name 'squatter' became (and has remained) synonymous with wealth, repression and injustice.

For them Barcroft Boake would coin the word 'money grub' in his haunting poem 'Where the Dead Men Lie', which appeared in the *Bulletin* on 19 December 1891:

Moneygrub, as he sips his claret
Looks with complacent eye
Down at his watch-chain, eighteen carat—
There, in his club, hard by:
Recks not that every link is stamped with
Names of the men whose limbs are cramped with
Too long lying in grave mould, camped with
Death where the dead men lie.

One of the greatest difficulties in developing the Amalgamated Shearers' Union was the assuredness of the squattocracy. The squatters' certainty that they were born to rule others was bolstered by their gentlemen's clubs and the belief in the brotherhood of the privileged class. Landowners have always known that to retain their acres they must have a club, even if there is no need for organisation in the industrial sense. This age-old free-masonry of landowners had taught many men to believe that this was how God meant life to be. An authoritarian 'gentleman', God was presented to them in their churches by the ruling-class brothers and actual blood-brothers of squattocracy.

Now that men were rising to deny much of what had been presented as Holy Writ, they would bring down upon themselves the righteous wrath of those who had lived comfortably within the established state of affairs and forced the swagman-shearer to a meek acceptance of his station in life. John Keith McDougall sardonically described these God-fearing men in 'Pompous Piebald Esquire':

When the blossoms come out and the sunshine is fair,
I drive to the church in my carriage and pair,
And the people I meet all respect my decree,
And humbly doff hats when they shake hands with me.

I have guiled them of old—I shall guile them again,
Though they slave for me hard in the sun and the rain;
Working hard with the spade, long hours with the axe,
To keep me immune from a land yielding tax.

I stick to my gold with a falcon-like clutch,
And the judgement to come doesn't trouble me much;
For the preachers assure me, when life here is done,
I'll be cleansed from all sin by the blood of the Son.

The state is my sword-blade, the Church is my shield;
I'm the master of earth and all things she doth yield;
And the million must cringe, with their brows in the mire,
To their lord, Pompous Piebald, the Boss and Esquire.[7]

•

The shearing seasons of 1892 and 1893 were comparatively quiet. Although there were no general strikes, there were several acts of arson—setting fire to shearing sheds and wool stockpiles. The targets for these acts were key figures in the 1891 strike. There was a case of a dozen free labourers at Terrick Terrick Station being poisoned when strychnine was added to the salt. The station was a large one, with 220,000 sheep, and its part-owner R. G. Casey had been prominent in the 1891 campaigns against the union.

By the end of 1893, London wool prices had fallen to a seven-year low. The Federal Council of the pastoralists decided to cut the shearing rate and severely undermine conditions. They refused a conference with the Australian Shearers' Union. The 1891 agreement, which they had signed, stipulated that no changes to wages or conditions could be made without negotiating with the union. The pastoralists reneged on their word and denied the decision they made, keeping it a secret from the Australian Shearers' Union until 20 March 1894.[8]

During May 1894, the newly formed Australian Workers' Union (AWU), comprising the ASU and the General Labourers' Union, issued a manifesto urging members to stand by the 1891 agreement. The shearers refused to accept the new terms imposed upon them and the pastoralists would not submit their case to arbitration, so a fresh strike developed.

The stage was set. Stoic mateship of the swagmen confronted the wealth, power, pomp and ceremony of the squatter.

Here in the 'lucky country', violent class conflict is often looked upon as un-Australian. It is commonly believed that the use of force is usually resorted to by small groups of extremists, never by the majority of 'decent' workers. Yet even a glance at Australian history reveals a cavalcade of riots, baton charges, shoot-outs, bashings of scabs, violent breaking-up of meetings, arson, police killings of strikers, setting up of street barricades, sabotage, drilling by armed militia, the suppression of dissent by the state and the repeated use of the army to crush strikes. These include the 1873 Clunes miners' riot, the maritime and shearing strikes of the 1890s, the New South Wales General Strike in 1917, the bitter struggles of the 1920s and 1930s depression years (with police shootings of waterfront strikers and coal miners at Rothbury, where two were killed and forty wounded), Ben Chifley using troops to break the coal strike in 1949, the 1975 Kerr coup, New South Wales Builders' Labourers' Federation's 'vigilantes' who destroyed scab building works, the 1982 storming of the Melbourne Club, state suppression of the Builders' Labourers' Federation, the Hawke Government's crushing of the pilots' strike, and more recently Patrick's assault on the wharfies.[9]

Even Labor Party historians tend to shy away from the extent of violence used by workers, often referring to it as spontaneous or poorly planned, yet these commentators persist in highlighting state violence against the same unionists. Also, rarely do we acknowledge that there has been mass public support for violence, which at times has made the way for huge social reform and change. The Eureka Stockade was massively popular on the goldfields and in Melbourne. World War I anti-conscription campaigns, street battles to halt the growth of fascism in the 1930s and militant protestors opposing the Vietnam War all received popular support.[10]

The shearers' strike of 1894 is one of the most violent industrial conflicts the country has seen, and in many areas was supported by the majority of the public. The arson and violence in most cases were not spontaneous or poorly planned, and most of the outrages were performed by militants and often criminals within the union movement.

During February 1894, at the same time the Pastoralists' Association had secretly decided to lower the shearing rate, Jim 'Shearblade' Martin was appointed as the general organiser of the Australian Labour Federation at their conference in Charters Towers. Shearblade had been jailed during the 1891 strike. The thirteen union leaders jailed at the Rockhampton trials in 1891 were released in November 1893. At a reception for the released prisoners, Shearblade made a speech on 20 November at Centennial Hall in Brisbane, where he talked of having revenge. He told the crowd that he could not say he believed in revolution or he might have to do another two years, but no power could prevent him from thinking that he believed in it. If the environments of workers' lives were such that they could not constitutionally get a fair share of the fruits of their labour, then they had a right to revolt. With the crowd cheering, Martin continued. If the Legislative Assembly was closed to the working men, then they must fight their battles on the plains of the country.

This was an admission by the union that there was obviously a growing criminal element within their ranks and an indication that the union were preparing themselves for a long and violent strike. Their determination to win this time would be the catalyst for the union's violent conduct in the forthcoming 1894 strike. The first step was to raise extra money for the strike fund.

A bank robbery was planned on 18 April, two months before the shearers' strike began. After the robbery, the proceeds were to be handed to a third man who would take the money to Queensland. Depending on the success of the robbery, several more heists were planned. Unfortunately for the union, the robbery was messed up.

After dismounting from the two finest-looking horses ever seen in the New South Wales town of Barraba, two robbers walked into the bank, drew their guns and demanded the money. The bank manager, Mr W. C. McKay, refused to hand over the money and was shot dead. The two killers fled empty handed.

A few days later during a huge man-hunt, the two horses used in the robbery were found lying dead at the bottom of a cliff, fourteen miles from Barraba. Their throats had been cut and any brands or markings on the horses had been hacked off. A few days later two men were arrested.

The first man arrested, about fifteen miles from Barraba in an exhausted condition, was Jack Cummins, a gun shearer and a delegate for the Shearers' Union. The second man arrested claimed his name was Joseph Anderson and that he was a sailor who had only been in the colony for nine months. Further investigation proved he was an ex-Sydney criminal, real name Alexander Lee. In 1885, he had been sentenced to seven years' imprisonment for attempting to murder someone at Circular Quay.

Cummins maintained his innocence to the gallows. Lee admitted that he was guilty, while at the same time declaring in a most emphatic manner that 'Cummins had no part in the murder'. A newspaper report at the time said Cummins stood tense in the dock, staring with fascinated intensity as Sir George Innes donned a small black square and sentenced them to death. Jack Cummins then declared to the hushed courtroom, 'And may the Lord have mercy on your soul too, for you have just condemned an innocent man to death.'

On the evening of the hanging, Cummins was visited by his younger sister for the last time. A small pen-knife was concealed in her mouth which she transferred in her final goodbye kiss. Later that night, Jack Cummins slashed his wrists with the pen-knife. Two warders noticed him twitching in bed, removed the blankets and found him in a pool of blood. They stopped the bleeding and managed to keep him alive, to be hanged in the morning.

A few minutes before the executioners entered Lee's cell, he was heard reciting 'Macpherson's Farewell' in a firm voice. Lee must surely have known the tradition of the poem. The Macphersons were a proud clan with an ancient tradition. Jamie Macpherson was hanged around 1700, amid allegations of political influence in his trial and execution. Macpherson's fame rests not with the way he lived, but the manner in which he died. According to tradition he read a farewell poem on the gallows, and then played a tune on his fiddle, while dancing. He offered the fiddle to anyone who could play, so he could perform his death dance on air, to the accompaniment of music. No one took up his offer so he smashed his fiddle, and was executed. Robert Burns wrote the lyric, apparently to Macpherson's own tune:

> Farewell, ye dungeons dark and strong
> Farewell, farewell to thee.
> Macpherson's rant will ne'er be lang
> On yonder gallows tree.
> Sae rantingly, sae wantonly
> Sae dauntingly gaed he
> He played a tune an' he danced aroon
> Beneath the gallows tree.

In the morning the gaol chaplain engaged in prayer with the men, before Howard the hangman entered the cells and pinioned them. The leg-irons were knocked off and white caps affixed to their heads.

At twelve minutes past nine, the chaplain emerged from the cell, followed by Cummins, wheeled in an invalid chair, and Lee walking with a firm step as they proceeded to the gallows. Before taking his stand on the drop, Lee said in a loud and distinct voice, 'Gentlemen, I declare that John Cummins is innocent of the crime for which this day he suffers. He is not the man who was with me at the Barraba bank, you're puttin' to death an innocent man.'

Cummins' brother and sister were in the crowd and called for his release. The hangman deliberately moved forward and pulled the white hoods over the prisoners' faces, and tightened the nooses. The rope around the neck of Cummins, who was seated in his wheelchair, caused him to gasp and make a gurgling sound as his hooded head fell to one side. Lee, defiant to the end, stood as firm as a rock.

Howard the hangman pulled the lever. With a dead muffled sound, the heavy trapdoor flew down, and the two men dropped together. Death was instantaneous for Cummins, with the weight of the wheelchair to which he was strapped immediately snapping his neck. It was a gruesome sight, Cummins in his wheelchair swinging from side to side with Lee beside him performing the death dance, with his muscles in spasms jumping and contorting his legs. After some seconds both men were swaying gently. The hanging was complete.

Details of the grotesque hanging of Lee and Cummins were printed in newspapers around the country. Ironically, the graphic accounts of the macabre scene had excited the imaginations of journalists and editors to the point where, by and large, they neglected to mention prevalent rumours that the failed bank robbery was to raise funds for the forthcoming strike.

The unionists had learnt from their mistake in 1891, when they had announced their intention to strike early in the season, allowing the Pastoralists' Association plenty of time to organise police and protect the non-union labour. But now in 1894 things were different; the strike began closer to the season, providing the unionists with a tactical advantage. The shearing season had to be finished in a few months and the squatters would not have enough time to organise non-union labour.

The intention and resolve of the union was made clear on 3 July. Early in the day, an attempt was made to burn the shed on Oondooroo Station, but the fire was extinguished before it took hold. Then the Ayrshire Downs shearing shed was burnt to the ground with gunshots being fired. Ayrshire Downs, north-west of Winton, was owned by the Darling Downs and Western Land Company. The Premier of Queensland, Sir Thomas McIlwraith, was a prominent shareholder in the company. A huge reward was offered and secret police began to infiltrate the unionists.

Within six weeks another five sheds in the district—Redcliffe, Cambridge Downs, Murweh, Eurongella and Casillis—were burnt to the ground by the striking unionists.

Two years later in 1896, Jim 'Shearblade' Martin was charged, found guilty and convicted to 15 years' hard labour for allegedly leading the men who set fire to the Ayrshire shed.[11]

The Burning of the *Rodney*

IT WAS NOW APPROACHING the end of August 1894, a few months before 'Waltzing Matilda' would be written. Paterson's time was being taken up writing such poems as 'How Gilbert Died', 'How the Favourite Beat Us' and 'A Voice from the Town' in preparation for *The Man from Snowy River and Other Verses*, which would be published within the year. Knowing that his fiancée, Sarah, then in Sydney with her aunt, had an invitation to visit her brother Frederick at Winton in Queensland, he would have been excited at the opportunity of getting back to the bush and creating some new ballads. There can be little doubt his attention was captured when thousands of shearers formed strike camps all along the Murray–Darling River system and at major rail-heads throughout western New South

Wales and western Queensland. Hundreds of armed police (troopers) were dispatched to the main areas of conflict.

The strike was organised and widespread: Queensland in the north, the whole of western New South Wales and parts of South Australia and Victoria. Almost without warning to the Pastoralists' Association the shearers set up large camps at central sites. As each property was to commence shearing, the union shearers would report to hear the conditions of the shed. They would then reject the conditions outright and return to the strike camps. Considering the average flocks were about 200,000 sheep the squatters were in a dilemma: sheep laden with a full year's wool, no income and the warmer weather approaching. 'The Strike of 1894' reflects on the tension along the river:

> Men were willing and strike-camps were filling,
> On the banks of the Darling River.
> The men on the land, who never dirtied their hand,
> With fear they began to shiver.[1]

Reports came in daily of shearing sheds being burnt, river-boats being stoned, fences burnt and scuffles at all major ports and rail-heads, where free labourers were being brought to the back country in an attempt to get the wool off.

These events portrays the level of violence that idealists within the working movement were prepared to carry out, and when analysed, give a comprehensive account of the escalating nature of the conflict and the utter determination of the union shearers to uphold their position.

One of the most violent events to make headlines in the *Sydney Morning Herald* on 26 August 1894 was the burning of the paddle steamer *Rodney* on the Darling River—the only act of 'inland piracy' recorded in Australia's history. To fully appreciate the events, we need to understand the importance of riverboat transport to the economic and social life of inland Australia. There were few roads—most passable only by bullock dray, horse, bicycle, or 'shank's pony' (walking). Huge quantities of cargo and produce were plied along the Murray, Darling and Murrumbidgee Rivers by paddle steamers. With broad beam and shallow draft, they were eminently suited to the ever-changing river. Throughout the shearers' strike, with owners desperate to commence shearing sheep heavily laden with wool, some paddle steamers were used to ferry non-unionists to the shearing sheds. Police were also ferried to these areas of conflict via the river systems.

The ultimate destination of the *Rodney* was Tolarno Station on the Darling River above Pooncarrie in western New South Wales, where more than 400 striking shearers had gathered, blocking all access to the station. This potentially explosive situation escalated when reports came through from Menindee of a boatload of special Sydney police being transported down the Darling from the north to arrest the unionists at Tolarno. At the same time, the *Rodney*, with its cargo of 'scab labour', was approaching from the south.[2]

The captain of the *Rodney*, Jimmy Dickson, was active during the 1891 shearers' strike, transporting non-union labour on his boat, so now that he was doing it again in 1894 the union shearers took a particular dislike to him. He was referred to as a 'double scab', and the unionists were determined to 'get him'.

> You've called me a bastard, What have I done?
> You scabbed you bastard in ninety-one,
> And what's more, you son of a whore,
> You scabbed again in ninety-four.[3]

When the *Rodney* embarked from Echuca with its cargo of fifty non-unionists under police protection, union shearers lined the banks of the Murray River and heckled the 'scab' shearers. Reports came in from Swan Hill, Mildura and Wentworth, as striking shearers attempted to hinder the *Rodney*'s progress along the Murray River and into the Darling, with its human cargo of non-unionists for the sheds.

Such was the national interest in the conflict that the journey of the ill-fated *Rodney* was played out daily, like a cheap pantomime, in the Sydney newspapers. The first report in the *Sydney Morning Herald* was on Friday 17 August:

> The steamer 'Rodney' sailed from Echuca for the Darling River today with 50 free labourers. There was a number of unionists on the wharf. Except [for] hooting everything

passed off quietly. The police were present under Inspector Larkin.

The *Rodney*, with steam up and under the control of Captain Dickson, pulled away from the old red-gum wharf and disappeared around the riverbend, with the sound of its whistle echoing across the river from bank to bank, amid the lofty river-gums. Two days later the *Rodney* was passing through Swan Hill:

> A Swan Hill telegram states that the steamer 'Rodney' passed through there yesterday with 57 free labourers on board. Strong efforts were made to capture some, but only one was captured. They are bound for the River Darling.[4]

When departing from Swan Hill, unionists lined the bank, yelling abuse and pelting stones at the free labourers. Two days later the *Rodney* had left the Murray River, and was heading north into the Darling. On the same day in the *Sydney Morning Herald*, along with a report on the *Rodney*, was an account of the progress of shearing at Peak Hill Station, where 80,000 sheep were to be shorn. The shearing had started under the 1891 agreement. The unionists had picketed the shed. Only seven shearers (scabs) had signed the agreement and commenced shearing. At this rate, it would be many months before the shed would complete the season. It was obvious to all that more non-union men would be needed. Some of these men were coming on the *Rodney*.

The next day news arrived indicating the mood of the authorities and the concentration of unionists along the Darling River.

> There are now 400 men in the union camp at Tolarno. All the approaches to the station are picketed. When the Sydney contingent of police, which passed here today on board steamer Lady of the Lake, arrives at Tolarno there will be thirty altogether. An attempt will then be made to arrest the rioters.[5]

Knowing that anyone convicted of burning a paddle steamer would be facing a jail term of between three and thirteen years, the striking unionists at Tolarno station moved quickly to intercept the *Rodney*, before the boatload of police arrived from the north.

One of the leading unionists in the strike camp was Joseph Benjamin Cummings. Unlike the stereotype of a shearer, he was a man with beautiful handwriting, a talent for poetry and an excellent singing voice. Cummings was a very good athlete and would later fight in both the Boer War and World War I. He neither smoked nor drank and was a gun shearer, who at one stage held a blade record for hand shears.[6] Cummings's daughter Thelma would later marry the famous bootmaker R. M. Williams. In his autobiography, *Beneath Whose Hand*, Williams commented on Cummings and his involvement in the burning of the *Rodney*:

> Thelma's father was a ring-leader of the attacking party. Eight men were captured and came to trial but the jury

found them not guilty. Thelma's father however, was on the run from that time. He continued to work under a variety of names; Thelma had been brought up under the name Cummings (or sometimes Davenport).[7]

Joe Cummings, along with other leading unionists, called the 400 men to assemble. After a short speech by Cummings, every man in the strike camp swore a secret oath never to reveal what was about to happen. History now tells us every man kept his word. Pieces of paper were drawn from an empty kerosene tin by each striker in the camp. Six of the tickets would bear a note stating that the drawer was to meet after nightfall at the place indicated on the ticket. All other unionists not selected were to leave the district as quickly as possible. One of the unionists not to be chosen was Robert Cameron, the father of The Hon. Clyde R. Cameron, who said that not being selected as one of the six to burn the *Rodney* was his lifelong regret.[8]

The men chosen were to go downriver, where at a certain bend they would find a steel cable. They were to tie it across the river at an oblique angle just below the waterline. When the bow of the *Rodney* hit the submerged cable, it would slew into the side of the river, be doused with kerosene and set alight.[9] One hundred years later, in 1994, near Polia Station, the wire marks were still visible in the tree where the steel cable remained fixed for many years.

Meanwhile, the *Rodney* continued northwards with its cargo of forty-four free labourers up the Darling River and past Wentworth. On the evening of Friday 25 August, they arrived at Syme's woodpile above Pooncarie and loaded the furnaces with enough wood for the ninety-mile dash up the Darling to Tolarno Station. The owners of Tolarno learned that the unionists in the strike camp had strung several miles of fencing wire, both under and above the waterline, to snag the boat as it passed. Fearing the *Rodney* being attacked if it proceeded further up the river they sent a rider to 'warn the skipper and advise him to turn and go downstream, but he would not, he turned into a billabong and put out his lights'.[10] At nightfall, approximately twenty-three miles north of Pooncarie, Captain Dickson pulled the *Rodney* into a billabong surrounded by marshy wetland, tying up to trees on the riverbank, with four guards posted and full steam up. He planned to wait overnight, and then continue early the following morning, in conditions offering greater safety.

At about four o'clock in the morning of 26 August, a small group of union men paddled out to the *Rodney* and climbed aboard. They had muffled the oars of the small rowing boat they used, turned their clothing inside-out and raddled their hair and faces with mud. They were unrecognisable. After a fight, they allowed the crew to leave the boat and row to safety. The scabs were left marooned on an island in the middle of the river. The union men cut loose the barge and left it to drift down the river—presumably not to damage the cargo it carried. They then poured kerosene over the decks and into the hold of the *Rodney* and burnt it to the waterline, before it slowly sank into the shallows.[11]

Captain Dickson would later confirm that armed men had crept through the water and threatened to shoot a man if he untied the rope holding the boat. When the alarm was given, the engine was put full speed astern, but was held fast by the rope. After the steamer was boarded by men at both ends, ten minutes' notice was given for all hands to leave the boat, which was immediately set on fire:

> As the flames rose, the attackers gave three cheers for the unionists at Polia Station. They watched the fire for some time, while a youth played 'After the Ball is Over' on his concertina, and the steamer began drifting downstream, first close to one bank, then close to the other, scorching the gum trees as she went. Then they left, taking some of the non-unionists with them, and 'maltreating others'. The 'Rodney' burned for several hours, then sank in the shallow water, clear of the channel, with her boiler and the remains of her paddle-boxes above the surface of the river.[12]

'After We Burnt the Rodney', set to the tune 'After the Ball is Over', records the night's event:

> After we burnt the *Rodney*, we danced on the river-bank,
> There we played an old tune until the *Rodney* sank,
> Many a heart was happy, if you could only see,
> We had a bloody great bon-fire, the night we burnt
>   the *Rodney*.[13]

Within days the burning of the ill-fated *Rodney* made headlines in the nation's newspapers:

PASTORALISTS AND SHEARERS
SERIOUS DEVELOPMENT OF THE DISPUTE
TROUBLE ON THE DARLING
A STEAMER BURNT AND SUNK
FOUR MEN WOUNDED

The shearing difficultly in New South Wales is assuming rather a serous character, especially in the Western districts, and several alarming rumours were current yesterday, particularly in political circles, in regard to outrages and the violence perpetrated by unionist shearers. The report received yesterday by the Government showed that the Darling country is in a very disturbed condition, and requests for further assistance had led to the dispatch of reinforcements of police.[14]

The burning of the steamer was followed by an outcry against lawlessness. Pastoralists talked of hanging the fire-bugs for piracy. At least one metropolitan newspaper advised the squatters to take up weapons. The New South Wales Government offered a reward for information that would lead to the conviction of the ring-leaders. Property owners and ships' captains armed themselves.

Tension increased when on the same day, further up the Darling River in the Grassmere woolshed at Nettalie Station near Wilcannia, shearing was about to commence with non-union labour. Because of the burning of the *Rodney* earlier in the morning, police were on hand to protect the free labourers. The *Sydney Morning Herald* reported the event as follows:

Riot At Nettalie Station Two Men Shot

A terrible affray is reported as having occurred at Grass-
mere woolshed, on Nettalie Station, last night. A mob of
unionists attempted to rescue the free labourers, and the
police had to resort to the use of firearms, resulting in
one unionist being shot dead and two others being badly
wounded. It is reported that one of the free labourers was
shot dead by a unionist . . .

Further details of the affray at Grassmere are at hand.
Two men were not shot dead as reported. But two union-
ists were shot with a revolver. Both are alive, but one is
in a critical condition. It appears that shortly before nine
o'clock last night about 100 unionists arrived at Grassmere
outside the men's hut. The police stationed there heard a
stampede of men. Senior Sergeant McDonagh came out
and the unionists informed him that they wanted to take
the free labourers, stating they were armed as well as the
police and were determined to have the men at any cost.
The sergeant replied that they would not be allowed to
do so. He was immediately assaulted and received a blow
on the head, felling him to the ground. The mob then
rushed the free labourers' hut, smashing the door in with
a battering ram. The police fired shots, as also did one of
the free labourers, who was armed with a revolver. Two
of the unionists were wounded in the affray. Shortly after
the shots were fired the unionists retreated, taking the
two wounded men.[15]

Word of the burning of the *Rodney* had reached the
Wilcannia strike camp, and knowing the Grassmere shed
had started shearing with non-union labour, the striking

unionists had gone into a frenzy. The leaders in the strike camp were concerned that press from the burning of the *Rodney* would act against the cause, so moved quickly to address the scab shearers at the Grassmere shed. A group of union shearers including Billy McLean and John Murphy had gone unarmed to interview the non-unionists.

> Billy led a band of good union men
> Out to the Grassmere Station,
> Where the black-leg shearers and policemen with guns,
> Awaited the confrontation.[16]

On reaching the shed, Billy was first to enter. Without warning he was shot and fell to the shearing shed floor. His mate John Murphy was also shot and fell beside him. The gang was then confronted by armed police guarding the shed and forced to retreat, carrying their wounded with them. McLean was in bad shape. The bullet went right through his lung. At first it was thought he was dead. The retreating unionists were pursued by six constables discharging their revolvers. McLean and Murphy were among eight men arrested and charged with riot.

> Billy was shot and Murphy they got,
> Ambushed at the shearing shed door.
> We never should forget, dags and sweat,
> Mixed with blood on the shearing shed floor.[17]

McLean was eventually stretchered into to court, charged with 'unlawful assembly' and convicted. He was sentenced to three years' hard labour and sent to Goulburn Gaol. Arthur Baker, the scab who'd shot the unarmed McLean, was congratulated by Judge Stephen and presented with a medal, 'The Abbott Cross', by the Pastoralists' Association.

Wounded in his lung, McLean developed tuberculosis in the damp cold of his Goulburn prison cell. With less than a third of his sentence served, he was released from gaol and sent home to his widowed mother, 600 miles away. No sooner had he reached home than he took to his bed, never to rise again, and died within days.

> They might fool you, but they'll never fool me,
> A hero he died, and a hero he will be,
> Few men will walk where he's gone,
> The Union wrote music, young Billy sang the song.[18]

William John McLean was the sixth of eleven children and was born on 22 October 1869. McLean lived at Koroit in the western district of Victoria. Much of the wool from the western and southern districts of New South Wales was transported by bullock dray to Port Fairy on the western Victorian coast, which at one time in the mid-1800s was second only to Sydney as the international port of Australia. McLean, and many other shearers, would hitch rides on these bullock drays or ride bicycles along the bullock tracks up to the Murray–Darling River systems. From there, they would be transported by riverboats to the shearing districts. They would travel up to New South Wales and Queensland at the commencement of the shearing season and work the sheds back down into Victoria.

Such was the union comradeship of the time that his mates, members of the Bourke branch of the Australian Shearers' Union, some 700 miles from McLean's home town, rallied to the aid of his mother and raised £90 for a monument which stands today at Tower Hill cemetery near Koroit.

Donald Macdonell, General Secretary of the Australian Workers' Union, wrote to his mate Henry Lawson and said:

> I want you to write the epitaph of Billy McLean, who between the blackleg who put a bullet in him, and the Government who prosecuted and imprisoned him, was done to death in the trouble of '94. We have collected enough cash to put a decent memorial over his mortal remains. Only one thing is needed to complete it and that is a verse of Henry Lawson's. You, perhaps, more than any other man, understand the straight bushman, with his loves and his hates; his strengths and his weakness, can voice these feelings. Let me have what I ask and so confer a big favour upon hosts of your outback friends and admirers, as well as upon your sincere friend.[19]

It is not known for sure if Lawson did write the memorial, but many believe the simplicity and dignity of the words on the monument indicate he may have. During the time McLean was shot, Lawson was working for the *Worker*, the union's daily newspaper in Sydney, as the provincial editor. His job was to sub-edit the news coming in directly from strike camps throughout the country. The work kept him in touch with what was happening at the centres of conflict. If there was a premeditated plot by the union to burn the *Rodney* then Lawson would surely have known about it and some evidence has been collected which suggests Lawson was present when the *Rodney* was burnt.[20] He was no stranger to the outback and had a lot of friends and connections with the union, so it is not entirely unexpected that he could have made another 'secret' trip outback.

Was he in some way connected with these events? Could that have been why Lawson was asked to write McLean's epitaph?

HIS FELLOW UNIONISTS
AND ADMIRERS
IN MEMORY OF THEIR COMRADE,
WILLIAM JOHN MCLEAN
WHO WAS SHOT BY A NON-UNIONIST
AT GRASSMERE STATION, N.S.W.,
DURING THE BUSH UNION STRUGGLE
OF 1894.
WHO DIED 22ND MARCH, 1896,
AGED 26 YEARS,
A GOOD SON, A FAITHFUL MATE,
AND A DEVOTED UNIONIST,
UNION IS STRENGTH.

On 28 August news reached Sydney that unionists had burned the paddle steamer *Rodney* on the Darling River and that two unionists had been shot at Grassmere. The pastoralists were alarmed. A manual issued in Queensland concerning the pastoralists' official view on how to treat striking unionists stated: 'Whenever necessity for firing upon offenders shall occur, it shall be at the leaders of riots or the assailants of the police, and, if possible with effect.'[21]

A few days later in a meeting between the Pastoralists' Association, the Colonial Secretary and Premier Reid, it was reported that Thomas Buckland, a miner turned pastoralist, when referring to the early days had stated: 'in 1839 and 1840 the owners of stations had to confront a similar trouble, and had through a determined co-operation been able to deal with it. The shining barrel of a revolver had done more in five minutes than the court could arbitrate upon in a decade.'[22]

In the days following the burning of the *Rodney* several men were arrested and eight men came to trial at Broken Hill. Almost thirty witnesses claimed the men were innocent and provided alibis. All prisoners were found not guilty. In a letter written by Mike Cummings about his father Joe, he states:

> After the sinking of the 'Rodney' an enquiry was held, but such was the Freemasonry amongst the Shearers that they all pretended to know nothing. My father along with others left the district pronto. He headed for Queensland and laid low, there was also much changing of names etc . . .[23]

Riverboats burnt, unionists shot and non-unionists under police protection. A secret ballot in the Tolarno strike camp, drawing lots from an empty kerosene tin. Changing of names, and a well organised get-away plan, sealed with an oath taken on their lives never to tell.

The 26 August 1894 was now etched into Australian history and like theatre, the events were publicly unfolding throughout the nation's newspapers. Nervous times indeed. One can only wonder how Banjo Paterson's creative imagination was being stirred by this social and class conflict. Every day in the Sydney newspapers he was reading about the civil insurrection in the outback, wondering where it would end and what might happen next . . . He didn't have to wait long.

A hastily built and heavily defended stockade around a temporary shearing shed at Dagworth Station. On the left are the three policemen. The centre policeman is Senior Constable Michael Daly, who was involved in the gunfight. Beside the policemen are the four Macpherson brothers, Angus, Gideon, Bob and Jack. The remaining two men are Weldon Tomlin, the shed overseer, and Henry Dyer, who were also involved in the gunfight. (State Library of Queensland)

12

Dagworth Burns

WITH THE EYES OF THE NATION already focused on the violent confrontation between the landowners and the unionists in the back-country, tension further escalated when only a week after the burning of the *Rodney*, the following article appeared in the *Sydney Morning Herald* on Tuesday 4 September 1894:

SERIOUS AFFRAY IN QUEENSLAND

ATTACK ON WOOLSHED

FORTY SHOTS FIRED

DEATH OF A UNIONIST

Affairs in the West have taken a serious turn, so serious, in fact, as to justify the statement recently made in the House by the Colonial Secretary that the strike had developed into an insurrection.

> At 8 o'clock on Sunday night Mr. Tozer, the Colonial
> Secretary, received a telegram from Winton stating that
> Dagworth shed had been burnt down by about 16 armed
> men, and that 40 shots had been fired. One constable
> was present at the time, as well as three brothers, Messrs.
> Macpherson [owners], and three station hands . . .

This incident would eventually thrust Bob Macpherson
and Samuel Hoffmeister onto the national stage. Little
did Paterson know he had the main characters for a ballad.

•

Dagworth was the eighth shearing shed to be burnt in
western Queensland within two months. The stakes were
getting higher and a resolution between the warring parties
had to be found. The press was awash with talks of civil
war and the government was enlisting special constables
and rushing them to the hotspots of union activity.

A few stations, notably Warrnambool and Lerida, had
already started shearing on the old agreement, made three
years earlier in 1891, as demanded by the union. If the
shearers' union could manage to persuade more landowners
in western Queensland to revert to the 1891 agreement, then
the renegade squatters would cave in and the strike would
be won. There was no money left in the strike funds. The
unionists were doing it tough, but so were the squatters,
who desperately needed the fleece off their sheep before the
heat and flies of the imminent summer were upon them.

A few weeks could make all the difference. The union must hold on. They must win the strike.

On 27 August, the day after the *Rodney* incident and the shooting at Grassmere, a large strike camp of more than 200 men assembled at the small township of Kynuna. The atmosphere was at fever pitch. News had just come through; another shearing shed at nearby Manuka Station had been burnt to the ground that morning. Manuka ran about 85,000 sheep and the shed had forty stands.

After a short conference with the strike committee in the Kynuna camp, the men were called to assemble. The union leaders addressed the rank and file. They delivered a powerful address assuring those present the strike could be won. They must hold their ranks. No one must leave the camp. The police would be out to arrest anyone suspected of burning the Manuka shed. The strike camp was the safest place to be. They finished with three cheers for the men responsible for burning the Manuka shed.

The next day brought renewed confidence in the Kynuna strike camp even though they were hearing rumours of other camps in the district beginning to disperse. Later that day dispatches arrived at Kynuna from the union secretary in Sydney. It seemed the press was turning against the union, raising concerns of prolific acts of arson that they suggested might escalate into civil war. The Colonial Secretary, Horace Tozer, recommended the adoption of the Peace Preservation Act in the Queensland Parliament. A special magistrate was appointed with extraordinary powers to impose law and order around Winton. The pastoralists were nervous. The unionists wanted to strike another blow before the government could legislate the new act.

One of the nearest sheds to the Kynuna strike camp was at Dagworth Station. Two weeks earlier, owner Bob Macpherson had announced he was to commence shearing under the new 1894 agreement. On 14 August, the union shearers had assembled at the Dagworth shed for the roll call. They demanded that Macpherson revert to the agreement made in 1891. Macpherson stood his ground. Not one unionist signed on to work under the new agreement.

How things had changed. Sheep had forced the Macphersons and their kin to leave their native Highland home. Now in Australia, sheep were their tenuous future, 80,000 of them. Under immense financial pressure, the Macpherson family was in debt to the banks for in excess of £100,000.[1] Bob Macpherson was in no position to tolerate union shearers waving red flags, telling him how to run his shed and demanding more money. This was his land and these were his sheep. He had taken all the risks. His very livelihood was at stake. Unionists with their ideals were not on Bob's agenda. He didn't have enough money to pay the banks. Why should a man who wants to work belong to a bloody union anyway? If he had work for a man, and that man wanted the work, then it was a contract between him and the worker, it had nothing to do with the bloody union.

The union didn't think so. If a man liked to join with other men and form a union, then he could submit in peaceable means and attempt to affect his wages and working conditions.[2] The Pastoralists' Association had refused the workers this basic right. Bob Macpherson belonged to the Pastoralists' Association, so when word reached the Kynuna strike camp that Bob Macpherson had mustered sheep ready to commence shearing on Monday 3 September with non-union labour, the unionists had their target.

Two prominent unionists among the sixteen men selected to attack Dagworth Station were John Tierney and Samuel Hoffmeister. Press reports alleged Tierney was the leader of the gang and that his voice was recognised during the raid. Hoffmeister, or 'Frenchy' as he was known, was a deeper, more politically driven individual, who often rode alone. Widely suspected of burning down both the Cassilis and Manuka woolsheds in the previous days, the Tierney–Hoffmeister gang mostly comprised men with criminal records.[3] It was decided the gang must not meet in the Kynuna camp among the rank and file. Another destination was selected. It would be a billabong, the Four-Mile Billabong, on the Diamantina River about four miles from the township of Kynuna. From there, in darkness, the gang would be able to follow the dry Diamantina river-bed to Dagworth Station.

Over the next two days the bush telegraph worked perfectly. Word of the plan to burn Dagworth successfully reached each member of the gang. One by one they arrived at the Four-Mile Billabong. Hoffmeister did not arrive at the camp until after sundown on the evening of Saturday 1 September.[4] Determined there would be no shearing at Dagworth on Monday, the plan had been to attack the Dagworth shed on Sunday night, but threat of rain forced their decision to move earlier. They would attack shortly after midnight that night, in the early hours of 2 September 1894. The night before had been a new moon—so the unionists were assured of complete darkness for their assault.

With two of his neighbours' sheds recently burnt, Macpherson suspected he would be next and was ready for trouble. He manned his shed with armed guards. Like other pastoralists in the area Macpherson had sought police presence at his property. Indeed, for five weeks now, a constable had been stationed there. At the Dagworth shed that Saturday evening were Bob Macpherson and about twenty men, including his brothers Jack and Gideon, overseer Henry Dyer, shed overseer Weldon Tomlin, and a policeman, Senior Constable Michael Daly.[5] There were no signs of what was to come. The night was quiet, with a gentle rustle of coolibah leaves in the light northerly breeze. They felt reasonably secure, confident that shearing would at last get under way in the morning. Their main concern, as always, was the dark cloudy night and the threat of rain. Due to this, 140 weaner lambs had been penned in the woolshed for shelter, should rain fall during the night.

On watch at midnight were Weldon Tomlin and police Senior Constable Daly, who was 'armed with a carbine and revolver and 59 rounds of ammunition'.[6] In the darkness of the night the attacking unionists had every advantage. At about 12.30 am, the unionists crept to within fifty yards of the shed and opened fire. Daly was joined by the Macpherson brothers and Henry Dyer, who was armed with a Winchester rifle. They returned fire on the attacking party. They continued firing, 'and then saw a match struck at the shed'.[7] Wool bales had been doused in kerosene. The attackers kept up continuous fire until the flames had reached the roof of the shed. Shortly before the match was struck, Daly heard a voice call out: 'Give it to the bastards. We have waited long enough for this and now we'll have it.'[8]

At the inquest on 6 September, Macpherson would describe what happened while watching his livelihood go up in flames, his sheep burning to death, with unionists continually firing at him:

> I was at the woolshed on the night of the 1st of September and had about 20 men. I have had the shed watched for about five weeks to protect it from being burnt by unionists. I was aroused about midnight by a volley of shots. I was in the hut nearest the shed, got up and procured a revolver from my brother after some time. Before that I heard a voice call out 'Hold up your hands or die' and afterwards 'Hold up your hands you bastards or die.'
>
> Dyer went away with Constable Daly and when I got a revolver I followed. When I saw a flash of 3 or 4 shots

about 40 yards away from the attacking party, I returned the fire and immediately heard a bullet whistle past me. I fired five more shots—the attacking party kept up a continuous fire. I could see Dyer, Daly and Tomlin returning the fire.

Before the shed was set fire to I heard the same voice say, 'Rally up boys and let them have it. You'll die or we'll die.' I saw the shed on fire. It was impossible to attempt to save it, in consequence of the incessant firing of the attacking party. About 140 lambs and other property were burnt in the shed. The firing continued on and off for ¾ of an hour and only ceased when the shed was fully at large. I attempted to save the lambs and some wool but was fired on by the attacking party and retired. It was too dark for me to see any of them. I think I recognised the voice and could identify it again. The shed was completely burnt all but a small corner.

When the shed was beyond being saved the unionists retreated to their horses, and followed the Diamantina riverbed back to their camp.

•

At first light Macpherson and Constable Daly mounted their horses and attempted to track the raiders. They had spent the night mopping up and shooting the injured, distressed sheep. Although the rain was sufficient to obliterate all tracks, they were able to ascertain that the unionists had travelled upstream towards Kynuna. The attackers had left several property gates open. There was little doubt they were headed to the Four-Mile Billabong. Macpherson was aware some unionists had gathered there during the last few days, although the main strike camp with more than 200 men was at Kynuna.

After returning to the scene of previous night's rifle battle, Bob Macpherson later told the inquest:

> I examined the place at daylight and saw several empty and full cartridges which I picked up from 10 to 30 yards from the shed, 26 were found. I saw melted bullets in the shed, and one taken out of an inner door in the hut nearest the shed—3 bullets were fired at the hut. If one man had been in his bunk, he would have been shot. In another hut fired at there were 14 men. In another hut fired at there was a woman and her two daughters . . .
>
> From the words used I think the attacking party were unionists. The words they used are commonly used by unionists. It was very dark. I could not see any there, nor do I know of any being wounded. It rained before daylight sufficient to destroy all tracks, which I searched for without success. The cartridges picked up were principally Winchester rifle and some Martini Henry and some revolver.

Macpherson and Daly gathered the evidence and rode twenty miles into Kynuna to enlist the aid of Constables Austin Cafferty and Robert Dyer who were stationed there. Some interesting news awaited them—union shearer Samuel Hoffmeister had reportedly committed suicide by the Four-Mile Billabong, four miles from Kynuna.[9]

•

Two days later, on 4 September, the *Sydney Morning Herald*
reported:

> There is hardly any doubt that this is the same gang that has
> been burning all the sheds. Information has been received
> from Winton that a man named Hoffmeister, a prominent
> unionist, was found dead about two miles from Kynuna.
> The local impression is that he was one of the attacking
> mob at Dagworth and was wounded there. There was seven
> unionists with Hoffmeister when he died. These assert that
> he committed suicide. In consequence of the seriousness
> of this last event, the Government is taking active steps
> to deal with persons found armed, and it is probable that
> a proclamation prohibiting the carrying of arms will be
> issued tomorrow. Dagworth is about 70 miles north-west of
> Winton, on the Upper Diamantina, near Ayrshire Downs,
> where the woolshed was burnt down some time ago.

So, Bob Macpherson, accompanied by the three policemen,
Daly, Cafferty and Dyer, rode out to inspect the body of
Samuel Hoffmeister, dead beside the billabong.

Following a postmortem, Hoffmeister was hurriedly
buried in a remote spot on Kynuna Station. The body has
never been found. The only people present at the burial
were Ernest Eglinton, the Police Magistrate, and Dr Francis
Wellford, who conducted the postmortem. Three days later
an inquest into Hoffmeister's death was conducted, which
resulted in a verdict of suicide by shooting.

Knowing he was going out to the Kynuna–Winton district with Sarah Riley in a matter of weeks, one can only imagine Banjo Paterson's intrigue as he read daily of these events back in Sydney. The verdict of suicide would never have been challenged, and Hoffmeister's death would have been locked away forever without question; that is, if Banjo Paterson had never written 'Waltzing Matilda'. The truth, like the water in the billabong where our swagman died, would have slowly disappeared. Just another forgotten death of a swagman.

The front cover of the *Bulletin* following the burning of Dagworth Station—
'the firestick policy of the western insurrection'.
(8 September 1894, State Library of New South Wales)

13

The Cover-Up

THE INQUEST into Samuel Hoffmeister's death was conducted by Police Magistrate Ernest Eglinton on 5 September 1894. Seven witnesses were called to give evidence, five of whom were striking union shearers arrested in the camp with Hoffmeister. They were Neil Highland, William Moody, Lewis Murray, James Spellacy and William Goode. The other two statements were taken from Senior Constable Austin Cafferty, one of the three policemen who rode out from Kynuna with Bob Macpherson. The final person to give evidence was Dr Francis Wellford, who conducted the postmortem on Hoffmeister's body.[1]

The five unionists arrested in the union camp all gave evidence alleging that Hoffmeister, whom they called 'Frenchy', had in 'mysterious circumstances' shot himself. None of the witnesses had seen him do it, but all claimed to have heard the shot or shots. The general thread of evidence claims those in the camp shared a meal together, after which Hoffmeister burnt a letter or some papers in the fire, went away behind a tent, stuck a gun in his mouth and 'blew his head off'. No-one could give any reason why he should take his own life. Hoffmeister did not leave a suicide note, and by all accounts, up until the time of his death appeared to be quite normal. There was no indication of depression, emotional upset or disturbance of mind.

There were a number of substantial and important contradictions in the evidence which seemed put-up, or poorly rehearsed. There was confusion over who owned the revolver and the position of the revolver. Police Senior Constable Austin Cafferty stated he had found fresh blood on the body, but it is difficult to imagine why there would be fresh blood, given the time it would have taken for Senior Constable Cafferty to have ridden out from Kynuna with the other two police and Bob Macpherson.

Neil Highland categorically denied that the deceased had slept in his tent. He also stated he heard shots (plural) when Hoffmeister shot himself—yet he had died from a single gunshot wound, the bullet entering at the roof of the mouth, penetrating the skull and the brain. Death was instantaneous.

William Moody gave evidence that Hoffmeister appeared to be in good health and sober. Frenchy was asleep in Highland's tent when Moody 'woke them up' in the morning. This was in total contradiction to the evidence given by Highland. Moody was adamant Hoffmeister had slept in

Highland's tent and accused him of lying. When Moody 'woke them up', Highland left the tent to cover up his saddle and Frenchy 'sang out "while you are there, cover my gear"'. One would think that a riding saddle and pack saddle becoming damp with light rain would not greatly trouble someone who was about shoot himself.

Moody then stated that Frenchy came from Highland's tent to the fire with an envelope in his hand, which he placed in the fire, saying, 'I'll burn this letter and then I am alright.' He then walked back towards Highland's tent alone. The next thing Moody heard was a gunshot. Moody, upon finding the body of Frenchy, called out, 'Frenchy has shot himself.' Someone replied, 'I don't believe a word of it.' It is clear the assertion of suicide was not accepted by at least one person from the camp, possibly an important witness.

Senior Constable Austin Cafferty gave evidence the body was lying six or seven yards from a tent where there was a camp of eleven men. Other witnesses had placed the body at between forty and fifty yards from the camp. It is patently obvious that very little inquiry was conducted with Senior Constable Cafferty into the death of Hoffmeister and nor, regrettably, was he cross-examined, but then, it is highly likely that Cafferty was the counsel assisting the coroner.

Doctor Wellford, a Government medical officer, expressed an unexplained and unsupported opinion that 'the wound was self inflicted'. He did not expand upon the opinion, nor offer any basis upon which he arrived at that opinion. One would think that his next observation, that the deceased had a meal shortly before he died, would be inconsistent with the deceased having shortly thereafter taken his own life.

The last witness was Mr William Goode, who observed Frenchy threw an envelope into the fire after dinner, and then heard him say something 'about it being alright now'. Frenchy walked away 'in the distance down the river'. Goode then heard a report of a shot. He and others went in that direction and found Frenchy dead. Goode identified the revolver as belonging to him but Highland said it was Hoffmeister's gun. This claim of ownership to the revolver was not pursued, either by the counsel assisting, nor by the coroner himself.

It is patently clear that Hoffmeister's death was not an accident, and according to evidence given in the inquiry, there were only two findings open to the coroner: either the deceased committed suicide as he so found, or the deceased was murdered by a person or persons unknown. A much more searching inquiry was needed before any finding as to the cause of death could be arrived at. As barrister Trevor Monti noted when interviewed by the author in 2007, 'There were far too many unexplained events surrounding the death to enable any finding at all to be made by the Coroner, let alone a specific finding of suicide.'[2]

Although it was obvious Hoffmeister and the other men in the union camp had burnt the Dagworth shed, mysteriously, none of them was charged with any offences. Strangely, they were not even questioned with regard to the gun battle and burning of the shed. The possibility of Hoffmeister and his mates being involved was certainly no secret, as printed in the national press: 'The local impression is that he was one of the attacking mob at Dagworth and was wounded there. There were seven unionists with Hoffmeister when he died.'[3]

A report despatched from Winton on 13 September commenting on the inquest was printed in the Brisbane *Courier* on 20 September and it also related Hoffmeister's death to the attack on Dagworth station:

> The enquiry into the death of Hoffmeister at a union camp at Kynuna resulted in a verdict of suicide. Found with him were a rifle and sixty-eight cartridges and a revolver and twenty empty cartridge shells. He committed suicide at a camp which had been formed four miles this side of Kynuna, some distance from the main camp, and about fourteen miles from the Dagworth shed. They gave as their reason for forming a camp there that the grass was better, but I am informed that there is good grass around the township. The significant part of the business is that there is a track from this camp to the woolshed, which forms something like one side of a triangle, and does not, therefore, go near the head station.

Police Constable Michael Daly, one of the three policemen who rode out to the union camp to examine the body of Samuel Hoffmeister, also placed Hoffmeister at the scene of the crime when giving evidence into the burning of the Dagworth shed:

> He [Hoffmeister] had a Martini sporting rifle with him
> and 68 rounds of ammunition. The rifle appeared to be
> recently used. He also had 29 exploded rifle cartridges,
> a revolver and 21 cartridges. I found a similar exploded
> cartridge case at the place where the men were firing
> on the shed . . . Hoffmeister was a unionist shearer and
> had his union tickets on his body, which was found in a
> unionist camp.[4]

A few days earlier, the Queensland cabinet had approved
a 1000 pound reward for anyone with information which
would convict persons involved with burning down a
shearing shed. Only five men in the camp were summoned
to testify at the inquest. Why weren't other unionists in the
camp questioned or charged? On 12 September the *Sydney
Morning Herald* reported that Hoffmeister had no known
motive to kill himself, and that seven unionists arrested
with Hoffmeister had criminal records. Yet the police just
let them go!

So, here we have a supposed suicide for no apparent
reason, a hastily buried body and an inquest with contradic-
tory, badly rehearsed evidence. Strange indeed!

There is little doubt that the organised criminal gang
comprising John Tierney and Hoffmeister was roaming the
country, and was responsible for setting fire to shearing
sheds. Hoffmeister's death would have been a blow to the
union's chances of winning the strike, leaving only Tierney
to lead the fire gang. But his death would have been a
major plus for the pastoralists, who were under extreme

pressure to end the strike. The stakes were high. Summer was approaching and the sheep were heavy with wool. Some members of the Pastoralists' Association were losing their determination and caving in to the Shearers' Union. And to confuse things even more, some of the sheds burnt in western Queensland were burnt by their owners, members of the Pastoralists' Union. This opportunism suggested the unionists were causing more trouble than they actually were, swaying public opinion and forcing the government to send more police. Then the station owners claimed insurance and refitted with new equipment.[5]

Eleven days later, on 13 September, John Tierney was arrested at the Tangorin strike camp near Hughenden, about 90 miles from Winton, where coincidentally on the same day, another shearer, John Corrigan, allegedly committed suicide by cutting his own throat with a razor.[6] Tierney was about thirty years of age and spoke with a strong Irish accent. He was described as a union leader and shearer. He was charged in Winton on 24 September with having:

> On the morning of 2 September, maliciously set fire to a woolshed at Dagworth, the property of Macpherson and Company . . . This offender, who has shorn in the Winton and Hughenden Districts, was a leader of a number of men by whom the Dagworth woolshed was burned, and several shots were fired on its defenders, evidently with intent to murder.[7]

A few days later, Tierney was brought before the bench in Winton and charged with arson and intent to murder at Dagworth Station. Police had gathered evidence against Tierney, and his voice had been recognised during the burning of Dagworth by Bob Macpherson. Surprisingly, he was discharged when police decided not to offer any evidence, and rather mysteriously Bob Macpherson claimed he was now unable to recognise Tierney's voice.

A few weeks later the Commissioner of Police, William Parry-Oakeden, submitted the first draft of his annual report. He described the Dagworth affray as a 'mysterious affair altogether'. Colonial Secretary Horace Tozer censored the commissioner's report, insisting the word 'mysterious' be removed.[8] When the commissioner submitted his final report on 8 November, his sanitised version read: 'the most serious offence being the determined attack on Dagworth woolshed, where over forty shots were exchanged, but fortunately none of the defenders were injured and no traces of the attacking party could be discovered next morning.'

End of story, no mention of an inquest, nothing about Hoffmeister's death and no mention of Tierney being charged. In subsequent confidential reports, the names of several men suspected of having been involved in the Dagworth fire were given, but no convictions were recorded.

There must now be serious doubt that Samuel Hoffmeister took his own life beside the billabong all those years ago. So the question must be asked—if our iconic swagman didn't take his own life, then who did?

Here was an undeclared war between striking unionists and station owners, with gun battles being waged between the two opposing sides. Hoffmeister was an extremely active and militant supporter of the trade unionists. There may well have been very good reason why the station owners would have wanted to see him dead.

Is it possible the swagman was shot by the squatter, or one of the three policemen, mounted on their thorough-breds? Or done in by his union mates? Was the death of our now famous swagman a cover-up by the Queensland police?

There are two other possible scenarios for Hoffmeister's death. The first is that Hoffmeister for some reason was shot by one of the unionists, most likely John Tierney, who was probably one of the other unionists in the camp but was not summoned to give evidence at the inquest. Why was there another apparent suicide at the Tangorin strike camp when Tierney was arrested? Why did the police decide to let Tierney go free for burning the Dagworth shed? Could Tierney have been a plant by the police to murder the fire-gang leaders? Or perhaps he had argued with Hoffmeister, who was claimed 'to be a bit barmy'. This might explain why the unionists in the camp fabricated the evidence.

A second, more plausible, explanation is that the unionists in the camp were confronted by Bob Macpherson and the three policemen. Having had his shearing shed burnt down, as well as being shot at the night before, Macpherson would have been rightfully looking for revenge. Could he or one of the three policemen have shot Hoffmeister? That would have given the unionists something to bargain with, gaining their freedom by claiming Hoffmeister had committed suicide, and not giving evidence against Macpherson and the three troopers.

Is it possible that in the middle of remote western Queensland some sort of deal was done, or an oath between those present was taken never to reveal how Hoffmeister died? As reported, he had no known motive to take his own life. However, Bob Macpherson and the police certainly had the strongest motive of all—to break the strike.

The Dagworth Station incident and death of Hoffmeister were a watershed in the end of the 1894 shearers' strike. Men were already defecting to the squatters and shearing under the old agreement. At Longreach the strike committee urged the men to vote. There ensued a volatile and stormy debate. In the end the men voted narrowly to call off the strike. Eventually the Charleville branch followed, then Winton, Hughenden, Tangorin and the Fifteen Mile Creek camp.

A correspondent for the *Sydney Morning Herald*, after visiting a shearers' camp on 12 September, made the following report:

> There is no doubt that the camp will rapidly melt away. Many of them have come long distances, at considerable expense, and they can ill afford to go home without handling the shears in two or three sheds.

After stating that the shearers had behaved, in the main, responsibly, the reporter then quotes one of the leaders thus:

'We are trying to teach the men that the victory of Labour can only be won at the ballot box, and the union is doing all it can to discourage outrages. If there is a repetition of violence, it will be the act of individuals, and not the organisation.'

•

By mid-October the strike was officially finished, although tension remained high throughout the area. On 5 November the local police searched the township of Kynuna for arms and ammunition. Among weapons found were three Winchester rifles, a revolver, two breech-loading guns, 2495 Winchester cartridges, thirty-three pounds of powder and large quantities of shot and detonators.[9]

At Dagworth Station, still under police protection, shearing didn't finish until shortly before Christmas, at least mid-December. A temporary shearing shed was set up in one of the huts on the property, with a barricade built around it for protection. Obviously, the Macphersons were still concerned about being attacked again, and in fact, during December three men attacked the shed, but they were driven off.[10]

A photo taken at the time shows nine men standing along a rough-hewn log fence, outside the temporary shearing shed. Six of these men were wearing moleskin trousers and shirts with sleeves rolled up, standing and mostly leaning on the fence. They were Henry Dyer, Weldon Tomlin, Jack Macpherson, Bob Macpherson, Gideon Macpherson and Angus Macpherson.[11] Beside them were three troopers grouped together on the left of the print, standing almost to attention, armed with rifles. The fence they were standing alongside was a crude barricade of logs strewn together, surrounding a corrugated iron shed.

Within two or three weeks of the photo being taken, Paterson would arrive at Dagworth Station. He surely would have seen the photo of the squatter with three policemen, and the temporary shearing shed still barricaded. He would meet and ride with Bob Macpherson on his property and may even have met the three policemen. This is the world in which Banjo Paterson found himself. He had been living in Sydney reading about events in the back-country, a violent socio-political war which had lasted for months. Now he would experience first hand what had occurred between the squatters and the swagmen, in the secretive and mysterious events of the 1894 shearers' strike.

14

Christina's Tune

THE SHEARING SHED WAS BURNT DOWN, 140 sheep were burnt to death, a swagman was found dead at the billabong by the squatter and three policemen, and there was possibly a cover-up of the swagman's death by the verdict of suicide. There and then, Banjo would write about a dead sheep, a swagman, a squatter, three policemen and an unexplained suicide. But for the very first time, Banjo would collaborate with another person to write not just a poem, but a song. While the events that occurred at Dagworth Station were utilised to construct the verses of 'Waltzing Matilda', the composition of a song required other elements: a chorus and a tune.

•

The person who would provide the assistance to Banjo for his new composition was Christina Macpherson. While the violent events of the 1894 shearers' strike were unfolding, Christina's life was also being affected by events that would eventually lead her to Banjo and the writing of their song.

Earlier in the year, during April and May 1894, Christina attended the Warrnambool races as a guest of her sister Margaret, who was married to Stewart McArthur (later Justice Sir Stewart McArthur) of Menningort, near Camperdown in western Victoria.

Christina had a marvellous country vacation with Margaret at Menningort, with its lovely cool climate and lush green pastures. It was a chance for some social interaction, soirées and of course the Warrnambool races, the greatest social event in western Victoria. This would be a welcome respite from her quaint city residence in Sutherland Road, Armadale, and a vast contrast to attending the pompous Madam Pfund's finishing school in St Kilda.[1]

The time-honoured Grand Annual Steeplechase, which is still a yearly event at the three-day Warrnambool May Race Carnival, was first run in 1872. A gruelling event, taking over six and a half minutes to complete, it is the longest horse race in Australia, a marathon distance of 5,500 metres with 33 jumps, more than any other horse race in the world.

This unique race leaves the racecourse proper, as the horses cross a road and two steeple-jumps and then race into the distant paddocks beyond. The excitement is magnified by the first half of the race being conducted in a clockwise direction, after which the skilful jockeys and horses negotiate an extremely dangerous downhill double jump, change direction and gallop towards the finishing line.

The Grand Annual Steeplechase at Warrnambool also has a rather extraordinary feature, in that thousands of patrons leave the racecourse to watch the race by climbing a hill outside the track, which offers a much better view of the steeplechase course. The view from this natural grandstand is far superior to any spot on the course proper. For the uninitiated it can be disconcerting when, 30 minutes before the main race, everyone begins to file out of the turnstiles away from the racecourse. But in Warrnambool, it's just part of the tradition to watch the jumps race from Scotchman's Hill.

While Christina was at the races she was taken by a 'new' march tune played by the Warrnambool Garrison Artillery Band, which she would memorise and later play by ear for Paterson at Dagworth. The tune was called 'The Craigielee March', a variant of an older Scottish song, 'Thou Bonnie Wood of Craigielea'.

Robert Tannerhill, a Scottish poet, originally wrote 'Thou Bonnie Wood of Craigielea' as a poem around 1790. Born in Paisley, he became known as the 'weaver poet'. His poetry and songs are recognised alongside those of Robert Burns. He died in 1810, drowning in a stream under the Paisley Canal. In a strange coincidence, more than 200 years later his poem would be attached to the most famous song ever written about an alleged drowning. Tannerhill's other famous poem, 'The Braes O' Balquihidder', is considered the original form of the enduring Scottish song 'Wild

Mountain Thyme', with its internationally popular chorus 'Will you go lassie go'.

The tune for Tannerhill's poem was written by James Barr. A gifted Scottish composer, born at Tarbolton in South Ayrshire, he was a good friend of Tannerhill and set several of his poems to music. 'Thou Bonnie Wood of Craigielea' was written in praise of the poet's hometown:

> The broom, the brier, the birken bush,
> Blooms bonnie o'er thy flow'ry lea;
> And a' the sweets that one can wish
> Frae Nature's hand are strew'd on thee.
> Thou bonnie wood o' Craigielea
> Thou bonnie wood o' Craigielea
> Near thee I pass'd life's early day
> And won my Mary's heart in thee.

The original Scottish air was rearranged into 'march time' for the Warrnambool Band, injecting some bounce into the original tune. Military bands were quite popular during the 1890s. The Warrnambool Garrison Artillery Band, resplendent in uniforms and spiked helmets, was formed at the Warrnambool Garrison, which featured several cannons, aptly situated on Cannon Hill above the town. All pointing towards the sea, they were expected to hold back any possible Russian invasion upon the town. Fortunately for Warrnamboolians, the invasion never came.

The new 'march' arrangement of 'Thou Bonnie Wood of Craigielea' was written by Thomas Bulch (originally

Bulshey), an Englishman born in Shildon, Durham, in 1860. Bulch was a prolific arranger of music, and used pseudonyms so people would not tire of his work and look elsewhere for variety. For the re-arranged 'The Craigielee March', he signed the name Godfrey Parker. His band was called 'Bulch's Model Band' until about 1900, when he handed it over to the city of Ballarat.

Regrettably, Bulch received little credit for his involvement in our national song. Even more regrettable was the treatment he received during World War I, when he opened his music shop in Sydney Road, Brunswick. The locals referred to it as 'The German's Music Shop' and vandalised his store because he displayed and sold band music, mostly printed in Leipzig, Germany, before the war began. During this time, two of his sons fought at Gallipoli for Australia, one being killed in France shortly before the shop was destroyed.[2]

The Warrnambool Racing Club programme of the 1894 Grand Annual Steeplechase Meeting listed the dance tunes played, the first tune being the 'March' called 'Craigielee'.

WARRNAMBOOL AMATEUR TURF CLUB

25TH APRIL, 1894.

HIS EXCELLENCY

THE GOVERNOR LORD HOPETOUN PRESENTS

MUSIC BY THE TOWN BAND ON TUESDAY 24TH

AND THURSDAY 26TH APRIL, 1894.

MARCH	'CRAIGIELEE'
SCHOTTISCHE	'THE ARGYLE'
MARCH	'JEANNIE GRAY'
WALTZ	'AFTER THE BALL'
FANTASIA	OP. 'BOHEMIAN GIRL'
QUADRILLES	'OLD TIMES'
GRAND MARCH	'BRAVE BARNABY'
SERENADE	'TWILIGHT WHISPERINGS'
MARCH	'THE JACOBITE'
GALOP	'O'ER THE DOWNS'

The 'march' tune was popular in the local area and stayed in the repertoire of the Warrnambool Band for many years. Many older Warnambool residents were familiar with 'The Craigielee March' tune and its association with the original 'Waltzing Matilda', as folklorist John Manifold wrote in his book *Who Wrote the Ballads*:

> As a very small boy in the Western District of Victoria in the 1920s, I distinctly heard it said (and I think I heard it said more than once): 'Banjo Paterson picked up the tune of "Waltzing Matilda" on the beach at Warrnambool.'
>
> I knew about Warrnambool and its beach; I had picked up shells and seaweed, and once a dead penguin, on the beach at Warrnambool myself. But I had never picked up a tune there; so the strange phrase stuck in my memory. What I have learnt since inclines me to believe that 'Craigielea' stayed in the repertory of the Warrnambool Garrison Artillery Band for many a year, and that regular visitors to Warrnambool came to identify the tune first

with Warrnambool and then with the Cowan 'Waltzing Matilda' as it became generally known. The old bandstand was quite close to the beach.[3]

Of course Banjo Paterson did not literally 'pick up the tune' on the Warrnambool beach, however what the *old* Warrnambool people were alluding to was that they, for many years, had heard the tune 'The Craigielee March' played on the bandstand near the Warrnambool beach.

The original song, 'Thou Bonnie Wood of Craigielea', was also well known in the Warrnambool area; it is likely Christina knew the song before she heard the altered 'march' tune at the Warrnambool races. The song would have been quite popular among the Scottish Australians living within the western district, and was probably played on homestead pianos at soirées and family gatherings. A meticulously handwritten copy (undated) of 'Thou Bonnie Wood of Craigielea' was unearthed by the Warrnambool Historical Society in 1994.

The name 'Craigielea' itself (Gaelic for field or meadow away from the wind underneath steep rugged rock) was a popular homestead name throughout the area. John Keith McDougall, the prolific western Victorian poet, would in later years write about his childhood home, a property on the eastern side of the Hopkins River at the foot of a rocky hill, in a poem titled 'Craigielea'. Either by design or chance, McDougall's poem can be substituted and sung perfectly to the tune 'Thou Bonnie Wood of Craigielea':

Bright shines the sun of Craigielea,
And blithe the birds are singing there;
The nestlings cheep in bush and tree,
And on the braes the flow'rs are fair.

The flow'rs are fair on Craigielea—
The yellow flow'rs that love the sun,
And butterfly and busy bee,
Are making love to ev'ry one.[4]

So 'Thou Bonnie Wood of Craigielea' had migrated from Scotland and found its way to Australia, where it became 'The Craigielee March'. At the races in Warrnambool, Christina Macpherson took the time to listen to 'The Craigielee March' and then transport the tune in her head to western Queensland. But the journey for the tune would not finish there; it would be transformed yet again, and in time travel to every corner of the globe. Amid the colour and excitement around her it's a wonder Christina heard the tune at all, and perhaps she may not have, if it wasn't for the fact that the 'The Craigielee March' is such a lovely, provocative little tune.

15

The Love Affair

CHRISTINA'S MOTHER, MARGARET, died in early December 1894. Her father, Ewan, wanting to unite his family after the death of his wife, took Christina and her sister Jean to join his sons at Dagworth Station in north-west Queensland. The Macpherson family had not been together for some years as the Macpherson boys, Bob, Jack and Gideon, had been living and working at Dagworth Station for about eleven years. The party was met at Winton by Bob Macpherson, who was to accompany them to Dagworth Station, near Kynuna, still a two-day trip away by horse and buggy.

During the stopover in Winton, Christina met an old school friend, Sarah Riley. Sarah was staying with her brother Frederick 'Whistler' Riley and his wife Marie, who had recently married and moved into their new home, 'Aloha', the first built in Vindex Street, Winton. The Rileys and Macphersons were good friends and neighbours, both having interests in nearby stations. Frederick Riley was the third son in the Riley family; all the sons were members of Riley, Chirnside and Company. Fred had been overseer on Vindex Station until he took up the management of Carandotta Station in 1889. Rheumatism forced him from the land and he started a commission agency in Winton in 1892.

Staying at Winton as a guest of the Riley family was Sarah's fiancé of eight years, Banjo Paterson, who was soon to have his first book of poems published. Paterson was introduced to Bob Macpherson, and both he and Sarah were invited to join the house party at Dagworth Station early in January.[1]

Ewan Macpherson, now an elderly man of seventy-four, would have been relieved and happy to unite his family so soon after the death of his wife. The recent events at Dagworth being printed in the nation's newspapers and the financial pressure of the strikes, combined with the death of his wife, would surely have been an enormous strain on him. The shearing would have just finished when the party arrived from Victoria and the stockade built around the temporary shearing shed would still have been in place.

As was the norm on western stations, neighbours would gather together for social occasions, often staying for days or weeks on end. Christina would have been excited to have her old school friend Sarah over for a lengthy stay. With the presence of Sarah's handsome fiancé, the conversation, emotions and social banter would have been running at fever pitch. Within two years Christina's sister Jean, who had travelled to Dagworth with Christina for the first time, would marry Samuel McCowan, at one time a member of Macpherson and Co. of Dagworth, who was now managing the adjoining Kynuna Station. It is highly possible their romance first blossomed at the house party in January 1895.

Nothing could have suited Banjo better than to be at Dagworth Station. Finally he was outback, like Lawson had been. Spending the days riding around the property with the squatter Bob Macpherson seemed like a step back in time to his childhood, when he galloped along pretending to be a bushranger or a mounted trooper. But here at Dagworth the story and events were real.

Here he had the chance to ride down to the Four-Mile Billabong, where Bob and three policemen had supposedly picked up the body of the swagman Hoffmeister; past the charred ruins of the shearing shed, burnt down by unionists during a gun battle; then on to the temporary shearing shed, still surrounded by a hastily built stockade—probably the only stockade built since Eureka. Banjo's inquisitive legal and poetic mind must have been sparked by such events.

And then, during one of the social evenings, the young and innocent Christina Macpherson played on a zither (a stringed instrument) what she could remember of a tune she had heard at Warrnambool races a few months earlier. The beautiful whimsical tune of an old Scottish song 'woke the Scot in Paterson'.[2] Banjo was entranced not only by the tune but also by its shy and attractive player. Banjo couldn't help but scribble down some words. Those words would later become a song—the original 'Waltzing Matilda':

Oh! there once was a swagman camped in the Billabong,
Under the shade of a Coolabah tree;
And he sang as he looked at his old billy boiling,
'Who'll come a-waltzing Matilda with me.'
    Who'll come a-waltzing Matilda, my darling,
    Who'll come a-waltzing Matilda with me?
    Waltzing Matilda and leading a water-bag—
    Who'll come a-waltzing Matilda with me?

Down came a jumbuck to drink at the water-hole,
Up jumped the swagman and grabbed him in glee;
And he sang as he put him away in his tucker-bag,
'You'll come a-waltzing Matilda with me.'
    Who'll come a-waltzing Matilda, my darling,
    Who'll come a-waltzing Matilda with me?
    Waltzing Matilda and leading a water-bag—
    Who'll come a-waltzing Matilda with me?

Down came the Squatter a-riding his thorough-bred;
Down came Policemen—one, two and three.
'Whose is the jumbuck you've got in the tucker-bag?
You'll come a-waltzing Matilda with we.'
    Who'll come a-waltzing Matilda, my darling,
    Who'll come a-waltzing Matilda with me?
    Waltzing Matilda and leading a water-bag—
    Who'll come a-waltzing Matilda with me?

But the swagman, he up and he jumped in the water-hole,
Drowning himself by the Coolabah tree;
And his ghost may be heard as it sings in the Billabong,
'Who'll come a-waltzing Matilda with me?'
    Who'll come a-waltzing Matilda, my darling,
    Who'll come a-waltzing Matilda with me?
    Waltzing Matilda and leading a water-bag—
    Who'll come a-waltzing Matilda with me?[3]

•

The first allusions to a relationship between Banjo and Christina appeared in *The Story of Waltzing Matilda*, published in 1944, when Sydney May referred to Paterson having 'sad memories' from his stay in Winton.

Sad memories? Were Paterson's memories of Winton and of the birth of 'Waltzing Matilda' entangled with some blazing row with Sarah over Christina, or vice versa? Paterson was highly attractive to women, and seldom out of girl trouble until he married Alice Walker in 1903.

Clement Semmler, writing in 1966, was much closer to the mark in *The Banjo of the Bush*. When referring to 'Waltzing Matilda' he writes:

> Vince Kelly has recalled that Paterson had a greater affec-
> tion for this ballad than most of his others; others have
> mentioned that Winton and Dagworth had 'sad memories
> for Paterson'. The reason, then, is surely simple. He did
> not marry Sarah Riley; he was a most handsome and
> eligible young man as we know, and my guess is that

John Manifold is not wide of the mark when he suggests
that a quarrel with Sarah over Christina Macpherson or
vice versa, could have explained most of his reluctance to
discuss the Dagworth days; the memory of it was better
locked away, like 'Waltzing Matilda' among its odds
and ends in a tin box. And since, in 1902, he met Alice
Walker of Tenterfield, and married her in 1903, this was
a further reason for him not to revive the song, nor the
memories and incidents associated with it.[4]

A more conclusive record of events at Dagworth Station
was given in 1995 by Dianna Baillieu, who knew her Aunt
Christina extremely well. There was no doubt in Dianna's
mind as to what had happened at Dagworth in January
1895. She was critical of Banjo's 'caddish behaviour', and
said the Macpherson brothers told Paterson 'never to darken
their doorstep again'. It really wasn't 'the done thing' to talk
about those sorts of affairs in her day, but the truth couldn't
hurt anyone now and besides, with all the confusion about
the writing of the song, Dianna was adamant that people
should know what really happened.

Dianna lived in a Toorak mansion, but her matter-of-
fact, no-nonsense way of talking was indicative of a woman
from the land. Her son Ted, the Victorian Liberal Premier,
commented on his mother's early days on the land in western
Victoria: 'resilient, a lot of self-sustenance, to this day she
won't turn the heater on. She's a penny saver.'[5]

After Dianna's father was killed in World War I she
returned with her mother from England and went to live

with her grandparents Stewart and Margaret McArthur at Menningort in the western district of Victoria. At the time, Christina lived in South Yarra and was 'pretty hard up, but not penniless by any means'. Before Christina died in 1936, she 'used to frequently get on the Camperdown train and about once a month come up to Camperdown and be met in the jinker'.[6]

Christina and Dianna developed a unique relationship; Dianna, about ten years old, was an only child on a large property, and a lonely great-aunt visiting from the city was a great joy, Dianna recalled:

> . . . so Aunt Chris used to come up and stay with my granny, her sister; and I used to like Aunt Chris very much; she used to play the piano. I got to know her, I was a solitary child living on a station with my mum and grand-parents, my grandfather was a judge and lived at the Melbourne club. He inherited Menningort with stacks of ghastly racing debts but made a conscious decision to hang in there, so Granny had a pretty austere time coping with the station, so Aunt Chris used to come up. I loved her, she was good fun . . . I knew Aunt Chris very well, and an aunt that comes up and plays the piano, and who is quite a jolly lady, is a great pleasure to a single child, as I was.[7]

Dianna explained how the story had been kept in the family for years and that like most young children, she got bored with family history: 'Dagworth and Waltzing Matilda were just one of those family things that used to get chatted about, around the table. It was just part of the family history; the broken romance with Sarah and the fact that it was over him making passes at Chris.'[8]

Although no letters between Christina and Banjo have been unearthed, Dianna was quite sure there was 'correspondence between Aunt Chris and Paterson after the "bust up", when the brothers told him to "get lost"! They didn't want to see him again because he was a "cad" and a "rotter" and all of that!' The belief that Banjo and Christina wrote to each other was also supported by Dianna's relative, 'old Leslie Macpherson', who is reported to have said: 'We understand there was correspondence between them after he was "chucked out". But it's still sad because she was mad about him, he must have been an attractive sort of bloke.'[9]

Dianna went on to say she honestly believed Christina never got over her affection for Banjo and what happened at Dagworth Station. Sadly, he was the only real love of her life, most likely her one and only fling. Christina never married, and as Dianna said:

> . . . it was very much a class society and a very small social society, where everybody knew each other; even though there was great distances, gossip would go around. It simply wasn't the thing to break off engagements and it certainly wasn't the done thing to get off with your fiancée's best friend. Things were serious then, that these days you wouldn't blink an eyelid at.[10]

Doctor Barrington Thomas overwhelmingly agreed with what Dianna had to say about Paterson. His great-aunt

Vivienne Riley (who had met Christina Macpherson) was adamant that Sarah had broken off her engagement with Paterson, not vice versa. He then revealed that it was part of the Riley family's oral history that when Paterson wrote 'an incident occurred at Dagworth which I prefer not to remember', he was referring to Sarah breaking off their engagement.

If Banjo's love for Sarah was fading by 1894, it certainly wasn't in 1891 when he'd written 'As Long As Your Eyes are Blue', revealing a love that Sarah surely returned:

> Oh, I love you, sweet, for your locks of brown
> And the blush on your cheek that lies—
> But I love you most for the kindly heart
> That I see in your sweet blue eyes—
>
> For the eyes are signs of the soul within,
> Of the heart that is real and true,
> And mine own sweetheart, I shall love you still,
> Just as long as your eyes are blue.

Banjo had been engaged to Sarah Riley for almost eight years. Maybe this suggests he was never going to marry her anyway. Maybe the secure lifestyle, partnership in a famous legal firm and idea of marrying into a distinguished family were wearing thin for the *Bulletin*'s chief bard and a famous poet on the threshold of publishing his first book. After all, he never really had any enthusiasm for his legal work. Was this his chance to take his turn with Clancy?

Dianna Baillieu further said:

He was a ladies' man, he flirted with Chris. I think perhaps writing the words to 'Waltzing Matilda' to her music was part of the flirtation. He probably meant nothing by it, but she had been lonely, sheltered and innocent. She put quite a wrong interpretation on it and as a result was very hurt. The Macpherson brothers did not like it at all, they were not impressed because Banjo was already engaged . . . I don't think Aunt Chris ever got over it, the poor thing.[11]

So, what has this to do with the song?

Clearly the verses of 'Waltzing Matilda' were influenced by the death of Samuel Hoffmeister during the 1894 shearers' strike. However, the chorus is out of context with the verses and seems to have been written with a completely different set of emotions. Is it possible this love triangle had some effect on the writing of 'Waltzing Matilda'? Could it have been written partly as a love song, eventually becoming an embarrassment to all concerned?

The original lyrics Banjo wrote for the chorus of his song were:

> Who'll come a-waltzing Matilda, my darling,
> Who'll come a-waltzing Matilda with me?
> Waltzing Matilda and leading a water-bag—
> Who'll come a-waltzing Matilda with me?

The term 'waltzing matilda' means 'to go walkabout with your tools of trade and the one you love—or whatever keeps you warm at night'. Undoubtedly it was a romantic expression from his heart—a flirtatious love song, and Banjo knew exactly what he was alluding to when he wrote 'Waltzing Matilda'. There is further evidence of this in his own original handwritten manuscript, where in the last line of the first verse he wrote:

Who'll come a-roving Australia with me.[12]

'Roving Australia' was then firmly scratched out and replaced with 'Waltzing Matilda'. This leaves little doubt as to what Banjo was trying to express to Christina Macpherson.

Who'll come *a-roving Australia*, my darling,
Who'll come *a-roving Australia* with me.

Banjo was never to go *a-roving Australia* with Christina, but he did write her a song.

•

So now after all these years, we can understand what Banjo was expressing. There is little doubt that had he not crossed out the phrase 'Roving Australia' but continued on using it in the song, we would not have a song called 'Waltzing Matilda', instead we would have a song titled 'Roving Australia'. The phrase can be substituted and easily sung in all versions of the song. Granted, it's not as poetic, but at least we would have known what he was alluding to. The master poet!

The extent of the affair between Banjo Paterson and Christina Macpherson is something no-one will ever know.

Sarah would most likely have been jealous with Banjo spending intimate time with Christina, writing words to fit an already existing tune. This process of writing can be repetitive and exacting, even for someone knowing and playing the tune themselves. In this circumstance, we have Banjo Paterson, who by all accounts was tone deaf, fitting words to a tune he didn't know. In a time before recordings were possible, Banjo would have needed Christina to play the tune many times for him as he fitted the words to it. They would have worked intimately together. And it must be said that Banjo did an articulate job in writing the original 'Waltzing Matilda' to the 'Craigielee March' tune; the syllables are note perfect. It truly is a composition by two people.

Whatever did happen was enough for Sarah to dump her famous fiancée. After eight years' engagement, the now thirty-two-year-old Sarah Riley, within a very small social circle, embarrassed and disgraced, was left with little prospect of ever marrying. The decision to dump her flirting boyfriend would not have been made easily.

There is conjecture as to how long Paterson was present at Dagworth Station, but several weeks after 'Waltzing Matilda' was written the Ramsay family, who part-owned Oondooroo Station, invited the Macphersons and Banjo, who was still a guest at Dagworth, to a house party and to watch a demonstration of some new fire-fighting equipment. They drove over across Sesbania Station, the old Bostock and Manifold property, in a jinker—apparently without

Sarah Riley. Awaiting them at Oondooroo were a piano and the trained baritone singer Herbert Ramsay, a cousin of the owners. The visit was prolonged as Christina sat at the piano playing, while Banjo wrote down the words for Herbert to sing. Bob Macpherson and Robert Ramsay joined in the spirit of things by asking Herbert to put on a costume as he sang 'Waltzing Matilda'.

Exactly how long it was after the song was written before Paterson was asked to leave is unclear. However, it would seem from the visit to the Ramsays and the impromptu performance of the song that things didn't blow up immediately.

Whatever the case may be, the humiliation and shame of the affair forced Sarah to leave Australia for London to wear her sackcloth and ashes. 'Her family was all-agog to see where Barty would look next.'[13] Like Christina, Sarah remained broken hearted and never married. This embarrassing affair caused Banjo Paterson to distance himself from the writing of 'Waltzing Matilda' and anything concerning his stay at Dagworth Station.

But it would seem Banjo moved on unscathed by the affair until further questions were raised about his secrecy with women friends within a matter of months. On 2 October 1895, his Aunt Nora in a letter to her eldest daughter Meta wrote: 'All the world says that Bartie Paterson is engaged to a Miss Alice Cape . . . a very musical young lady, but he has not said a word about it to his relations . . . Bartie has so many lady friends.' Later it was suggested that competing with horses might be too much for Alice and his other numerous lady friends, including a divorcée whose name went round the family in whispers.[14]

Australia's favourite poet was a love rat who wrote 'Waltzing Matilda' with the help of a woman he was wooing while he was engaged to her best friend. The disgrace of this love-triangle, in such a small social circle, was devastating.

16

The 'Jolly Swagman' Song

BANJO AND CHRISTINA'S SONG became very popular around the Winton area, but was essentially still a local song. However, there is little doubt the shearers in the area, knowing full well who the song was written about (Hoffmeister), learnt and sang the song as they travelled through the country, singing it by campfires, around billabongs and in pubs.

The first official performance of 'Waltzing Matilda', three months after it was written, was at the North Gregory Hotel in Winton, on 6 April 1895. It was sung by Herbert Ramsay at a banquet attended by the Premier of Queensland, Hugh Nelson, and his ministerial party. Then, as John Manifold records in *Who Wrote the Ballads*: 'In May, the Winton Races took place. The Dagworth party and the Oondooroo party joined forces again, and sang "their" song all over Winton. It became the rage. People made manuscript copies of the words—did anyone write down the tune, I wonder?'[1]

Fortunately Christina Macpherson did write down the tune and words at the Winton Races, where the small social group that Dianna Baillieu had referred to had gathered again. It seems they were attempting to transplant the Warrnambool May Race Meeting into Winton as well, which was a premier social event for the area. The Winton races were conducted over two days at the end of May—Warrnambool had raced at the beginning of the same month. The results in Winton seemed like a 'who's who' from the western district of Victoria. On the first day, Meteor from Warrnambool Downs won the President's Plate. The winner of the Ladies' Bracelet was Rainbow, owned by C. P. Bell, formerly a Warrnambool resident, from Ayrshire Downs. The Maiden Plate was won by Orlando, from Oondooroo Station, owned by the Ramsays and the Manifolds, while the Flying Handicap was won by Valor, from Vindex Station, owned by the Rileys and Chirnsides.

The theme continued on the second day. The first race was won by Happy Boy, owned by Bill Riley, and the Maiden Plate by Dodger, from Warrnambool Downs, with Merlin from Oondooroo Station winning the Leviathan Stakes. The races were conducted for the very first time with the use of 'an electric starting machine, which performed as good as could be expected, and everyone was loud in its praises'.[2]

Among the visitors at the races were Mr and Mrs W. B. Bartlam from Townsville. The Bartlams were related to John Bostock, the former Warrnambool resident who was now a steward for the Winton Racing Club and foundation councillor of the Winton Shire. By this time, four months after the song was written, 'Waltzing Matilda' had already gained favour with the locals. Christina was encouraged to hand-write copies of 'Waltzing Matilda' for interested people, one of which she gave to Mrs Bartlam. This manuscript was handed down through the Bartlam family, while the song itself was used as a lullaby to sing the Bartlam children to sleep at night.[3]

This particular handwritten manuscript was sent to local historian Richard Magoffin by the Bartlam family in November 1971 and provided conclusive proof of how 'Waltzing Matilda', the original version, was first written— thus ending a debate about the origins of the song, which in some academic circles had been raging for several years.

However, the song was never officially published, and although popular in some areas, had it not been for a simple twist of fate, it may well have disappeared from Australian history forever.

'Waltzing Matilda'—the 'jolly swagman' song, as we know it today, which is sung around the world more than any other Australian song—was rearranged by Marie Cowan in 1903, eight years after the original song was conceived by Banjo and Christina in January of 1895.

During 1902, Paterson, needing some extra cash and on the point of marriage, sold to the publishers Angus & Robertson some unwanted verse. Among this 'old junk' was a copy of the text (without tune) of 'Waltzing Matilda'. Angus & Robertson then sold the musical rights in 'Waltzing Matilda'—that is, they sold the right to set it to music and perform it as a song—to James Inglis & Co., the proprietors of Billy Tea. It seems that Mr Inglis had notions in advance of his time, and proposed to use 'Waltzing Matilda' to advertise his product. But evidently this idea came to nothing. According to member of the firm who later published the music, 'They [Inglis & Co.] had one or two settings made, but these were not satisfactory, and it was then that Marie Cowan was invited to try her hand at it.' (Mrs Cowan was the wife of the general manager of Inglis & Co.; not a professional composer but a gifted amateur.) The late Mr Cowan confirmed that before copies of the edition were issued to the public, he had sent a copy to Banjo Paterson who telephoned him, saying, 'Your song received, very satisfactory, Marie Cowan has done a good job, good luck to her.'[4]

Had it not been for James Inglis and Co. wanting to develop a commercial to advertise their product Billy Tea, quite possibly 'Waltzing Matilda' may never have been heard of again, or at least, the song would never have gained the popularity it enjoys today.

Marie Cowan was quite offended when music was published with her name as the composer; she was adamant that she had only rearranged the song. That being said, the Billy Tea Company considered her version satisfactory, and decided to issue an edition of the song in sheet music form, for national distribution. A free copy was given away with every packet of Billy Tea. Possibly it was the first-ever singing commercial!

There are various ways Marie Cowan could have known of the original song. She could easily have obtained a copy of 'The Craigielee March', as the tune would have been circulated and been performed by various bands. The original song was also sung by soldiers at the Boer War. From there 'Waltzing Matilda' found its way back to Sydney, either via soldiers who lived in Sydney, or via returned servicemen travelling through Sydney on their way back to western Queensland. Perhaps Marie Cowan had heard the song then.

However, the most likely scenario is that Marie Cowan actually had a handwritten copy of 'Waltzing Matilda'. In Christina Macpherson's letter to Thomas Wood in 1931, describing how 'Waltzing Matilda' was written, she states that Paterson wrote to her asking for a copy of the tune, which she sent to him, and that he had passed it on to a musical friend. Did it finally finish in the hands of Marie Cowan? It would seem so. Either way, the tune was slightly changed and today, the Cowan arrangement of 'Waltzing Matilda' is known by all Australians and throughout the world.

Once a jolly swagman camped by a billabong,
Under the shade of a coolibah tree,
And he sang as he watched and waited till his billy boiled,
'You'll come a Waltzing Matilda with me.
Waltzing Matilda, Waltzing Matilda,
You'll come a Waltzing Matilda with me.'
And he sang and he watched and waited till his billy boiled,
'You'll come a Waltzing Matilda with me.'

Down came a jumbuck to drink at the billabong,
Up jumped the swagman and grabbed him with glee.
And he sang as he shoved that jumbuck in his tucker bag,
'You'll come a Waltzing Matilda with me.'
Waltzing Matilda, Waltzing Matilda,
You'll come a Waltzing Matilda with me.'
And he sang as he shoved that jumbuck in his tucker bag,
'You'll come a Waltzing Matilda with me.'

Up rode the squatter mounted on his thoroughbred
Down came the troopers, one two three
'Whose that jolly jumbuck you've got in your tucker bag?
You'll come a Waltzing Matilda with me.'
'Waltzing Matilda, Waltzing Matilda,
You'll come a Waltzing Matilda with me.'
Whose that jolly jumbuck you've got in your tucker bag?
'You'll come a Waltzing Matilda with me.'

Up jumped the swagman and sprang into the billabong,
'You'll never catch me alive' said he;
And his ghost may be heard as you pass by that billabong,
'You'll come a Waltzing Matilda with me.
Waltzing Matilda, Waltzing Matilda,

You'll come a Waltzing Matilda with me.'
And his ghost may be heard as you pass by that billabong,
'You'll come a Waltzing Matilda with me.'[5]

So now we have two slightly different songs: The original Macpherson–Paterson song and the popular Cowan version. Let us stay with the Cowan version a little longer.

When Marie Cowan set 'Waltzing Matilda' to a slightly different tune she also changed some of the original lyrics.

The first line Banjo penned in the original song was:

Oh! there once was a swagman camped in the billabong . . .

Marie Cowan changed it to:

Once a jolly swagman camped by a billabong . . .

This slight alteration to the lyric was to change the character of the original song. It was thought the image of Billy Tea would be enhanced if the song was happier, or 'more jolly', giving the impression that the tea would help to make the drinker feel that way.

A small change, it would seem. But the once hard-done-by swagman—who travelled hundreds of miles through the outback on foot, from shed to shed, looking for work, enduring spartan conditions for little pay while working under the rule of an overbearing landowner—had, with the quick stroke of a pen, become 'jolly'. Not only that, but the jumbuck became 'jolly' as well. The whole tone of the song was changed, and with it, the character of all Australia's itinerant workers . . . forever.

Interestingly enough, the other most significant phrase that was changed from Banjo's lyrics was the first line of the chorus:

Who'll come a-waltzing Matilda, my darling.

It was very simply changed to:

Waltzing Matilda, Waltzing Matilda.

Again this would seem a rather minor change, but fortunately for Banjo Paterson, it removed any reference to the song being in part a love song. On the surface these would seem two very trivial alterations to the lyrics, but they drastically changed the nature of the song.

The coincidence of the song being rearranged in 1903, on the eve of Banjo marrying Alice Walker of Tenterfield, also provides some intrigue. Paterson, guarding against his embarrassing past romantic affair, did what any discreet, guilt-ridden husband-to-be might do. On learning of the changes Marie Cowan had made, with an apparent lack of interest he wished her the best of luck.

Due to the wider publication and success of the new Cowan version, the original Macpherson–Paterson song all but disappeared without trace. Some writers on the origins of 'Waltzing Matilda' went as far as to claim that Banjo Paterson had not written the song at all, and that he doctored up an 'old bush song'. But there is no old bush song anything like 'Waltzing Matilda'. Other than a couple of orally collected stories from some 'old timers'—mainly E. J. Brady saying (at the age of seventy-seven) that he used to sing it in the bush when he was a boy, dating the song to before 1895—there is no evidence at all. Among Paterson's papers there is a list of songs and their origins that he compiled himself for *Old Bush Songs*. 'Waltzing Matilda' is not included.

These writers, though earnest in their attempts to find the truth, did not at the time have the crucial piece of evidence that solved the mystery—that being Christina Macpherson's handwritten manuscript, which no-one knew existed until 1971.

Previous writers on the history of 'Waltzing Matilda', such as Sydney May, *The Story of Waltzing Matilda* (1944); John Manifold, *Who Wrote the Ballads* (1964); and Harry Pearce, *On the Origins of Waltzing Matilda* (1971), did not know of the original manuscript. The dilemma that faced these writers was trying to marry two quite different songs and stories, like trying to fit a square peg into a round hole.

On one hand, there was the popular Cowan version of 'Waltzing Matilda', and on the other hand, there was Christina Macpherson having said that she played a tune to Banjo Paterson. She had heard the tune at the Warrnambool races, and of course, Banjo himself had stated that at Dagworth Christina had played him a little Scottish tune, which he put words to and called 'Waltzing Matilda'. But at the time there was no song, and little evidence of this so-called 'Craigielee' tune. Most writers dismissed the 'Craigielee' version; but not all of them. John Manifold, one of Australia's foremost folklorists, wanted to believe that the 'Craigielee' version did exist. He had family connections to the song, and didn't realise how close to the truth he was when in 1964, he wrote in his book *Who Wrote the Ballads*:

> My father learnt Waltzing Matilda by ear on Sesbania station, adjoining Oondooroo, as it was, shortly before the printed version began to achieve popularity. He used a tune that differed from the printed [Cowan] tune only to the extent of a bar or two; but it did differ; and that is how I have inherited a slight feeling of distrust and hostility to the Cowan version.[6]

Not only were Manifold's feelings about the song correct, but as a young boy, he probably met Christina Macpherson, and may even have heard her play the original 'Waltzing Matilda'. Dianna Baillieu was the same age as John Manifold and as a young girl living at Menningort, near Camperdown, she would visit the nearby Manifolds at the magnificent Purrumbete homestead to play with John's elder sister. During these years Christina often stayed at Menningort, and would almost definitely have visited the Manifolds as well. John Manifold eventually became Dianna's first boyfriend, and later on she affectionately corresponded with him in England, while he was studying at Cambridge. Dianna and her girlfriends, who were all rather envious of his scholastic and artistic ability, gave him the nickname of 'The Suckling', being the youngest in the Manifold family. 'In fact,' Dianna said, 'I was still corresponding with him when he met that woman from the blue stocking brigade whom he married, and eventually became a communist.'[7]

Another author who put in an extraordinary amount of work trying to unravel the mystery, as though it were a Sherlock Holmes detective story, was Harry Pearce. His research on the origins of the term 'Waltzing Matilda' was substantial, but again, as regards the origins of the tune, he was working with the wrong clues. In his book *On the Origins of Waltzing Matilda* Pearce wrote: 'Richard Magoffin, who has a station at Nelia, in the Waltzing Matilda country, has become interested in the origins of the song and collected evidence he says that will prove it is based on "Craigielee".'[8]

Evidence Magoffin did have; and of course this evidence was Christina's handwritten manuscript sent to him by the Bartlam family. After that specific manuscript resurfaced, another similar copy in Christina's handwriting was uncovered from her personal belongings. These two manuscripts are now national treasures.

The earlier writers on the origins of the tune for 'Waltzing Matilda' never had these crucial manuscripts and, although earnest in their attempts to uncover the facts, did much to confuse the issue. Unfortunately, some writers continue to regurgitate an old myth that 'Waltzing

Matilda' may have been written as a parody of an allegedly older English song, 'The Bold Fusilier'. This is simply not true. No-one has ever found this supposed old English song; it does not exist. In fact the opposite is the case; the 'Bold Fusilier' song is a parody of our 'Waltzing Matilda', which the English soldiers heard during the Boer War and World War I.

Many commentators on the subject have had limited musical knowledge and therefore cannot readily perceive the relationship between the different versions of 'Waltzing Matilda'. It simply is not possible to understand the subtle nuances of 'Thou Bonnie Wood of Craigielea' and 'Waltzing Matilda' unless they are learnt note by note, and performed. Traditional or trained musicians recognise a direct and easily understood musical transition from the original song 'Thou Bonnie Wood of Craigielea' to the re-arranged 'Craigielee March' played at Warrnambool, then to Christina Macpherson's handwritten manuscripts of 'Waltzing Matilda', and finally to the Marie Cowan version, the popular 'jolly swagman' song we sing today. There is no other tune in question.

Since the 1970s, a third version of 'Waltzing Matilda' has become quite popular via the work of modern, revivalist 'bush bands'. This version contains the original lyrics as written by Banjo and Christina, and when played a little slower than the usual 'bush band' tempo, this song is very similar to the original. Several years after 'Waltzing Matilda' was written, Bob Macpherson had a relationship with Josephine Penne, who was a French pianist living in Cloncurry, Queensland. Although they never married, together they had a son. Bob Macpherson supplied Josephine with the original lyrics, and possibly tried to orally transmit the original tune as best he could. This song was collected many years later by one of Australia's leading folklore collectors, John Meredith. It became known as the Buderim version. Richard Magoffin, however, had learnt this version of the song from his father in the 1940s and maintains it always was, and still is, the 'Cloncurry' version. Australians now know that song as the 'Queensland' version.

Some years after Christina's death in 1936, among her belongings was found an unopened letter. The letter was addressed to Dr Wood (c/o Mrs J. C. Manifold at Talindert, near Camperdown in western Victoria). Dr Thomas Wood had been writing about music in Australia and had mentioned 'Waltzing Matilda'. Christina wrote him a letter and for reasons unknown never posted it.

> In reading your impressions about music in Australia I was interested to note that you had mentioned Waltzing Matilda and thought it might interest you to hear how 'Banjo' Paterson came to write it. He was on a visit to Winton, North Queensland and I was staying with my brothers about 80 miles from Winton. We went in to Winton for a week or so and one day I played (from ear) a tune, which I had heard played by a band at the Races in Warrnambool, a country town in the Western District of Victoria. Mr. Paterson asked what it was. I could not

tell him and he then said he thought he could write some lines to it. He then and there wrote the first verse. We tried it and thought it went well, so he then wrote the other verses. I might add that in a short time everyone in the District was singing it . . .[9]

(Christina mentions the song was written in Winton. However, the song was reworked and polished in Winton after it was written at Dagworth Station.)

Her recollections were also confirmed by Paterson himself, when in the early 1930s, speaking on ABC radio about artesian water in western Queensland, he not only referred to Hoffmeister's death but also Christina's tune: 'The shearers staged a strike and Macpherson's woolshed at Dagworth was burnt down, and a man was picked up dead . . . Miss Macpherson used to play a little Scottish tune on a zither and I put words to it and called it "Waltzing Matilda".'

The Christina Macpherson manuscripts, supported by oral and written documentation, prove conclusively that the original song 'Waltzing Matilda' was written to a variation of the Scottish song 'Thou Bonnie Wood of Craigielea'.

17

And His Ghost May Be Heard

AFTER PATERSON'S TRIP to western Queensland he returned to Sydney, and for the rest of 1895 put his mind to the task of preparing poems for his forthcoming book. *The Man from Snowy River and Other Verses* was published by Angus & Robertson in October 1895. The first edition sold out within a week and the book went through four editions and 6000 copies in six months, making Paterson second only to Rudyard Kipling in popularity among living poets writing in English. 'The Banjo' became our first real pop star, becoming a household name, the first person to achieve national popular status in Australian history.

The Times in England compared 'The Banjo' to Kipling—who personally sent a letter congratulating Paterson and encouraged him 'to write more about the man who is born and bred on the land'. Thousands of copies were sold in the United Kingdom, providing many people there with their first glimpse of Australian bush life.

Paterson had mastered the Australian ballad which depended on several elements:

> excitement, preferably with a touch of the ironic or cynical; a genuine feeling for love of the land, with the inner certainty that the land healed itself and that inevitably, with patience and courage to await it, rebirth followed after drought-death; as a corollary of this, some elements of gloom and melancholy brought on by environment; and interwoven in all this, the dominant Australian characteristic to 'give it a go' and take a risk.[1]

Although Banjo would continue to write, in some sense he was burnt out and became more conservative with age. His creative writing would never reach the height of his earlier works. Although his letters from South Africa during the Boer War are considered by some to be his finest descriptive writing work, they never captured the public imagination like his poetry of the early 1890s.

Another major influence on his life had always been the long and distinguished military involvement of his mother's lineage. His great-grandfather, Major Edward Darvall, served under Wellington in India and then took part in defending English soil from a threatened Napoleonic military invasion. Among his great-uncles was a major-general in the British Indian Army and an attorney-general of New South Wales, who was a prominent figure in the Sydney establishment.

When the Boer War broke out in 1899, Paterson immediately seized the opportunity to experience action. Finally, he gave up his job as a solicitor. Unable to enlist because of his deformed arm, he became a war correspondent for the *Sydney Morning Herald*. Sailing with the First Contingent of New South Wales Lancers, he rode with them to join General John French's cavalry division, to defend the Cape Colony against Boer incursions from the Orange Free State. Here, Lord Roberts, with Kitchener as his Chief of Staff, planned to encircle the Orange Free State of Bloemfontein. Paterson continued to ride with the Lancers on a journey of more than 500 miles, into enemy territory.

During the gruelling ride almost two-thirds of the division's horses collapsed or were destroyed. Paterson completed the ride on his favourite saddle horse that he had brought from Australia, leading a packhorse and cart-horse to carry supplies. After Bloemfontein was taken he travelled another 300 miles across the Vaal to occupy Johannesburg and then on to Pretoria. Afterwards he rode south with squadrons to hunt down Boer guerrilla resistance fighters before returning to Australia in July 1900. His highly descriptive and prolific first-hand dispatches from the front were published in the *Sydney Morning Herald*.

Paterson was then sent to China in 1901 with the intention of covering the Boxer Rebellion, but he arrived after the uprising was over. He went to England to visit Kipling (whom he had met during the Boer War) before he returned to Australia. By 1902 Paterson had left the legal profession for good. The following year he was appointed Editor of the *Evening News* in Sydney, a position he held until 1908, when he resigned to take over a property in Wee Jasper. At almost forty years of age, in 1903 he married Alice Walker in Tenterfield, and they had two children, Grace (born in 1904) and Hugh (born in 1906).

During World War I Paterson again sailed to Europe, hoping for an appointment as war correspondent. Instead, he was attached as an ambulance driver to the Australian Voluntary Hospital in France. On hearing that back in Australia they were recruiting cavalry, he returned home. His reputation preceded him and he was commissioned as a lieutenant to the 2nd Remount Unit of the AIF. Within weeks he was promoted to captain, in charge of supplying horses for the Light Horse and Field Artillery in Sinai and Palestine. Few men knew horses well enough to accomplish the task. Horses were sent in mobs of a thousand at a time and hastily prepared for action.

With the Turks advancing, the demand for horses increased and the remount divisions were amalgamated. Banjo was promoted to Major Paterson, managing the supply of horses until the Turks were forced out of Jerusalem and defeated. Within two weeks the Germans capitulated in France, bringing the war to an end in November 1918. The horses Paterson had looked after for several years could not return home, and the order was given to destroy them, a decision that physically sickened him. It broke his heart—it broke every soldier's heart—shooting their best friends, who had carried each rider through deserts and gunfire, and slept with them at night to keep them warm. More than 50,000 horses were sent from Australia during the war, and only one was brought back home. Eric Bogle in his song 'As If He Knows', written in 2001, remembers these magnificent animals:

> And all along the picket lines beneath the desert sky
> The Light Horsemen move amongst their mates
>   to say one last goodbye
> And the horses stand so quietly
> Row on silent row
> It's as if they know

Back in Australia Paterson returned to journalism, working for the *Sydney Sportsman* and as a freelance journalist. After his retirement in 1930 he published various books, none of which would reach the acclaim of his first book of poems. He was created a Commander of the British Empire (CBE) in 1939, for service to Australian literature. Two years later, on 5 February 1941, at the age of seventy-four, with a secure reputation as Australia's principal folk poet, Andrew Barton Paterson, 'The Banjo', died from heart failure. On the evening of his death, the author and broadcaster Vance Palmer, in a tribute to Paterson, aptly said:

He laid hold both of our affections and imaginations; he made himself a vital part of the country we all know and love, and it would not only have been a poorer country but one far the less united in bonds of intimate feeling, if he had never lived or written.[2]

During his life, Paterson showed little respect for his critics. He learnt to ride with the Monaro horsemen; he needed the approval of no-one else. Banjo was a commentator, a cultural conversationalist. Rather than commit characters to history books or allow them to become museum pieces, he used his craft to keep them alive. He loathed scabs, politicians, lawyers and the law. He championed ordinary Australians, the bush workers, the underdogs of the city and country, the outlaws Gilbert and Dunn, the horse thief Andy Reagan, the out-of-luck jockey and the down-at-heel drover.[3] To pretend he was not socially and politically minded is ridiculous, as his poem 'On Kiley's Run' reminds us:

> The owner lives in England now
> Of Kiley's Run.
> He knows a racehorse from a cow;
> But that is all he knows of stock:
> His chiefest care is how to dock
> Expenses, and he sends from town
> To cut the shearers' wages down
> On Kiley's Run.[4]

When Christina Macpherson died on 27 March 1936, she had received no recognition at all for her part in the creation of our national song. Banjo, at least, lived long enough to know 'Waltzing Matilda' had found its way into the hearts of many Australians. How bemused he would have been had he been alive eleven years later in 1952, when 'Waltzing Matilda' was played at the Helsinki Olympic Games, as Marjorie Jackson stood on the winners' podium after receiving her gold medal. The Games organisers thought, as many people overseas still think today, 'Waltzing Matilda' was our national song. The Australian officials may have privately agreed, but in the end they insisted on 'God Save the Queen'.

After World War II, Australia knew it needed and deserved an anthem of its own. 'God Save the Queen' meant nothing to the majority of Australians. The only other Australian song that Australians were singing was 'Waltzing Matilda'. But the idea of a song about a suicidal sheep-stealing swagman being sung as our anthem was not universally accepted.

In 1974, eventually it was decided to hold a national poll to select a new national anthem. Four songs were put forward. 'Waltzing Matilda' was one of them and it finished second in the voting, with the numbers as follows:

'Advance Australia Fair'	2,940,854
'Waltzing Matilda'	1,918,206
'God Save the Queen'	1,257,341
'Song of Australia'	652,858

By the very nature of its lyric, 'Advance Australia Fair' has done little to unite Australians in voice. Perhaps by indoctrinating the young and impressionable we may find some acceptance for the song in future generations, but it still won't say anything about who we really are. There are two differing patriotic cultures at work in Australia today, as Matthew Richardson has described:

> One is serious, straightforward and strident. Its colours are blue, white and red. Its annual celebration is Australia Day; and its song is 'Advance Australia Fair'. It is promoted by certain political leaders, primary school teachers and by commercial sponsors and Federal Government initiatives. It is the same as patriotism overseas.
>
> The other kind is sardonic, complicated, subtle and pervasive. Its colours are green and yellow. Its annual commemoration is Anzac Day. Its song is 'Waltzing Matilda'. It involves normal Australians being themselves and needs no promoters. It is uniquely Australian.[5]

The opposition to certain pompous, irrelevant lines in 'Advance Australia Fair' has been well documented and will continue to strike discord with many Australians. But the current policies for dealing with boat people make an absurdity of the lines:

> For those who've come across the seas,
> We've boundless plains to share.

This is a most deceptive piece of false advertising. How can we have a national anthem that is so misleading? Perhaps this jingoistic song is better understood by reading some of the other verses written by its author, the Scotsman Peter McCormick. And, Australians all, let us rejoice that we don't have to sing them:

When gallant Cook from Albion sail'd,
To trace wide oceans o'er,
True British courage bore him on,
Till he landed on our shore.
Then here he raised Old England's flag,
The standard of the brave;
With all her faults we love her still,
'Britannia rules the wave!'
In joyful strains then let us sing
'Advance Australia fair!'

Should foreign foe e'er sight our coast,
Or dare a foot to land,
We'll rouse to arms like sires of yore
To guard our native strand;
Britannia then shall surely know,
Beyond wide ocean's roll,
Her sons in fair Australia's land
Still keep a British soul.
In joyful strains then let us sing
'Advance Australia fair!'

Before the Bledisloe Cup match in 1999 against New Zealand, the 107,000-strong crowd in the Telstra stadium in Sydney responded to the culturally iconic and confronting haka with a stirring rendition of 'Waltzing Matilda' and everyone knew the words. It represented the spirit of our nation, which is as relevant today as when the song was written, and in fact, 'Waltzing Matilda' has helped keep that spirit alive. Perhaps now, with a better understanding of 'Waltzing Matilda', it may be considered at some point in the future as a possible anthem. Be that as it may; no matter how you try, one simply cannot imagine Australian soldiers, at any time in the past or in the future, charging into battle singing 'Advance Australia Fair'!

•

In 1901, when the Australian Parliament was formed at the Royal Exhibition building in Melbourne, the ceremony finished with 'Rule Britannia' and 'God Save the King', reflecting our ties with Victorian England. One hundred years later at the centenary of the Parliament, when wanting to have music that reflected our own unique cultural footprint, composer Peter Sculthorpe chose 'Waltzing Matilda' to start the ceremony. The lilting version of 'Waltzing Matilda' sung by Bruce Woodley to the original tune, like the best interpretations of any national song, made the hair stand up on the back of Australian necks. The song was older than the Parliament itself.

Unfortunately, Paterson sold the lyrics to 'Waltzing Matilda' to Angus & Robertson in 1902 and, as companies merged and were bought and sold, the copyright eventually passed to the current owner, Carl Fischer Music, who registered the song in the United States in 1941. Copyright and the collection and payment of royalties are possibly among the most confusing and complicated areas of international law, but, in brief, this means that the rights for 'Waltzing Matilda' are owned by Carl Fischer Music in the territory of the United States and the company collects royalties for recordings and live performances of the song in that territory. In Australia, though, the work has passed out of copyright and entered the public domain, so we are free here to perform 'Waltzing Matilda' whenever and wherever we like.

It should be noted that Carl Fischer Music does not own an original composition. When the company registered the rights in 1941, the music was said to have been 'composed' by Marie Cowan. We now know that is not correct. Marie Cowan did not compose the song; she merely rearranged an already existing song. Her work was not original. Carl Fischer's hold on the copyright might possibly fall into the category of 'possession is nine tenths of the law'. By acquiring the rights to the words it seems they have assumed the rights to the music as well. To my knowledge no-one has ever challenged their claim in court; a test case would have to be mounted for all the legal ramifications to be aired and understood. No doubt the real authorship by Christina Macpherson would become a crucial point in any such case.

What a pity Banjo was embroiled in an affair and became so reluctant to discuss 'Waltzing Matilda'. His silence has allowed debate to fester for more than one hundred years. At least he continued to receive recognition for his composition, whereas his silence meant that poor Christina went to her grave with nothing—no recognition and no payment.

'Waltzing Matilda' was written at a pivotal time in Australia's short and colourful history. The shearing strikes of the 1890s were made up of a series of violent events spread over three years. In context, this social and class war rivals any major single historical event in Australian history, such as the Eureka Stockade or the bushranging exploits of Ned Kelly. To coin a phrase, this is Australia's culturally defining trilogy. Each one of these historical events took place in a brief forty-year period, from 1854 to 1894, when an Australian identity was being forged. All possess the same underlying social democratic ideologies: freedom from too much authority and a country free of the old-world class system. These were not rebellions. Rebellions usually involve the taking of power or the claiming of land. These were all fights for social democracy and a right to have a say in Australia's future; something we would later simply call 'a fair go'.

Here in 'the lucky country' there seemed a chance for social classes to converge like nowhere else in the world. A new society, Australian! Some called it an experiment, comprising mostly ex-convicts, disengaged Europeans and gold diggers, all infused with an intangible ethos that we would later term 'mateship'.

The idea of humans being born free but spending their lives as slaves to institutions, metaphorically shackled to daily life, was resisted in Australia, where freedom was a priority. The key to freedom was personal choice. Wordsworth had written about it in Europe, in Australia Lawson was writing about it, and so was Banjo Paterson.

The shearing strikes of the 1890s, which have received little attention in Australian history as taught, may have remained obscure, except for Banjo Paterson writing 'Waltzing Matilda'. Ironically, Paterson is often referred to as the 'squatters' poet', yet his song of a sole swagman confronted by a squatter and three policemen continually reminds Australians of our working-class struggles and attitudes against unwarranted authority.

During the 1890s, poets and story-tellers found a unique Australian voice, while artists looking through fresh eyes discovered soft pastel colours and dazzling light. Here in Australia, a scattered gathering of people from all corners of the British Isles and Europe embraced a new spirit and created their own nation. Politicians debated unionism, federation and the possibility of independence, a republic! It is only fitting that we have an anthem as a continuous reminder of that passionate phase of Australian history. Did Banjo Paterson write 'Waltzing Matilda' purposefully, calling for a fair go, exploiting this new revolutionary class convergence?

I don't think so. 'Waltzing Matilda' was a spontaneous composition. Spontaneity, as songwriters know, is the subconscious surfacing freely. Many songwriting students spend days staring at a blank piece of paper trying to write about a predetermined subject. Often, when they least expect it, sometimes in the middle of the night or the middle of a conversation, words will flow from their mind like a torrent. Often these words are about a completely different subject, something that has been in the back of their mind for who knows how long, waiting to be given birth. Virtually overnight their song will be written as a spontaneous reaction to deeper thoughts. 'Waltzing Matilda' was written like that.

For centuries many songs of protest, like the treason songs written during early Australian settlement, were written as allegories, to disguise the subject matter of the song and prevent the writers and singers of these songs being convicted of treason.

In the same simple tradition, many Australians, and people throughout the world, think 'Waltzing Matilda' is a simple song about a petty thief stealing a sheep. It is a common misconception, which more than likely prevented the song being selected as the national anthem in the 1970s. But it is not a simple song! Written in simple language, yes, but vividly pictorial, displaying many of our national characteristics and created during an intense socio-political time, which embroiled the lives of many well-known Australian families from opposite ends of the political spectrum. Here we have the master poet at work, spontaneously continuing an oral tradition that was centuries old—penning a quintessential Australian song as an allegory, basing it on real events, and creating an Australian story that could not have been written in any other country. As with the nursery rhymes of old, shrouded in mystery and allegory, the truth is just below the surface.

The swagman was Samuel Hoffmeister, a union shearer camped by the Four-Mile Billabong, under the shade of a coolibah tree, contemplating his boiling billy. Jumbuck is an Aboriginal word meaning 'white mist', often pronounced 'jumboc' or 'gumboc', and is how the Aboriginal people referred to the flocks of sheep invading their natural hunting grounds. These jumbucks represented the wealth and power that only belonged to a minority of Australians at the time. The squatter was Bob Macpherson, who rode up with three policemen to arrest the sole swagman for attempting to steal his symbolic jumbuck. Then Paterson's swagman mysteriously jumped into the waterhole, but the story doesn't end there, because Banjo knows his ghost will be heard singing, if we happen to be interested enough to pass by that billabong and listen.

And here we have another fascinating twist. The last verse that Banjo wrote was:

> But the swagman, he up and he jumped into the water-hole,
> Drowning himself by the Coolabah tree,
> And his ghost may be heard as it sings in the billabong,
> 'Who'll come a-waltzing Matilda with me?'

The second line eventually became:

> You'll never catch me alive said he.

It is thought that over time this line was substituted by the shearers and bushmen who were singing 'Waltzing Matilda' and knew the true story behind the song. This folk osmosis has all the hallmarks of earlier treason songs, like 'The Wild Colonial Boy' and 'Bold Jack Donahue'.

During 1995 at the centenary celebration in Winton, the then Prime Minister Paul Keating commented:

> I don't think there's any doubt that the words describe a class struggle. If ever there was a class struggle in Australia it was in its most virulent form in the 1890s. It is not hard to see the song as an affirmation of the idea of the fair go, which still strikes a powerful chord in Australia and I think will always do. I think we can interpret 'Waltzing Matilda' as a celebration of our rebellious nature. But the truth is none of these things come into mind when I hear it sung . . . a national song is not to be interpreted intellectually. It comes to you emotionally. When you hear it, if you don't come to understand the force and emotionalism of it, the sense of the nation, the thing it's become to the rest of us, then there's no way of understanding it. I wonder what in fact the writer of the words actually meant, and what the spirit was about, and about the ghost of the swagman. I think the trick in it is that the song is the ghost of the swagman, and 100 years later we're still hearing the ghost as loud as it was heard when it was written.

Over the years numerous writers and commentators have investigated 'Waltzing Matilda'. Some have claimed the song for the left side of politics, while the conservatives would like us to believe that the words of 'Waltzing Matilda' have 'no real meaning'.[6] Few, if any, have given any credence to the love affair between Paterson and Christina Macpherson and the resulting silence from Paterson about the song's creation. Now, this deeper understanding of the events and people surrounding the writing of the song takes it from a frivolous ditty to a ballad with immense social and cultural meaning. A story that will excite the imaginations of all Australians, because 'Waltzing Matilda' belongs to us all.

And his ghost may be heard . . .

Bibliography

Adam-Smith, Patsy, 1982, *The Shearers*, Thomas Nelson, Melbourne

Adams, Francis, 1886, *Australian Essays*, W. Inglis, Melbourne

Armstrong, Mick, 2007, *Burning the* Rodney, Socialist Alternative, Melbourne

Blainey, Geoffrey, 2003, *Black Kettle and Full Moon*, Penguin Books, Camberwell

Broome, Richard, 1984, *The Victorians, Arriving*, Fairfax, Syme & Weldon, McMahons Point

Burrows, R., & Barton, A., 1996, *Henry Lawson, A Stranger on the Darling*, Harper Collins, Sydney

Cavendish, R. (ed.), 1982, *Legends of the World*, Orbis Publishing, London

Clark, C. M., 1981, *History of Australia, Volume V: The People Make Laws*, Melbourne University Press, Carlton

Clune, Frank, 1936, *Roaming Round the Darling*, Angus & Robertson, Sydney

Critchett, J., 1990, *A Distant Field of Murder*, Melbourne University Press, Carlton

Davey, Gwenda Beed and Seal, Graham (eds), 1993, *The Oxford Companion to Australian Folklore*, Oxford University Press, Melbourne

Dengate, John, 2011, *Oaths*, unpublished, author's collection

Dingle, Tony, 1984, *The Victorians, Settling*, Fairfax, Syme & Weldon, McMahons Point

Dutton, Geoffrey, 1985, *The Squatters*, Viking O'Neil, Ringwood

Edwards, Ron, 1976, *The Big Book of Australian Folk Song*, Rigby Limited, Sydney

Fahey, W., & Seal, G. (eds), 2005, *Old Bush Songs*, ABC Books, Sydney

Forrest, Peter & Sheila, 2008, *Banjo and Christina*, Shady Tree, Darwin

Harris, A., 1847, *Settlers and Convicts – Recollections of Sixteen Years' Labour in the Australian Backwoods by an Emigrant Mechanic*, London, republished 1969, Melbourne University Press, Melbourne

Hayes, Barbara (ed.), 1987, *Folk Tales and Fables of the World*, David Bateman Ltd, Buderim

Haynes, Jim (ed.), 2008, *The Book of Australian Popular Rhymed Verse*, ABC Books, Sydney

Kempster, Chris (ed.), 1989, *The Songs of Henry Lawson,* Viking O'Neil, Ringwood

Kiddle, Margaret, 1961, *Men of Yesterday: A Social History of the Western District of Victoria, 1834–1890,* Melbourne University Press, Carlton

Lawson, Henry, 1896, *In the Days When the World Was Wide and Other Verses*, Angus & Robertson, Sydney

Leurs, Margaret, 1987, *Laureate of Labor: A Biography of J. K. McDougall, Socialist and Poet*, Banyan Press, Sandy Bay

Lindsay, N., 1965, *Bohemians at the* Bulletin*,* Angus & Robertson, Sydney,

Magoffin, Richard, 1973, *Fair Dinkum Matilda,* Mimosa Press, Charters Towers

Magoffin, Richard, 1983, *Waltzing Matilda: Song of Australia,* Mimosa Press, Charters Towers

Manifold, John, 1964, *Who Wrote the Ballads: Notes on Australian Folksong,* Australian Book Society, Sydney

May, Sidney, 1944, *The Story of Waltzing Matilda,* Smith and Paterson, Brisbane

McDonald, Graham, 2010, *The Matilda Discography*, National Film and Sound Archive, Canberra

McDougall, J. K., 1923, *The Trend of Ages and Other Verses*, Labor Call Print, Melbourne

McDougall, J. K., 1930, *Grass and Gossamer and Other Verses*, The Industrial Printing and Publicity Co., Melbourne

McDougall, J. K., 1936, *The Golden Road and Other Verses*, The Industrial Printing and Publicity Co., Melbourne

McDougall, J. K., 1939, *Beasts of the Blood Trail and Other Verses*, The Industrial Printing and Publicity Co., Melbourne

McDougall, J. K., 1948, *Shadows in the Sun and Other Verses*, The Industrial Printing and Publicity Co., Melbourne

McHugh, Evan, 2004, *Outback Heroes,* Penguin, Camberwell

Meredith, John, 1983, *Duke of the Outback,* Red Rooster Press, Ascot Vale

Meredith, John & Anderson, Hugh, 1967, *Folk Songs of Australia,* Ure Smith, Sydney

Merritt, John, 1986, *The Making of the AWU,* Oxford University Press, Melbourne

Molony, J., 1987, *History of Australia,* Penguin Books, Ringwood

Mudie, Ian, 1961, *Riverboats*, Rigby, Sydney

Osborne, Richard, 1886, *The History of Warrnambool, 1847–1886*, Chronicle, Prahran

Palmer, Vance, 1954, *The Legend of the Nineties,* Melbourne University Press, Melbourne

Paterson, A. B., 1895, *The Man from Snowy River and Other Verses,* Angus & Robertson, Sydney

Paterson, A. B. (ed.), 1905, *Old Bush Songs,* Angus & Robertson, Sydney

Paterson, A. B., 1983, *Singer of the Bush: A. B. 'Banjo' Paterson: Complete Works 1885–1900,* Lansdowne Press, Sydney

Paterson, A. B., 1983, *Song of the Pen: A. B. 'Banjo' Paterson: Complete Works 1901–1941,* Lansdowne Press, Sydney

Pearce, H. H., 1971, *On the Origins of Waltzing Matilda,* Hawthorn Press, Melbourne

Perry, Roland, 2004, *Monash: The Outsider Who Won a War,* Random House, Sydney

Prentis, Malcolm, 2008, *The Scots in Australia,* University of New South Wales, Sydney

Priestly, Susan, 1984, *The Victorians, Making Their Mark,* Fairfax, Syme & Weldon, McMahons Point

Raddick, Therese (ed.), 1989, *Songs of Australian Working Life,* Greenhouse, Elwood

Randell, J. O., 1983, *Teamwork: A History of the Graziers' Associations of Victoria and Riverina,* Livestock Grain Producers' Association of New South Wales, Sydney

Richardson, Matthew, 2006, *Once a Jolly Swagman: The Ballad of Waltzing Matilda,* Melbourne University Press, Melbourne

Roderick, Colin, 1993, *Banjo Paterson: Poet by Accident,* Allen & Unwin, North Sydney

Roderick, Colin, 1991, *Henry Lawson: A Life,* Collins/Angus & Robertson, North Ryde, NSW

Roderick, Colin (ed.), 1970, *Henry Lawson: Letters 1890–1922,* Angus & Robertson, Sydney

Roderick, Colin (ed.), 1984, *Henry Lawson, The Master Story-teller,* Angus & Robertson, Australia

Sayers, C. E., 1972, *Of Many Things: A History of Warrnambool,* Olinda Books, Olinda, Victoria

Sayers, C. E. & Yule, P. L., 1969, *By These We Flourish: A History of Warrnambool,* Warrnambool Institute Press, Warrnambool

Scott, Bill (ed.), 1976, *Complete Book of Australian Folklore,* Ure Smith, Sydney

Scott, Bill, date unknown, *On Becoming Australian,* author's collection

Semmler, Clement, 1965, *A. B. (Banjo) Paterson,* Lansdowne Press, Melbourne

Semmler, Clement, 1966, *The Banjo of the Bush,* Lansdowne Press, Melbourne

Semmler, Clement, 1969, 'Some Notes on the Literature of the Shearers' Strikes of 1891 and 1894', *International Social Science Journal,* Vol. XXI, No. 3, United Nations Scientific and Cultural Organisation, Place de Fonteroy, Paris

Spence, W.G., 1909, *Australia's Awakening,* Worker Print, Sydney

Spence, W.G., 1961, *History of the A.W.U.,* The Worker Trustees, Sydney

Stone, D., & Garden, D., 1978, *Squatters and Settlers,* Popular Books, Frenchs Forest

Stuart, Julian, 1967, *Part of the Glory,* Australasian Book Society, Sydney

Svensen, Stuart, 1989, *The Shearers' War: The Story of the 1891 Shearers' Strike,* University of Queensland Press, St Lucia

Svensen, Stuart, 1995, *Industrial War: The Great Strikes 1890–94,* Ram Press, Wollongong

Tritton, Duke, 1964, *Time Means Tucker,* Akron Press, Arncliffe

Ward, Russel, 1958, *The Australian Legend,* Oxford University Press, Melbourne

Williams, R.M., & Ruhen, O., 1984, *Beneath Whose Hand: The Autobiography of R.M. Williams,* Pan Macmillan, Sydney

Notes

Chapter 1   Australia's Song for the World

1. Clement Semmler, *The Banjo of the Bush*, Lansdowne Press, Melbourne, 1966, p. 98.
2. Graham McDonald, *The Matilda Discography*, National Film and Sound Archive, Canberra, 2010.
3. Sheryl Allen, *Waltzing Matilda—Unravelling the Mystery*, Landmark Property Australia, 2010, No. 33, p. 5.
4. Carolyn Ford, 'Waltzing Matilda Turns 100', *Herald Sun*, 15 October 1994.

Chapter 2   The Backdrop for a Song

1. Francis Adams, *Australian Essays*, W. Inglis, Melbourne, 1886, p. 33.
2. Dennis O'Keeffe, 'The Ghost of Yick Yung', *Waltzing Down the Years*, CD, Larrikin Entertainment, Sydney, 1996.
3. John Monash, letter to Leo Monash, 9 May 1883. Reprinted in Roland Perry, *Monash: The Outsider Who Won a War*, Random House Australia, Milsons Point, 2004, p. 21.

Chapter 3   Clancy and the Man from Snowy River

1. Vance Palmer, *The Legend of the Nineties*, Melbourne University Press, Melbourne, 1954, p. 52.
2. Clement Semmler, *The Banjo of the Bush*, Lansdowne Press, Melbourne, 1966, p. 87.
3. A. B. Paterson, *The Man from Snowy River and Other Verses*, Angus and Robertson, Sydney, 1895, p. 10.
4. ibid.

5. ibid., p. 1.
6. ibid., p. 2.
7. ibid., p. 3.
8. ibid., p. 4.

Chapter 4   There Once Was a Swagman

1. *Shorter Oxford English Dictionary on Historical Principles*, 3rd ed., Clarendon Press, Oxford, 1990, p. 2206.
2. *Australian Concise Oxford Dictionary*, 3rd ed., Oxford University Press, Melbourne, 1997, p. 1377.
3. Colin Roderick (ed.), *Henry Lawson, The Master Story-teller*, Angus and Robertson, Sydney, 1984, p. 499.
4. Ron Edwards, *The Big Book of Australian Folk Song*, Rigby Ltd, Sydney, 1976, p. 338.
5. Russel Ward, *The Australian Legend*, Oxford University Press, Melbourne, 1958, p. 221.
6. Letter from The Reverend Richard Johnson, 1790, reprinted in Bill Scott, *On Becoming Australian*, date unknown.
7. ibid.
8. Ward, p. 107.
9. John Dengate, *Oaths*, unpublished, 2011, author's collection.
10. Gwenda Beed Davey and Graham Seal (eds), *The Oxford Companion to Australian Folklore*, Oxford University Press, Melbourne, 1993, p. 187.
11. Ward, p. 54.
12. Edwards, p. 186.
13. Jim Haynes (ed.), *The Book of Australian Popular Rhymed Verse*, ABC Books, Sydney, 2008, p. 149.
14. Ward, p. 136.
15. Sidney Baker, 'The Drum', 1959, reprinted in Bill Scott, *On Becoming Australian*, date unknown.
16. D. Stone and D. Garden, *Squatters and Settlers*, Popular Books, Frenchs Forest, 1978, p. 144.
17. ibid.
18. John Meredith, *Duke of the Outback*, Red Rooster Press, Ascot Vale, 1983, p. 69.
19. Edwards, p. 17.

Chapter 5   Up Rode the Squatter

1. Margaret Kiddle, *Men of Yesterday: A Social History of the Western District of Victoria, 1834–1890*, Melbourne University Press, Carlton, 1961, p. 100.
2. Geoffrey Dutton, *The Squatters*, Viking O'Neil, Ringwood, 1985, p. 65.
3. ibid.
4. *Shorter Oxford English Dictionary on Historical Principles*, 3rd ed., Clarendon Press, Oxford, 1990, p. 2096.
5. Dutton, p. 5.
6. ibid., p. 127.

7. Mary A. McManus, *Reminiscences of the Early Settlement in the Manaroa District* as printed in D. Stone and D. Garden, *Squatters and Settlers*, Popular Books, Frenchs Forest, 1978, p. 127.

8. Dutton, p. 5.

9. ibid., p. 66.

10. J. O. Randell, *Teamwork: A History of the Graziers' Associations of Victoria and Riverina*, Livestock Grain Producers' Association of New South Wales, Sydney, 1983, p. 10.

11. Kiddle, p. 52.

12. Julian Stuart, *Part of the Glory*, Australasian Book Society, Sydney, 1967, pp. 51–3

13. A. B. Paterson, *The Man from Snowy River and Other Verses*, Angus and Robertson, Sydney, 1895, p. 57.

14. A. Harris, *Settlers and Convicts: Recollections of Sixteen Years' Labour in the Australian Backwoods by an Emigrant Mechanic*, London, republished by Melbourne University Press, Melbourne, 1969, p. 215.

15. Niel Black's journal, reprinted in Kiddle, p. 131.

16. Kiddle, p. 127.

17. *Victorian Year Book*, 1902–3, p. 203, reprinted in D. Stone and D. Garden, *Squatters and Settlers*, Popular Books, Frenchs Forest, 1978, p. 78.

18. John Keith McDougall, *The Trend of Ages and Other Verses*, Labor Call Print, Melbourne, 1923, p. 73.

19. Margaret Leurs, *Laureate of Labour: A Biography of J. K. McDougall, Socialist and Poet*, Banyan Press, Sandy Bay, 1987, p. 27.

20. ibid., p. 7.

21. Kiddle, p. 244.

22. Cuddie Headrigg was a character in Sir Walter Scott's novel *Old Mortality*, published in 1816 (first series of 'Tales of My Landlord').

23. Leurs, p. 32.

Chapter 6 The Banjo

1. Clement Semmler, *The Banjo of the Bush*, Lansdowne Press, Melbourne, 1966, p. 36.

2. A. B. Paterson, *The Man from Snowy River and Other Verses*, Angus and Robertson, Sydney, 1895, p. 38.

3. Therese Raddick (ed.), *Songs of Australian Working Life*, Greenhouse, Elwood, 1989, p. 37.

4. A. B. Paterson (ed.), *Old Bush Songs*, Angus and Robertson, Sydney, 1905, p. 5.

5. Henry Lawson, *In The Days When The World Was Wide and Other Verses*, Angus and Robertson, Sydney, 1896, p. 33.

6. Semmler, *The Banjo of the Bush*, p. 36.

7. Paterson, *The Man from Snowy River and Other Verses*, p. 59.

8. Semmler, *The Banjo of the Bush*, p. 38.

9. Paterson, *The Man from Snowy River and Other Verses*, p. 4.

10. A. B. Paterson, *Singer of the Bush: A. B. 'Banjo' Paterson: Complete Works 1885–1900*, Lansdowne Press, Sydney, 1983, p. 258.
11. Semmler, *The Banjo of the Bush*, p. 42.
12. Colin Roderick, *Banjo Paterson: Poet by Accident*, Allen & Unwin, North Sydney, 1993, p. 7.
13. Paterson, *The Man from Snowy River and Other Verses*, p. 10.
14. Paterson (ed.), *Old Bush Songs*, p. 12.
15. Semmler, *The Banjo of the Bush*, p. 50.
16. Paterson, *The Man from Snowy River and Other Verses*, p. 35.
17. Roderick, *Banjo Paterson: Poet by Accident*, p 50.
18. Paterson, *Singer of the Bush*, p. xxiii.
19. Semmler, *The Banjo of the Bush*, p. 62.
20. ibid., p. 19.
21. ibid., p. 61.

Chapter 7   The Old Billy Boiling

1. A. B. Paterson, 'Looking Backward', *Sydney Mail*, 28 December 1938.
2. C. E. W. Bean, 'The Dreadnought of the Darling', reprinted in Clement Semmler, *The Banjo of the Bush*, Lansdowne Press, Melbourne, 1966, p. 18.
3. Clement Semmler, *A. B. (Banjo) Paterson*, Lansdowne Press, Melbourne, 1965, p. 10.
4. Duke Tritton, *Time Means Tucker*, Akron Press, Arncliffe, 1964, p. 84.
5. Henry Lawson, *In The Days When The World Was Wide and Other Verses*, Angus and Robertson, Sydney, 1896, p. 47.
6. Tritton, p. 21.
7. Russel Ward, *The Australian Legend*, Oxford University Press, Melbourne, 1958, p. 260.
8. Patsy Adam-Smith, *The Shearers*, Thomas Nelson, Melbourne, 1982, p. 116.
9. Dennis O'Keeffe, 'William Spence', *Waltzing Matilda*, CD, Heritage Recordings, Warrnambool, 1994.
10. J. O. Randell, *Teamwork: A History of the Graziers' Associations of Victoria and Riverina*, Livestock Grain Producers' Association of New South Wales, Sydney, 1983, p. 7.
11. ibid., p. 4.
12. Julian Stuart, *Part of the Glory*, Australasian Book Society, Sydney, 1967, p. 44.
13. Clement Semmler, 'Some notes on the literature of the shearers' strike of 1891 and 1894', *International Social Science Journal*, Vol. XXI, No. 3, 1969.
14. *The Worker*, Brisbane, 16 May 1891.

Chapter 8   Warrnambool to Winton

1. Margaret Kiddle, *Men of Yesterday: A Social History of the Western District of Victoria, 1834–1890*, Melbourne University Press, Carlton, 1961, p. 474.
2. ibid., p. 470.
3. A. B. Paterson, *Song of the Pen: A. B. 'Banjo' Paterson: Complete Works 1901–1941*, Lansdowne Press, Sydney, 1983, p. 498.

4. Richard Osborne, *A History of Warrnambool, 1847–1886*, Chronicle, Prahran, 1886, p. 141.
5. C. E. Sayers, *Of Many Things: A History of Warrnambool*, Olinda Books, Olinda, 1972, p. 8.
6. Kiddle, p. 201.
7. ibid., p. 220.
8. Malcolm Prentis, *The Scots in Australia*, University of New South Wales, Sydney, 2008, p. 34.
9. Sidney May, *The Story of Waltzing Matilda*, Smith and Paterson, Brisbane, 1944, p. 36.
10. ibid., p. 25.
11. Richard Magoffin, *Fair Dinkum Matilda*, Mimosa Press, Charters Towers, 1983, p. 59.

Chapter 9   Australia for the Australians

1. R. Cavendish (ed.), *Legends of the World*, Orbis Publishing, London, 1982, p. 172.
2. Colin Roderick, *Banjo Paterson: Poet by Accident*, Allen & Unwin, North Sydney, 1993, p. 89.
3. ibid., p. 29.
4. ibid., p. 50.
5. ibid., p. 63.
6. A. B. Paterson, *Singer of the Bush: A. B. 'Banjo' Paterson: Complete Works 1885–1900*, Lansdowne Press, Sydney, 1983, p. 72.
7. ibid., p. 67.
8. ibid., p. 67.
9. A. B. Paterson, 'Looking Backward', *Sydney Mail*, 28 December 1938.
10. Vance Palmer, *The Legend of the Nineties*, Melbourne University Press, Melbourne, 1954, p. 60.
11. Letter from Emily Barton to Aunt Nora, 18 October 1888, reprinted in Colin Roderick, *Banjo Paterson: Poet by Accident*, Allen & Unwin, North Sydney, 1993, p. 64.
12. Clement Semmler, *A. B. (Banjo) Paterson*, Lansdowne Press, Melbourne, 1965, p. 79.
13. ibid., p. 81.
14. Roderick, *Banjo Paterson: Poet by Accident*, p. 76.
15. *Bulletin*, 9 July 1892.
16. *Bulletin*, 23 July 1892.
17. *Bulletin*, 6 August 1892.
18. *Bulletin*, 18 August 1892.
19. *Bulletin*, 10 October 1892.
20. Semmler, *A. B. (Banjo) Paterson*, p. 86.
21. R. Burrows & A. Barton, *Henry Lawson, A Stranger on the Darling*, HarperCollins, Sydney, 1996, p. 18.

22. Henry Lawson, letter to Mrs Emma Brooks, 21 September 1892, reprinted in R. Burrows & A. Barton, *Henry Lawson, A Stranger on the Darling*, HarperCollins, Sydney, 1996, p. 21.
23. Jim Haynes (ed.), *The Book of Australian Popular Rhymed Verse*, ABC Books, Sydney, 2008, p. 372.
24. Henry Lawson, *In The Days When The World Was Wide and Other Verses*, Angus and Robertson, Sydney, 1896, p. 47.
25. ibid., p. 90.

Chapter 10   The Fight Begins

1. Ron Edwards, *The Big Book of Australian Folk Song*, Rigby Ltd, Sydney, 1976, p. 137.
2. Patsy Adam-Smith, *The Shearers*, Thomas Nelson, Melbourne, 1982, p. 120.
3. D. Stone and D. Garden, *Squatters and Settlers*, Popular Books, Frenchs Forest, 1978, p. 168.
4. Clement Semmler, 'Some notes on the literature of the shearers' strike of 1891 and 1894', *International Social Science Journal*, Vol. XXI, No. 3, 1969.
5. A. B. Paterson, *The Man from Snowy River and Other Verses*, Angus and Robertson, Sydney, 1895, p. 57.
6. Semmler, *International Social Science Journal*.
7. Margaret Leurs, *Laureate of Labour: A Biography of J. K. McDougall, Socialist and Poet*, Banyan Press, Sandy Bay, 1987, p. 24.
8. John Keith McDougall, *The Trend of Ages and Other Verses*, Labor Call Print, Melbourne, 1923, p. 99.
9. John Merritt, *The Making of the A.W.U*, Oxford University Press, Melbourne, 1986, p. 226.
10. Mick Armstrong, *Burning the* Rodney, Socialist Alternative, Melbourne, 2007, p. 2.
11. Stuart Svensen, *Industrial War: The Great Strikes 1890–94*, Ram Press, Wollongong, 1995, p. 94.

Chapter 11   The Burning of the *Rodney*

1. Dennis O'Keeffe, 'The Strike of 1894', *Wrought Iron Australians*, CD, Heritage Recordings, Warrnambool, 1992.
2. *Sydney Morning Herald*, 23 August 1894.
3. Frank Hardy, oral interview, 1992, author's collection.
4. *Sydney Morning Herald*, 20 August 1894.
5. *Sydney Morning Herald*, 23 August 1894.
6. Mike Cummings (son of Joseph Cummings), letter to Dennis O'Keeffe, 6 August 1995, author's collection.
7. R. M. Williams and Ruhen, O., *Beneath Whose Hand: The Autobiography of R. M. Williams*, Pan Macmillan, Sydney, 1984, p. 13.
8. The Hon. Clyde R. Cameron, AO, Letter to Dennis O'Keeffe, 25 May 1995, author's collection.
9. ibid.

10. Letter collected by John Meredith from Mrs Fitzy-Wolquist of Botabalar Vineyard, Mudgee. Written by her grandmother, who was living on Tolarno Station, 29 August 1894.
11. Ian Mudie, *Riverboats*, Rigby, Sydney, 1961, pp. 215–16.
12. ibid.
13. Dennis O'Keeffe, 'After We Burnt The *Rodney*', *Wrought Iron Australians*, CD, Heritage Recordings, Warrnambool, 1992.
14. *Sydney Morning Herald*, 28 August 1894.
15. ibid.
16. Dennis O'Keeffe, 'The Strike of 1894'.
17. ibid.
18. ibid.
19. 'The Union Buries Its Dead', *The Worker*, 27 October 1900.
20. Don Beian, interview with Mick Ryan, 1972, author's collection.
21. Colin Roderick, *Henry Lawson: A Life*, Collins/Angus and Robertson, North Ryde, 1991, p. 117.
22. ibid.
23. Mike Cummings, letter to Dennis O'Keeffe, 6 August 1995.

Chapter 12 Dagworth Burns

1. Peter and Sheila Forrest, *Banjo and Christina*, Shady Tree, Darwin, 2008, p. 62.
2. Julian Stuart, *Part of the Glory*, Australasian Book Society, Sydney, 1967, p. 44.
3. Stuart Svensen, *Industrial War: The Great Strikes 1890–94*, Ram Press, Wollongong, 1995, p. 76.
4. Magisterial inquiry before E. Eglinton re. *The Death of Samuel Hoffmeister 2 September 1894*, Department of Justice Queensland, 5 September 1894.
5. Magisterial inquiry before E. Eglinton re. *The burning of the Dagworth wool-shed on September 2 1894*, Department of Justice Queensland, 6 September 1894.
6. ibid.
7. ibid.
8. ibid.
9. Richard Magoffin, *Waltzing Matilda: Song of Australia*, Mimosa Press, Charters Towers, 1983, p. 47.

Chapter 13 The Cover-up

1. Magisterial inquiry before E. Eglinton re. *The Death of Samuel Hoffmeister 2 September 1894*, Department of Justice Queensland, 5 September 1894.
2. Trevor Monti, barrister, Owen Dixon Chambers East, memorandum re. *The Inquest into the Death of Samuel Hoffmeister*, 14 August 2007, author's collection.
3. *Sydney Morning Herald*, 4 September 1894.
4. Magisterial inquiry before E. Eglinton re. *The burning of the Dagworth wool-shed on September 2 1894*, Department of Justice Queensland, 6 September 1894.

5. Letter collected by Dennis O'Keeffe from Cynthia Butcher, 1992. Written by her mother Lexie from information passed on to her by her mother, Harriette Higginson, who visited Dagworth Station when Paterson was staying there.
6. Stuart Svensen, *Industrial War: The Great Strikes 1890–94*, Ram Press, Wollongong, 1995, p. 76.
7. *Queensland Police Gazette*, September 1894.
8. Svensen, *Industrial War*, p. 77.
9. Richard Magoffin, *Fair Dinkum Matilda*, Mimosa Press, Charters Towers, 1983, p. 90.
10. ibid.
11. Peter and Sheila Forrest, *Banjo and Christina*, Shady Tree, Darwin, 2008, p. 77.

Chapter 14 Christina's Tune

1. Sidney May, *The Story of Waltzing Matilda*, Smith and Paterson, Brisbane, 1944, p. 26.
2. Letter from Greg Brown to Dennis O'Keeffe, 8 December 1998, author's collection. Greg Brown is the great-great-grandson of Thomas Bulch. It was his great-grandfather who was killed in France during World War I.
3. John Manifold, *Who Wrote the Ballads: Notes on Australian Folksong*, Australian Book Society, Sydney, 1964, p. 124.
4. John Keith McDougall, *The Golden Road and Other Verses*, The Industrial Printing and Publicity Co., Melbourne, 1936, p. 55.

Chapter 15 The Love Affair

1. Sidney May, *The Story of Waltzing Matilda*, Smith and Paterson, Brisbane, 1944, p. 14.
2. John Manifold, *Who Wrote the Ballads: Notes on Australian Folksong*, Australian Book Society, Sydney, 1964, p. 118.
3. Christina Macpherson, 'Waltzing Matilda', handwritten manuscript, 1895, National Library of Australia.
4. Clement Semmler, *The Banjo of the Bush*, Lansdowne Press, Melbourne, 1966, p. 99.
5. *The Age*, 24 June 2006.
6. Dianna Baillieu, interview with Dennis O'Keeffe, 22 August 1995, author's collection.
7. ibid.
8. ibid.
9. ibid.
10. ibid.
11. Dianna Baillieu, interview with Robyn Holmes, National Library of Australia, 20 September 2006.
12. A. B. Paterson, early draft and signed manuscript of 'Waltzing Matilda', reproduced in *Singer of the Bush: A. B. 'Banjo' Paterson: Complete Works 1885–1900*, Lansdowne Press, Sydney, 1983, p. 251.

13. Colin Roderick, *Banjo Paterson: Poet by Accident*, Allen & Unwin, North Sydney, 1993, p. 88.
14. ibid., p. 89.

Chapter 16   The 'Jolly Swagman' Song

1. John Manifold, *Who Wrote the Ballads: Notes on Australian Folksong*, Australian Book Society, Sydney, 1964, p. 120.
2. Richard Magoffin, *Fair Dinkum Matilda*, Mimosa Press, Charters Towers, 1983, p. 162.
3. ibid., p. 151.
4. Manifold, p. 121.
5. Marie Cowan, revised version of 'Waltzing Matilda', James Inglis & Co., 1903.
6. Manifold, p. 124.
7. Dianna Baillieu, interview with Dennis O'Keeffe, 22 August 1995, author's collection.
8. H. H. Pearce, *On the Origins of Waltzing Matilda*, Hawthorn Press, Melbourne, 1971, p. 114.
9. Letter to Doctor Wood from Christina Macpherson, c/o Mrs J. C. Manifold, Talindert, Camperdown, Victoria, Dianna Baillieu collection, Melbourne.

Chapter 17   And His Ghost May Be Heard

1. Clement Semmler, *A. B. (Banjo) Paterson*, Lansdowne Press, Melbourne, 1965, p. 34.
2. *Sydney Morning Herald*, 5 February 1941.
3. Clement Semmler, *The Banjo of the Bush*, Lansdowne Press, Melbourne, 1966, p. 100.
4. A. B. Paterson, *The Man from Snowy River and Other Verses*, Angus and Robertson, Sydney, 1895, p. 38.
5. Matthew Richardson, *Once a Jolly Swagman: The Ballad of Waltzing Matilda*, Melbourne University Press, Melbourne, 2006, p. 170.
6. Peter Forrest quoted in Sheryl Allen, *Waltzing Matilda—Unravelling the Mystery*, Landmark Property Australia, No. 33, 2010, p. 5.

Index

1st Battalion, Royal Australian
    Regiment 2
2nd Remount Unit, AIF 262

'A Bush Toast' 166
'A Bushman's Song' 168–9
A Convict's Tour to Hell 44
'A Dream of the Melbourne Cup' 104
Adams, Francis 16
'Advance Australia Fair' 265–7
'After We Burnt the Rodney' 189
'All Among the Wool' 164
Allen, Peter 3
Amalgamated Shearers' Union
    of Australia, see Australian
    Shearers' Union; Australian
    Workers' Union
'An Answer to Various Bards' 157–8
Ararat, land distribution in 79
Archer, Frederick 132
Archer, Thomas 132
Archibald, J.F. 104, 153–4, 158
Arthur, George 61–2
'As If He Knows' 263
'As Long As Your Eyes are Blue' 239

Astley, William 44–5
auf der Walz 8
Australia (film) 5
Australia for the Australians 145–9
Australian character traits 49–50
Australian Concise Oxford Dictionary
    38
Australian Labour Federation 117–18
Australian Miners' Union 114
Australian Parliament Centenary 268
Australian Shearers' Union 115–18,
    167
Australian Workers' Union 173
Ayrshire Downs 180

Baillieu, Dianna 236–7, 239–40,
    254–5
Baillieu, Ted 236
Baker, Arthur 193
Baker, Sidney 49–50
'Banjo' pseudonym 104
'Banks of the Condamine' 55–6
Barr, James 226
Barraba bank robbery 176
Barrett, Thomas 40

Bartlam, W.B. 247
Barton, Emily 95, 97, 100, 151
Battle of Muar ix–x
Bean, C.E.W. 108
Bedford, Randolf 125–6
Betts, Edward Marsden 'Teddy' 100
'billy' (tea can) 111–12
Billy Tea, song given away with 249
Binalong school 90
Black, Niel 71, 130
Bledisloe Cup Match 1999 267–8
Boake, Barcroft 171
Boer War 261
Bogalong races 91–3
Bogle, Eric 263
Bostock, John 247
Bostock family 133
Bourke, NSW 159–60
Bourke, Richard 66
Brady, E.J. 253
Buckland, Thomas 196
Buderim version 256–7
Bulch, Thomas 226–7
bullockies 85–7
Burns, Robert 178
bushrangers 90–1, 138–9

Cafferty, Austin 207–8, 211–13
Cameron, Robert 187
Cape, Alice 243
Carl Fischer Music 6, 268–9
Carr, William Picken ix–x
Casey, R.G. 173
Castle Hill rebellion 43–4
catarrh in sheep 77
Charles Gavan Duffy Land Act 78
Chifley, Ben 174
China, Paterson travels to 261–2
Chinese labour, hostility to 167–8
Chubby Checker 5
'Clancy of the Overflow'
    first publication 28–9, 104–5
    Lawson's parody of 156–7
    on city life 96
    popularity of 35–6
Clermont–Barcaldine protests 119–22

Cloncurry version 256–7
Cobb & Co coaches 88–9
Cole, Nick 134–5
Commonwealth Games Brisbane
    1982 2
convicts, in settlement of Australia
    40–2, 65–8
copyright issues 268–9
Corrigan, John 217
Cowan, Marie 247–52, 269
'Craigielea' (poem) 229–30
'Craigielea,' name used for homesteads
    229
'Craigielea' tune 142
'Craigielee March' 13, 225, 256
Crooked R brand 70
Cummings, Joseph Benjamin 186–7,
    196
Cummins, Jack 176–9

Dagworth Station, Queensland
    Macphersons' purchase of 137–8
    Paterson's stay at 233–4
    shearing at 221
    shearing shed burnt 112, 199–209
Daley, Victor 47
Daly, Michael 204–7, 215–16
Darvall, Edward 260
Dawson, Peter 4
Dickson, Jimmy 184–5, 188–9
Duffy, Charles Gavan 78
'Dummy' (convict servant) 68–9
'dummying' 78–9, 149–50
Dutton, Geoffrey 61, 64–5
Dyer, Henry 204–5, 208, 221
Dyer, Robert 207–8

Eglinton, Ernest 208, 211
Eliza (ship) 44
Employers' Federation 118
Eureka Stockade rebellion 18–19,
    47–8

Fairbairn, George 122
Farrell, John 19
Fitzgerald, Robert 60

floggings of convicts 66, 70
'Flower of Scotland' 16
foot-rot in sheep 77
Forrest, Peter 6
Four-Mile Billabong 203–4
'free contract' doctrine 125
'Freedom on the Wallaby' 126–8
'From the Wreck' 72

Galvin, Patrick 44
German immigrants 9–10
Gilbert, John 90–1
Gladesville, NSW 98–100
'God Save the Queen' 265
Goode, William 211, 214
Gordon, Adam Lindsay 72
Gordon, Jim 160
Grand Annual Steeplechase Meeting
    224–5, 227–8
graziers, see squatters
Griffith, Samuel 119, 169

Hahndorf, German immigrants in 10
Handwerksbuch 8
Harding, George Rogers 123–4
Harrington, Edward 141
Helsinki Olympic Games 1952 265
Highland, Neil 211–12
Hoffmeister, Samuel 'Frenchy'
    alleged suicide of 14–15, 24,
        112–13, 207
    cover-up of death 211–16
    in song 273
    involvement in arson 203–4
horses
    Paterson's love of 100–1
    racing at Bogolong 91–3
    racing at Warrnambool 224–5
    racing at Winton 246–7
    use in World War I 262–3
'How Gilbert Died' 90–1

Illalong station 83–4
'In Defence of the Bush' 155–6
Indigenous Australians, treatment of
    70–2

Innes, George 177
Irish political rebels 42–3, 47–8

James Inglis & Co, buys rights to
    song 3–4, 248–9
'Jim Jones of Botany Bay' 46
'John Brown's Body' 15
Johnson, Richard 41
Jondaryan station 118
'jumbucks' 273
Jumna (boat) 118

Kanaka labour in Queensland 167–8
Keating, Paul 7–8, 274
King, Jonathan 6
Kipling, Rudyard 259–60
Kyuna camp 201, 221

Lalor, Peter 18–19
Lambing Flat, NSW 89–90
'Landlordism and Land Trusts' 80–1
Laureate of Labour 79
Lawson, Henry
    bush travels 158–63
    'Freedom on the Wallaby' 126–8
    literary style 60
    McLean memorial 194
    'Out Back' 111
    Paterson on 107–8
    Paterson's rivalry with 153–5
    political interests 19, 150
    'The Roaring Days' 89
    'The Romance of the Swag' 38
'Lazy Harry's' 161
Lee, Alexander 176–9
Leurs, Margaret 79
Lindsay, Daryl 4
Lindsay, Lionel 105
Lindsay, Norman 109, 144

Macdonell, Donald 194
MacKillop, Mary 2
MacNamara, Francis 44
Macpherson, Angus 222
Macpherson, Bob
    implicates Tierney in arson 218–19

in song 273
Josephine Penne and 256–7
meets Christina at Winton 231–3
moves to Dagworth station 142
photograph of 221–2
Scottish origins 136–8
shearing policy 202–8
visits Ramsays 243
Macpherson, Christina
  befriends Sarah Riley 164
  birth of 136
  collaborates on 'Waltzing Matilda'
    138, 223–4, 242, 257–8
  correspondence with Paterson 238
  death of 264–5
  makes copies of song 247
  meetings with Dianna Baillieu
    237–8
  Paterson's feelings for 13–14, 25
  travels to Queensland 132
  visits Menningort 254
Macpherson, Ewan 137, 139, 232
Macpherson, Jamie 177–8
Macpherson, Jean 233
Macpherson, Robert 59
Macpherson family 136–8, 177,
  204–7, 221, 231
'Macpherson's Farewell' 177–8
Magoffin, Richard 247, 255, 257
Manifold, John 228–9, 245–6, 253–5
Manifold family 135–6, 246
Manuka Station, NSW 201
Martin, James 'Shearblade' 123, 175,
  180
Masters and Servants Act 1846 (Qld)
  170
mateship 40, 50–1
Matilda (name), Teutonic origins 9
May, Sydney 235, 253
McArthur, Stewart 224
McArthur family 133–5
McCaughey, Samuel 161
McCormick, Peter 267
McCowan, Samuel 233
McDonald, Alice 140

McDougall, John Keith 72–5, 80–1,
  172, 229–30
McGuiness, Paul 133
McIlwraith, Thomas 180
McKay, W.C. 176
McLean, William John 'Billy' 24,
  192–5
McManus, Mary 64
Melbourne, immigration to 134
Melbourne Club 78
Menningort, Victoria 224
Meredith, John 257
Mills, Ali (Arjibuk) 5
Mitchell, Thomas 129
Monash, John 19–20
Montgomery, Alex 19
Monti, Trevor 214
Montreal Olympics 1976 2
Moody, William 211–13
Morant, Harry 19
'Morgan' 141
Morgan, Daniel 'Mad Dan' 138–41
Mulga Bill 94
Murphy, John 192–3
Murray, Lewis 211
mythology 27–8

national anthem, competition for
  265–7
nationalism, growing sense of 21, 151
Nelson, Hugh 245
Nettalie Station riot 190–2
New South Wales 22–4, 46
Nielsen, Shaw 60

Old Bush Songs 86–8, 97–8, 253
'Old Jacob' 68
'Old Pardon, the Son of Reprieve'
  92–3
Olympic Games Atlanta 1996 6
Olympic Games Sydney 2000 2
'On Kiley's Run' 83–4, 144, 264
On the Beach 5
On the Origins of Waltzing Matilda
  253, 255
On the River 98–9

Once a Jolly Swagman 5
Oondooroo station 136, 180, 246
oral legends 107
'Out Back' 111, 162

Palmer, Vance 27, 263–4
Pardon (horse) 91–3
Parry-Oakeden, William 218
Part of the Glory 68–9
Pastoralists' Association, see also
    squatters
    'agreement' by 23
    and strike of 1894 202–3
    cuts shearing rate 115, 175
    formation of 117–18
    hires non-union labour 121
    on indentured labour 167
    reaction to unrest 195–6
    shearing sheds burnt by 217
Paterson, Andrew Barton 'Banjo'
    as war correspondent 261–2
    early life 83–105
    in Bulletin 28–9
    Lawson's relations with 127–8,
        153–5
    literary career 153, 181, 259–60
    meets Christina Macpherson 232
    military career 262–3
    on bush songs 87–8
    original version of song 13, 258
    overseas travels 261–2
    personal life 108–9, 144–5, 151–2,
        163–4
    political interests 145–9, 271
    relations with women 143, 235–6,
        243
    retirement and death 263–4
Paterson, Andrew Bogle 83–4
Paterson, Grace 262
Paterson, Hugh 262
Paterson, Rose Isabella 83–4
Peak Downs rioters 119–22
Peak Hill Station, NSW 185
Pearce, Harry 253, 255
Penne, Josephine 256–7
Pitt-Tozer, William 132

political prisoners 41–4
'Pompous Piebald Esquire' 172
Port Phillip Immigration Society 67

Queensland
    Indigenous Australians in 72
    parliamentary structure 167–9
    settlement of 129–31
    shearers' strikes 119–21
    squatters in 63–4
    union activism in 22–4, 166–9,
        172–3
'Queensland version' of Waltzing
    Matilda 256–7
Quinlan, John 140, 142

Ramsay family 242–3, 245–6
Reid, George 196
Richardson, Matthew 266
Rieu, André 6
Riley, Frederick 164, 231–2
Riley, Sarah Ann
    at Dagworth station 14, 25
    befriends Christina Macpherson
        164
    breaks engagement 242–3
    engagement to Paterson 152
    meets Christina at Winton 231
Riley, Vivienne 239
Riley family 246
Rodney (steamer) 24, 181–97
Rouse, Richard 70
Rutherford, John 140
Rutherford, Margaret 136
Ryan, Thomas Joseph 133

'Salt Bush' 94
Sandy Creek camp 119–22
'scab' (sheep disease) 76–7
Scotland, migrants from 136–7
Sculthorpe, Peter 268
Semmler, Clement 235–6
shearers
    1891 agreement with 173–6
    1894 strike 11, 14–16, 182
    arson attempts 180, 200

attitudes to unionism 165–6
class warfare by 270
return to work 220–1
wives of 54–5
working conditions 51–4
Shearing in the Bar 54
sheep 76–7, 273
shepherds 51
Siebell, Harry 19
Sir Edward Manifold Stakes 135
'Song of Australia' 265
Spellacy, James 211
Spence, William G. 51–2, 113–15,
125
sports, Australian interest in 33
squatters, see also Pastoralists'
Association
move into Queensland 130
origins of 59–81
Paterson's attitude to 149–50
payment of shearers 115
treatment of swagmen 111–12
workers exploited by 170–2
Street, John William 151–2
Stuart, Donald 68
Stuart, Julian 68–9, 122–4
'swag' 9, 37–8, 52–3
swagmen 37–40, 56–7, 111–12
'Sweeney' 163
Sydney, colonial 96–7, 148
Sydney Cove 40–2
Sydney Grammar School 95
Sydney Rowing Club 99

Tales of the Old Regime 44–5
Tannerhill, Robert 225
Tasmania 46, 61–2, 72
Taylor, George 122
Temple, David 115–16
Terrick Terrick station, Queensland
173
'The Amateur Rider' 101
The Animals Noah Forgot 84
The Australian Legend 49
The Banjo of the Bush 235–6
'The Bold Fusilier' 256

'The Braes O' Balquihidder' 225–6
'The Broken-Down Squatter' 86
The *Bulletin* 17–18, 28, 103–4
'The Bushfire' 103
'The Bushman's Song' 70
The Daily Worker 194–5
'The Death of Ben Hall' 138–9
The Dreadnought of the Darling 108
'The Great Northern Line' 85–6
'The Height of Fashion' 154
'The Hypnotist' 103
The Legend of the Nineties 27
'The Man from Ironbark' 105
'The Man from Snowy River' 105
The Man from Snowy River and
Other Verses 29–36, 181, 259
'The Old Bark Hut' 97–8
'The Old Bullock Dray' 86
'The Old Squatter's Soliloquy' 72–5
'The Old Tin Trunk' 160
'The Overflow of Clancy' 156–7
'The Roaring Days' 89
'The Romance of the Swag' 38
'The Springtime It Brings on the
Shearing' 39
The Squatters 61
The Story of Waltzing Matilda 235,
253
'The Strike of 1894' 182
Thomas, Barrington 238–9
'Thou Bonnie Wood of Craigielea'
13, 225–6, 229–30, 256, 258
Tierney, John 203, 216–19
Tolarno station, NSW 183
Tolpuddle Martyrs 43
Tomlin, Weldon 204, 221
Toorale Station, NSW 161–3
Tozer, Horace 201, 218
Tritton, Harry 'Duke' 54, 109–10
typhoid fever 101

unionism 21–2, 113–16, 173–4
'Up the Country' 155
US Army 1st Marine Division 2

Van Diemen's Land (Tasmania) 46,
    61–2, 72
Victoria
    land distribution in 79–80
    landholders move into Queensland
        130–1
Villers-Bretonneux 33
Vindex station, Queensland 232, 246

Walker, Alice 14, 252, 262
'Waltjim Bat Matilda' 5
'Waltzing Matilda'
    changes to words and music 251–2,
        273–4
    creation of 234–5
    first official performance 245
    lyrics of 250–1
    'Queensland version' 256–7
    significance of 3–6
    sung in battle ix–x

Ward, Russel 49
Warrnambool, Victoria 131, 224–8,
    246
Warrnambool Downs, Queensland
    132–3
Wellford, Francis 208, 211, 213
Welsh Chartists 42
'Where the Dead Men Lie' 171
'Whiteboys' 44, 48
Who Wrote the Ballads 228–9,
    245–6, 253–4
'Wild Mountain Thyme' 225–6
Williams, R.M. 186–7
Williamson, John 3
Winton, Queensland 131–2, 246–7
Wood, Thomas 257–8
Woodley, Bruce 268
World War I, Paterson's service in
    262–3